INTERNATIONAL BUSINESS AND THE MANAGEMENT OF CHANGE

International Business and the Management of Change

Euro-Asian perspectives

Edited by

MALCOLM TREVOR
Nagoya City University, Japan

Avebury

Aldershot · Brookfield USA · Hong Kong · Singapore · Sydney

Published by
Avebury
Academic Publishing Group
Gower House
Croft Road
Aldershot
Hants GU11 3HR
England

Gower Publishing Company
Old Post Road
Brookfield
Vermont 05036
USA

A CIP catalogue record for this book is available from the British Library and the US Library of Congress.

ISBN 1 85628 193 0

Printed in Great Britain by Billing & Sons Ltd, Worcester

Contents

v

Introduction

This is a more timely moment to look at international business and the management of change in a Euro-Asian context than could have been imagined even five years ago.

In 1957 the signature of the Treaty of Rome marked the beginning of the European Economic Community. In a comparable manner, 1992 marks a major step along the way to making the Single European Market a reality: something that has not been discussed with more attention than in business circles in Japan. Back in 1957 the Harvard Business Review reported that many US corporations had worked out pan-European strategies but had found that they had had to modify them because of the many national differences in standards, markets and procedures that continued to exist even after the Treaty of Rome had come into force. But in 1992 and thereafter the situation will have changed, which presents businessmen with both opportunities and risks. In other words, companies must manage change if they want to be competitive.

The return of Hong Kong to China in 1997 is likewise concentrating managers' minds. In the 1960s many Japanese businessmen were looking at the huge Chinese market and its pent up demand as a kind of Eldorado: only to be disappointed by China's lack of hard currency, the difficulties of doing business with the bureaucracy of a so-called 'planned' economy and the paradoxical strength of the Chinese position in being able to play off one foreign competitor against another.

The political, if not economic, reintegration of Germany has been accomplished with a speed that surprised many people and some are talking of Eastern Europe as another golden business opportunity. The momentous changes in Europe indeed present businessmen with fresh opportunities but the challenges and uncertainty are also considerable. There is, for example, the appalling condition of industry and infrastructure, not to mention pollution, in Eastern Europe and such problems as the work ethic and the introduction of proper systems of managerial control, such as cost accounting. As always, there will be winners and losers and the winners will be those companies that are future-oriented and able to change to meet the new conditions, with both the insight and the ability to commit the right resources to the right projects at the right time.

Again, the changes in the relations between the superpowers and the situation inside the USSR will make themselves felt in the business field. A 'peace dividend', if there is one, would for example allow the USA to reduce its military expenditure and to transfer not only funds but also skilled personnel to civilian research. This could be expected to have a favourable impact on the competitive performance of US companies — and hence on the US trade balance and the value of the dollar. This in turn could be expected to reduce calls for protectionism and to expand, not contract, world trade.

I first came to Japan in late 1962. If there was an expression 'kokusaika' (internationalisation) then, I never heard it. Now it is constantly discussed, though not perhaps always with much precision. What it means for Japanese, European and other companies is nevertheless crucial. How far, for instance, does the internationalisation of business, whether in manufacturing industry or in the commercial and financial sectors presuppose the internationalisation of personnel, personnel management and organisational structures? The future competitiveness of companies that intend to be global players largely depends on them finding workable answers to these questions.

Yet as Dr. Kenichi Ohmae of McKinsey so ably pointed out in his book 'Triad Power. The Coming Shape of Global Competition' — which is here already! — there is a paradox. Companies must be alive to their global competitors, while at the same time being closer to local markets, customers and societies than they were before. They need, to use Dr. Ohmae's term, to become 'insiders'. This is what Toyota is doing at Fremont in California, what Yamazaki Mazak is doing at Worcester in England and what BMW, ICI and other European firms are doing in Japan.

Apart from the classic entrepreneurs, who are by definition risk-takers, many managers seek to reduce or control uncertainty. They do not welcome change. Certainly change is not always convenient or easy but, as the Greek philosopher Heraclitus and traditional Buddhist philosophy both teach, change is an inescapable fact of life. Companies must therefore manage change and it is to be hoped that the contents of this volume will make a positive contribution to this process.

One of the best observations on the management of change comes from Peter Drucker, who one might think had had more influence on business in Japan in the post-1945 period than in the USA itself. 'Management is not just a creature of the economy; it is a creator as well. And only to the extent to which it masters the economic circumstances, and alters them by conscious, directed action, does it really manage' (Quoted from 'The Practice of Management', Pan Books, London, 1968: a bestseller in Japan under the title 'Gendai no Keiei').

On behalf of the Euro-Asia Management Studies Association (EAMSA), I should like to thank all those who have made this volume possible and who supported the preceding conference held in Nagoya. Those whose hard work contributed to the success of this meeting are too numerous to mention individually but special thanks are due to the following: Nagoya City, for kindly making the City's new and magnificently equipped conference building available. Nagoya City University, for help and encouragement. Toyota Motor Corporation, for most generous financial support and for kindly hosting a plant visit and meeting with busy top management that was much appreciated. Yamazaki Mazak Corporation for generous financial support and senior management participation. The Daiko Zaidan for financial support. Brother Industries for administrative support and senior management participation and, last but not least, our good colleagues Professor Y. Hoshino of Nagoya City University and Professor Y. Teramoto of the University of Tsukuba, without whose great expenditure of time and effort the conference would not have succeeded.

Dr. Malcolm Trevor
Chairman, EAMSA
Professor of International Personnel Management
Nagoya City University
Japan

PART 1:

THE GLOBALISATION OF COMPETITION

1 Accessibility of non-European multinationals to EEC 1992 and the automobile technology market

SUNG-JO PARK
FREE UNIVERSITY, BERLIN

'Free 1992' for all automobile producers?

Despite all pessimistic predictions concerning the development of demand in the automobile industry, the integration of EEC 1992 seems to have encouraged automobile producers.[1] The large American automobile firms General Motors and Ford are building up logistic centres fitting the needs of Europe; the Japanese — after having successfully built up transplants in the USA — are aiming at expanding and increasing the number of their transplants in Europe, thus trying to build up a trilateral network of production and distribution. Smaller newcomers such as Korea, China etc. are also eager to prepare for 1992 by being very concerned about the technology of the European automobile industry.

The European automobile producers (VW, Renault, Fiat) have long since withdrawn from their American transplants and are concentrating on Europe instead. Lacking a unified strategy, it seems as if European automobile producers intend to face the growing competition either by liberalisation (West Germany) or by protectionism (France, Italy, Spain).[2]

Optimism concerning EEC 1992, which backs up the internationalisation strategies of the Japanese automobile producers, is, apart from the typical characteristics of the European automobile market such as the variety of car segments and automobile production technologies,[3] based on a higher increase of demand in Europe compared to North America (see Table 1 by U. Jürgens), which will increase all the more given the removal of tariff and non-tariff barriers after 1992.

Table 1 Estimated demand in the automobile industry for the 1990s

	Number of new registrations (1000 Units)	DRI (1988)	Ward's (1987)	Ssangyong (1989)	Wildemann-Delphi Report (1988)
		1987-1993	1987-1997	1988-2000	1987-1995
Western Europe	12,330	− 1.95%	+ 10.50%	+ 18.28%	—
West Germany	2,916	− 8.80%	—	—	− 7.00%
EEC	11,251	+ 0.80%	—	—	− 9.73%
North America	11,284	+ 4.74%	+ 6.90%	+ 11.35%	+23.00%
Japan	3,275	+ 6.78%	+ 36.40%	+ 9.16%	+ 3.00%
Asia Oceania	1,325	+46.65%		+213.84%	—
Africa Middle/Near East	1,168	+38.18%	+200.00%	+ 51.11%	—
South America	970	+38.45%	+ 72.70%	+ 51.11%	—
TOTAL	32,657	+ 8.79%	+ 16.90%	+ 27.00%	—

Cf. U. Jürgens 'Zur Situation der bundesdeutschen Automobilindustrie Ende der achtziger Jahre: Gefährdungspotentiale für die künftige Entwicklung', Berlin 1989.

Because of the EEC's strong potential of demand — compared to the other continents (including the Eastern Bloc countries) — and the vast variety of production and demand structures, the American and Japanese multinationals are very concerned to expand their market shares in the EEC (for 1988, Ford's share amounted to 11.2 per cent, GM's share to 10.3 per cent and Japanese firms' share to 9.2 per cent).

The building up of Japanese transplants in the USA dates back to the early 1980s, when the Americans started to operate import quotas and Voluntary Restraint Agreements (VRA). The present production capacity of the North American transplants is estimated at 1.5 million cars rising to 2.4 million by 1995, whereas for Western Europe, the actual capacity is still less than 300,000 cars but will exceed 1 million by 1995. It can be assumed that by the mid-1990s the production capacity of the Japanese transplants[4] will be about 3.5 millions (cf. Table 2).

A few years ago, the Koreans for the first time exported their cars to EEC countries (Great Britain, Benelux etc.), but in contrast to their experience in North America, they failed to be very successful. From 1990 onwards exports will be extended to EFTA countries (Switzerland and Finland). According to estimates by European experts, the Korean automobile industry, whose yearly production of 1 million units is already taking sixth place in the world, will, despite these modest beginnings have 2 per cent of the German market in the 1990s.[5]

Taiwan, Malaysia, Jugoslavia and others already show the first signs of entering the EEC market and the possibility of importing the VW 'Golf' from the People's Republic of China in the 1990s is already being discussed in certain circles.

Table 2   Transplants of Japanese automobile companies in North America and Western Europe (private cars and light trucks)

	Start of production (Year)	Production 1989/90 (number of cars)	Final assembly (number of cars)	Type	Investments
North America					
USA					
Honda	1982	360,000	510,000	Accord, Civic	US$ 1.7 bill.
Nissan	1983	228,000	400,000	Sentra, Pickup	US$ 750 mill.
Toyota/GM	1984	200,000	280,000	Corolla	US$ 1 bill.
Mazda	1987	240,000	240,000	MX-6, Ford Probe	US$ 550 mill.
Toyota	1988	100,000	200,000	Camry	US$ 1.1 bill.
Diamond Star (MMC/Chrysler)	1988	Pilot line	240,000	Coupé, Sedan	US$ 600 mill.
Subaru-Isuzu	1989	—	240,000	Subaru, light trucks	US$ 500 mill.
Canada					
Honda	1986	120,000	80,000	Accord	CN$ 200 mill.
Toyota	1988	50,000	50,000	Corolla-Derivate	CN$ 400 mill.
Suzuki/GM	1989	200,000	200,000	Chevrolet Sprint, Forsa, Pontiac, Firefly Samurai	CN$ 615 mill.
TOTAL		1,558,000	2,440,000		US$ 7.196 bill.
Western Europe					
Nissan U.K.	1986	75,000	400,000	Micra, Bluebird	US$ 960 mill.
Nissan/Motor Iberica	1980	80,000	200,000	Priv. cars/trucks New inv. up to 92	US$ 760 mill.
Mitsubishi/ UNIVEX Portugal	1989	6,400	10,000	trucks	?
Isuzu/GM	1989	55,000	60,000 (?)		?
Honda/Rover	1990	40,000	?	Concerto/R-8	?
Toyota/VW Joint Venture (FRG)	1989	15,000	15,000	HiLux pickup	?
Toyota Derbyshire/GB	1992	—	200,000	Carina II	US$ 1.2 bill.
Suzuki/Land Rover Santana (Suzuki=20%)	?	—	120,000	Vitaras/priv. cars	?
TOTAL		291,000	1,005,000		US$ 2.920 bill.
GRAND TOTAL (North America and Western Europe)		1,849,000	3,445,000		US$ 10.116 bill.

Compiled by U. Jürgens (1989)

EEC strategies of non-European countries

As to non-European multinationals, there are different strategies towards EEC countries —

USA (Ford/General Motors):–	Early transnationalisation strategy after World War II → building up of transplants and outsourcing structure; localisation of management and building up independent logistics centres for Europe (product cycle strategy)
JAPAN (Nissan, Honda, Mitsubishi, Toyota, Mazda, etc.):–	Building up of a distribution network and after-sales service for sales in the 1960s and 1970s → after reaching a market share of 10 per cent, building up of marketing centres and centres for homologation and evaluation; → building up of production sites in the mid-1980s (market expanding and production site strategy)
NIES (e.g. South Korea):–	Building up the distribution network and after-sales service for sales in some European countries in the mid-1980s and access to European automobile technology (technology transfer strategy)

American multinationals: Ford and General Motors[6]

The different strategies towards the EEC are closely linked to the development level of the product and production method technology of the respective country. Having started the building up of their own production centres at a very early stage, the American multinationals could operate on the basis of a highly developed product and production process technology, thus reaching transnationalisation i.e. Europeanisation in a very short time. It corresponds with Vernon's product cycle theory, so that consequently they have almost been regarded as domestic automobile producers.

During the last years Ford and General Motors (GM) have built up their own logistic centres (Ford of Europe, GM Europe) to which the research and development centres of Ford in Cologne and of GM in Rüsselsheim (both in West Germany) are closely linked. Ford is said to be the most internationalised automobile company in the world, having almost identical structures of production in North America and Europe. Ford has regarded the European market as a unity ever since. There is, for example, border-crossing inter-connected production at four points in Europe, for example in the case of the 'Fiesta', which shows that a decentralised production structure (assembly at three different places) and, in the case of some components, parallel production is favoured.

Therefore a flexible capacity utilisation is necessary, which means that in the case of the 'Fiesta' only Dagenham is working to capacity whereas the other places of production are not. The advantage of this method is that one can react flexibly to market tendencies and, if there is a strike at one plant, at once make use of other capacity. Already during the 1970s, Ford computerised the whole production process in Europe and in the 1980s linked the R&D, the outsourcing, the production capacity and the production process together with the sales and financial systems. In particular, the section responsible for outsourcing has been built up upon a special information system, thus being able to take care of the whole material supply and production control. The project for the 1990s is to introduce the '5-days-supply' system first in order to end up with JIT, which is already the case for the Saarlouis plant.

Early in 1988, GM built up its European logistics centre (GM Europe) in Zürich. Decision making concerning the EEC lies with the Strategy Board (consisting of members of the executive board of Opel and Vauxhall), which decides in detail upon the automobile type, production run, production location, sales markets and the necessary investments. Special importance is paid to the R&D division of Opel Rüsselsheim, where the planning, research and development of all cars to be built outside Europe are undertaken.

As to what concerns the EEC market, GM is using a product mix strategy, producing apart from the 'Kadett' (1985), 'Omega' (1987), 'Senator' (1987) and others the upper middle class car Opel 'Vectra/Vauxhall' competing with the Renault 21, Peugeot 405, Nissan Bluebird and VW Passat. The revitalized R&D section has added to GM's image of 'technological innovation'.

Another factor is the newly founded European Sourcing Committee, where the departments for R&D, quality control and material purchase are canalised for mutual information exchange. In this committee, there are four teams consisting of Material Purchase for Spain, GM Continental Vauxhall and Opel, the Advanced Purchasing Team, which together with the R&D section records all parts necessary for cars of the future and finally the Material & Product Control Team, which supervises the production process and the quality control in the sub-contracting companies. The so-called Creative

Team has been established by GM Europe and is providing the sub-contracting companies with concrete guidelines for production strategies.

Apart from strict selection, the new sourcing strategy also caused the diversification or globalisation of the parts suppliers, with the result of GM Continental recently being able to save 22 per cent of the costs.

Remarkable is the fact that GM is transferring its management experiences of the joint venture with Toyota in NUMMI to Western Europe. Because GM's European managers were said to be bureaucratic and hierarchically orientated, thus lacking dynamic creativity, GM tried successfully to overcome this lethargy and to introduce completely new communication structures between management and employees. As a consequence, a new type of GM industrial relations has been created which made possible for example the nightshift in Spain and the 10-hours shift of GM Continental.

It is obvious that the research and development activities of both multinationals are completely focused on the EEC and on markets outside the USA in general. As a matter of course, they also make good use of the possibilities they are given to gain access to basic and applied research.

Within the EEC a decentralised spread of the outsourcing policy of GM and Ford is not difficult to achieve, because part producers or suppliers are not necessarily dependent on an automobile maker, as the relations between the maker and the suppliers are mainly open and very often horizontal; whereas in Japan the relation between one producer and its various sub-contracting companies is closed and vertical. Therefore in Europe there is the possibility of gaining easy access to the technology of the sub-contracting companies. In other words, concerning the transfer of technology, the European sub-contracting companies are more or less autonomous. The second and much more important method to gain access to basic and applied research is to make use of universities and of research institutes linked to them, based on close cooperation between universities and industry.

Japanese multinationals

Motives for the establishment of research centres[7]

As to R&D activities, Japanese multinationals have recently made stronger efforts, paying special attention to the following:–

Japanese multinationals do not carry out basic research but try to adapt to the market trends of the respective country as quickly as possible, paying attention to trends in technology, trying out conditions for environment protection and developing new product designs.

According to this concept, JETRO (Japan External Trade Organisation) has grouped six strategies as follows:

8

(i) Localisation of product development:
Companies: Otsuka, Kao, Sony, Nissan, Honda

(ii) Increase of outsourcing and development of product design:
Companies: Nissan, Sony

(iii) Quick adaptation to the needs of the consumers:
Companies: Yoshida Kogyo

(iv) Stronger emphasis on the technological level of the company in general:
Companies: Sony (lacking qualified engineers in Japan), Nissan (ditto)

(v) Recruiting qualified local personnel:
Companies: Hitachi

(vi) Collection of market trend information:
Companies: Otsuka, Kao.

In most cases, Japanese multinationals have built up their research institutes in Germany, as the following examples show:

Company	*Place of R&D activities*
Sony	Stuttgart (Fellbach)
Mazda	Frankfurt (Oberursel)
Mitsubishi Automobile	Frankfurt (Trebur)
Honda	Offenbach
Murawa	Nürnberg
Toshiba	Regensburg
Canon	Gießen
Epson	München
Otsuka	Frankfurt
NEC	München
Mitsubishi Electronic Europe	Ratingen (Düsseldorf)
Fujitsu	Frankfurt, München, Ottobrunn
Panasonic	Hamburg
Yazaki	Köln
NGK Insulators Inc.	Ratingen (Düsseldorf)
Wako Chemicals	Neuss
Bando Chemical Ind.	Mönchengladbach
Hitachi	Cambridge (Engand)
Nissan	England and Brussels
Shimazu	Duisburg
Okuma	Krefeld
Takeda Chemicals	Frankfurt
Kao	Berlin
Fuji	Kleve

Asked why so many Japanese research centres concentrate on Germany, the following answers have been given:–

(i)   Regarding geographical situation, infrastructure and especially economic power, Germany forms the centre of Europe

(ii)   Germany is said to be one of the most liberalised countries in Europe (e.g. concerning the automobile industry)

(iii)   Although labour legislation is strict, the recruiting of qualified personnel is easy

(iv)   The economic, institutional and social infrastructure is developed to the greatest extent

(v)   Concerning the promotion of foreign investment, Germany offers the most incentives (compared to other EEC countries)

Regarding the promotion of foreign investment, different regions in Germany have recently offered foreign companies their own High Technology park, with good chances of access to the basic research of the universities. The High Technology park Bietigheim close to Stuttgart has been reserved for the Japanese[8] and the region of Baseweiler near Aachen for the Koreans.[9]

M & A strategy

Japanese multinationals frequently use the M & A strategy. As one of the first, Sony took over the Wega company at Fellbach near Stuttgart. The M & A strategy has been applied to companies with a good distribution network but which got into trouble because of inefficient production management.

Thus the M & A strategy of the Japanese or East Asians (for example the Korean firm Tongil) is aimed at companies possessing research and development potential. An example is Dainippon Ink & Chemicals Inc. (DIC), which assured its basic research by buying Hartmann Druckfarben GmbH in Frankfurt, the producer of offset printing plates for Polychrome GmbH in Osterode, and by the takeover of the European Inmont research laboratory in Berlin. The Japanese are now carrying out basic research in the field of polymers at DIC Berlin GmbH & Co. Research and Development Laboratory Europe KG. Matsushita Electric Works Ltd. has recently taken over SDS Relais AG at Deishofen near Munich, including a strong development division of eight experts for super-modern technology.

The M & A strategy is particularly backed up by the fact that the export successes of the Japanese multinationals in the fields of consumer electronics, office automation, automobiles etc. are mainly due to quick adoption of technology, mass production and rational pricing policies, where special attention has always been paid to applied research. In other words, the need for qualified 'creative' personnel becomes stronger. A member of the executive board of Fujita, for example, acknowledges that by 1990 Japan will be lacking 500,000 software engineers. Accordingly there is a need to use European and especially German programmers and information technologists.[10]

Access to basic research

In Western Europe, Japanese multinationals have seldom worked with universities or other institutes where basic research is being carried out (except for Nissan in England). But this is slowly going to change, especially after it was recognised that Japanese multinationals are able to work together with well known institutes like MIT, Princeton, the University of California etc.; so that various research projects at MIT, Caltec or Columbia University are now financed by Japanese multinationals. A typical example is NEC Corporation, which last year built up a research centre in Munich; where 50 qualified research workers will not only work on the design and market acceptance of current products but also on future ones. NEC is interested in intensive cooperation with the Max Planck Society but Japanese multinationals in general are developing more contacts with this Society, the Fraunhofer Institute, the smaller research centres in Karlsruhe and Jülich and university institutes[11] as well as with the regional technology parks.[12]

Access to European technolog and (automobile) markets requires constant consumer-oriented research and development in two respects: firstly, how to learn quickly from the extremely diversified technology market of the automobile industry, in order to accelerate the diversification of the Japanese car segments, and secondly, how to meet the needs of consumers and market trends by product planning, car body design, evaluation, and research engineering, and how to prepare for homologation and authorization procedures.

Lack of vertical diffusion of technological innovation in Japan

The diversified technologies within the automobile industry and the diversity of cars linked to it, require a diffusion of technology which is accompanied on the one hand by a suitable innovation process and on the other by the demand of different car segments. The car segments of different countries are shown in Table 3 below.

It is easy to recognize that Japan is weak in the upper automobile classes, but concentrated first on the small car segments and afterwards on the lower middle class. Thus, the accent has been shifted from bottom to top. Nowadays the Japanese are trying to gain access to the upper class with models like the 'Lexus', 'Infiniti' etc. But obviously the quality of these Japanese cars needs to be improved a lot.[13] It seems as if automobile technology in this sector is yet not as developed as in Western Europe.

11

Table 3 Structure of the automobile market in selected countries in 1986 (Share of market segments* concerning all new registrations in per cent)

	West Germany	Italy	France	Great Britain	USA**	Japan
Upper Class	1.1	0.2	0.1	0.8	9.3	2.5
Upper Middle Class	13.3	4.4	7.4	6.0	13.5	
Middle Class	54.1	25.6	38.8	44.2	30.9	
Lower Middle Class	19.1	21.7	22.6	25.6	29.9	97.5
Small Cars	12.4	48.1	31.0	23.3	16.1	

*　Definition of market segments by swept volume. Upper Class: over 3,000 ccm; Upper middle Class: 2,000–3,000 ccm; Middle Class: 1,500–2,000 ccm; Small Cars: under 1,200 ccm.

**　Data not fully comparable because of lacking swept volume definition. Upper Class: Luxury; Upper Middle Class: Full size; Middle Class: Intermediate; Lower Middle Class: Compact; Small Cars: Subcompact (cf. Ward's Automotive Reports).

In Western Europe, especially West Germany, technological innovation is first carried out in the upper car segments and then applied to the lower ones. The reasons are that consumers of upper class cars are a lot more demanding than those of small cars. They are also willing to pay more for technological innovation in the sectors of comfort, security etc. because of their higher income. Thus it is easier to introduce technological innovation at the upper end of the market. Drivers of 'big cars' are more inclined to accept price increases due to technological innovation than drivers of 'small cars'.[14] W. Diez has represented German technological innovation concerning fuel injection schematically as follows:

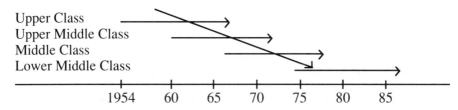

It becomes clear that after the maturity and standardisation of the new technology in the upper segments, it will spread to the lower ones as well.

For Japan, the diffusion of technological innovation is as follows:

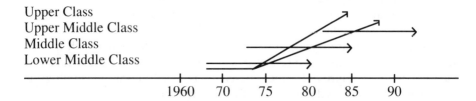

In other words, it is characteristic that Japanese multinationals, because of a lack of consumers in the upper class car segments, try out technological innovation first in the USA and then in Western Europe or supply the market from the beginning with such classes of cars. Thus the question arises, if and to what extent the Japanese automobile industry can win American or Western European drivers of 'big cars' as their customers. At least for Europe, the Japanese automobile industry is said to have only a slight chance.

Establishment of research and development centres in Europe

The newly established research centres of the Japanese multinationals are called R&D Centres. But there is a different meaning behind the appellation R&D.[15] In July 1989, Toyota and Nissan established R&D centres in Brussels, and in February 1989, Mitsubishi Motor Europe in Trebur near Frankfurt. Honda started in July 1989 with the building of a new R&D centre at Offenbach. What all these centres have in common is, firstly, the date of establishment, being very close to each other, taking into account EEC 1992, and secondly, localisation, putting the accent on Brussels and Frankfurt. Finally, there is the accent on market observation and adjustment, design development, automobile evaluation, and preparation for homologation and approval, including the EEC emission restrictions. But there are of course variations.

As to Nissan and Honda, there seem to be similar motives for the establishment of R&D centres. These two companies have long had production units in Europe. Nissan owns two production sites (Newcastle, England, and Spain) and Honda has been cooperating for ten years with Austin Rover, the former British Leyland. Up to 1986, Nissan had assigned all advance work, regarding e.g. the necessary parts, to European sub-contracting companies, providing Japanese blueprints, specifications and design. But the costs were out of all proportion. The establishment of the Design Company in Newcastle as well as the Nissan European Technology Centre in Brussels are part of the strategy to localise advance work and the specification of Nissan outlines at European sub-contracting companies and to improve their quality.

The other companies' motives refer more to the advance adjustment of technical developments and needs, which will be created by coming EEC restrictions for example, with the automobile concepts and product planning of the Japanese mother company. In addition, the argument of establishing oneself better in the European market by better marketing has also been put forward. Honda has even adopted a Gen-Ba Philosophy, believing itself to be at the 'scene of action', where the basic impulse of scientific curiosity and research has been functioning as a motor over two and a half thousand years. Honda meets European scepticism concerning the future of the auto-mobile and motorbike sector with its company philosophy of Gen-Butsu, meaning 'Look at the things as they are and deal directly with the prob-lems'. Even if the other companies are not so quick in making a philosophy out of it, it is commonly known that all of them are trying to learn and profit from European efficiency and quality orientations.

Interestingly, the research and development activities of Japanese auto-mobile producers are concentrated on only two regions: Brussels and Frank-furt am Main. According to a study on Toyota, neither research nor devel-opment activities are being carried out in their technology centres. Their activity is restricted to homologation and approvals. Nissan is at the moment carrying out tests on an automobile prototype. Both technology centres in Brussels put the emphasis on the quick assimilation of future technical restrictions and development of the EEC market.

Honda, Mitsubishi and Mazda, having established themselves in the Frankfurt region, emphasize the importance of having the leading competi-tors in automobile making close by for their research and development activities. Honda and Mazda have firmly supported integration, thus for them not only close contact with competitors but also with a good number of companies and institutions working in the automobile business are of importance, because qualified personnel can most easily be hired there. The distribution company Honda Deutschland GmbH, already established by 1961 in Offenbach and employing 320 staff, has been decisive for maintain-ing Offenbach as the company site.

Mitsubishi Auto Deutschland GmbH, being a general importer and dis-tributor, has had a similar approach to the establishment of the Mitsubishi R&D centre.

With an investment of DM 5 billion, Mazda distinguishes itself from the other companies. The architecturally interesting building, with its long cor-ridors more reminiscent of a spacious Buddhist temple than of a research and development centre, shows a long-term company strategy for Europe.

The presence of a number of Japanese banks and the easy availability of Japanese capital is obviously an important factor in choosing Frankfurt. The city leads in the increase in the number of Japanese in Germany and the greater proportion of the employees of Japanese companies also live there, even if their places of work are spread throughout the region.

Regarding traffic connections, the Frankfurt region is taken to be the centre of Germany as well as of Europe. German motorways generally have no speed limits and are an ideal testing ground for cars: something not found in Japan with the same length. There are also two car racetracks near Frankfurt: the Hockenheimer Ring and the Nürburgring. Thus the Japanese say that for the German motorways above and the two racetracks it is worth being in Frankfurt.

The employment structure says a lot about the quality and external con-trol of research and development work. Although the numbers of employees are close to each other (average 37 employees), the companies differ concerning personnel policy. While Nissan and Honda are taking great care of the best integration possible of their employees in the European environment, Mitsubishi seems to shut itself off from the outside world. Mazda, still at the building-up stage and dominated by the Japanese, will, according to future company trends, probably tend to be the group aiming at the best integration possible.

A general view of the functions of R&D and/or technology centres is as follows:

Table 4 The functions of R&D and/or technology centres

	Nissan	Mazda	Mitsubishi	Honda
Market research	*	X	*	X
Marketing	X	X	O	X
Product planning	*	X	O	X
Engineering/technical research	X	X	X	X
ABE/Homologation	X	X	X	X
Car evaluation	X	X	X	X
Final test/motorway test driving	X	X	X	X
Emission test	X	X	X	X
Technical development	X	(planned)	O	O
Styling/design	X	X	O	X
Assistance for European production units	X	O	O	O

Legend: X = Activity named explicitly by the company
O = Activity denied explicitly by the company
* = Activity not named by the company

Nissan has relations with universities and other institutions especially in England and the Benelux countries. Mazda considers that no automobile company can exist without cooperation but could not give information on cooperation with German companies because it was currently being established or negotiated. Mitsubishi did not give much information but stated that they did not have any cooperation with other companies and institutions. Taking into account the peripheral nature of the site and the strong dependency on the Japanese mother company, the manager interviewed himself called the research work being carried out relatively isolated. Honda still carries out scientific cooperation with European universities and other institutions through its specialised engineering departments in Japan, for the moment excluding the R&D centre. The legally independent company is not able to accept external research commissions — a situation which can be observed at the other R&D centres too.

In simplified form, the question about the R&D centres is: Are Japanese automobile producers really doing research work in Germany? Japanese Technology and R&D centres are a novelty in Europe. Almost simultaneously the big Japanese automobile companies have established such institutions in recent weeks. But they are the result of years of effort in the fields of homologation and approval activities.

By establishing these centres, new fields of work have been created in Europe such as product planning, car body design, evaluation, or research engineering aimed at optimizing Japanese cars' marketability to European consumers. But for the time being, research work is basically concentrated on evaluation, with Germany highways being used as test tracks for prototypes. Apart from this, the companies regard the assignment of Japanese engineers to Europe for limited periods of time as necessary for gaining product understanding; but critical research work is still carried out in Japan. The R&D centres play the role of sensitisers, i.e. of accustoming Japanese engineers to the European automobile market and its demands, which differ markedly from the Japanese domestic market. Especially because of different driving behaviour and different or lacking speed limits, there are different requirements regarding technology and comfort for European consumers, especially in Germany. Thus none of the companies interviewed is carrying out real research and development.

Korean multinationals

Korean multinationals have started out in different conditions, although as concerns access to the EEC market, they show a development similar to the Japanese multinationals by building up productions sites while simultaneously exporting consumer goods, followed by durable consumer goods. In the survey carried out on Korean companies in the EEC,[16] most of them stated they were quite content with the business situation and intended to expand. Asked about their strategies for 1992, the following items were mentioned:

–   product-orientated decentralisation of branches and joint operations of branches in the same product group.

–   building up of a 'pan-European plan for marketing'.

–   M&A strategy and founding of joint ventures.

–   selling of goods bearing their own trademark.

Looking at these strategies, the motives are: securing and expanding the market, intensifying overseas investment and above all securing the independent technology potential for an independent production system. The motivation of all NIC multinationals interested in the EEC market could be summed up under this common denominator. This is especially the case for the automobile industry of South Korea, Taiwan and other newcomers. As to capital participation and technology transfer, the Korean multinationals are mainly linked to Japanese and American automobile multinationals; and so are the Taiwanese.

For the Koreans, capital cooperation with American multinationals mostly means handing over certain management competences to the American partner, while technology transfer from Japanese multinationals results in severe restrictions concerning sales in international markets. Japanese companies recently started not to transfer any more technologies to NIC multinationals. Thus Korean and NIC multinationals are now trying to free themselves from technological dependency on Japanese companies as soon as possible (cf. Table 5).

Another factor is the dependency on automobile exports to North America. In 1987 Korean multinationals exported up to 86 per cent to this region (including 81 per cent to the USA).

Table 5   The technological dependency of Korea — status of technical licencing and joint ventures

Country Classification	Japan	US	UK	W. Germany	France	Others	Total
Technical Cooperation (No.)	177	45	27	20	5	12	286
Ratio (%)	61.9	15.7	9.4	7.0	1.8	4.2	100
Joint Venture (No.)	55	31	2	9	—	4	101
Ratio (%)	54.4	30.7	2.0	8.9	—	4.0	100

Source: Korea Automobile Manufacturers Association (KAMA),
Korean Automotive Industries, Seoul, 1989, p. 19.

The export of automobiles to Europe was less than 20,000 units in 1988. Accordingly, the Korean automobile industry is trying to reduce the total export dependency on the USA in favour of the EEC. In this context the double question arises of how first to get rid of the technological dependency on Japan and the USA, and then how to offer cars meeting European standards.

One well-known Korean combine is focusing on joining the EEC technological scene. The most important factor is to gain direct access to European automobile technology by establishing a research centre in Germany; thus being able to produce 'one's own cars' independently. But it is important to start with importing technology and production equipment as before, as shown in Figure 1 below.

As to the import of technology, Britain takes the leading place, having famous engineering institutions which are not related to particular automobile producers and that can therefore freely carry out technology transfer.

But for the import of equipment, Germany is the leader, followed by Austria and Denmark. Thus it becomes clear that the technology potential of medium-sized companies is very powerful in Central Europe. Therefore the Korean combine favours Germany as a site.

Thus for the Korean multinationals neither the building up of production centres, as in the case of American multinationals, nor the securing and expansion of the market, as in the case of Japanese multinationals, is decisive: direct access to automobile technology in Western Europe has the highest priority. Accordingly, by gaining access to the EEC technology market, the circle Tokyo–USA–EEC for technological independence and future globalisation strategy would be closed. Obviously, with its strong export success and investments, the Hyundai combine has concentrated on its globalization strategy in Canada (cf. Table 7), whereas the Kia combine puts more emphasis on the strategy of technological independence, having established research centres in Tokyo, Detroit, Los Angeles, and Frankfurt (?).

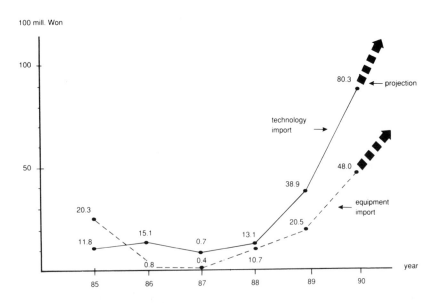

Figure 1   Import of technology and production equipment

18

Table 6   Technology and equipment imports from Europe by a Korean combine (Unit: Won 100 Mill.)

Technology imports	1985	1986	1987	1988	1989	1990	Sum	Technology suppliers
Germany	—	—	—	2.2	12.2	16.5	30.5	GATRAG, TEVES, ZF, TUV, BOSCH, etc.
Britain	11.8	12.6	7.6	10.9	23.3	66.9	133.1	LAD, LOTUS, RICARD, VATEL, etc,
Italy	—	—	—	—	1.9	0.3	2.2	IED
Austria	—	2.5	2.1	—	1.5	5.6	11.7	AVL
TOTAL	11.8	15.1	9.7	13.1	38.9	89.3	177.9	

Equipment imports	1985	1986	1987	1988	1989	1990	Sum
Germany	20.0	—	0.2	5.1	15.0	26.6	74.9
Britain	0.2	0.5	—	1.8	0.8	2.8	6.1
Denmark	0.9	0.2	0.2	1.6	3.6	2.8	9.3
Switzerland	0.2	0.1	—	0.1	—	1.6	1.9
Netherlands	—	—	—	0.2	0.6	—	0.8
Austria	—	—	—	0.9	0.5	11.9	13.3
France	—	—	—	1.0	—	—	1.0
TOTAL	26.3	0.8	0.4	10.7	20.5	48.7	107.3

Table 7   Overseas investments by a Korean automobile producer (the Hyundai Combine)

Classification	Products	Capacity	Investment	Number of employees	Country
Car assembly plant	Passenger cars	100,000 units	US $ 325 mill.	2,000	Canada
Automobile parts plant	Aluminium wheels	300,000 EA	US $ 20 mill.	250	Canada

Source: KAMA, op. cit., p. 19.

Conclusion

In 1989, the author conducted an empirical study on the access of Japanese companies to European high tech in Germany, Italy, France and Belgium. The opinions of many experts interviewed concerning Japanese strategy could, in accordance with the German magazine *Der Spiegel* — a magazine the author does not always agree with — be formulated as follows:

> The Japanese take international technology policy as a self-service shop. They do not participate in basic research jointly conducted by several nations but make use of the findings of others . . . and transfer them into profitable products. Foreign investments of Japanese firms have not . . . been integrated into local markets but have served as arms of the mother company for security or increasing exports.[17]

It is evident that Japanese multinationals are well advanced with their preparations for EEC 1992 in the context of their globalisation strategies, having adjusted themselves to the future market developments and technology in Europe. But there is still the question of how far in the long run Japanese multinationals are willing to integrate themselves into the EEC market, like American multinationals. The fact that Japanese multinationals have their European sourcing mainly concentrated on their Japanese sub-contracting companies, which also invest in Europe, should not make people too optimistic. The transnationalisation, or Europeanisation, of American multinationals has already reached the stage where these companies are naturally regarded as 'European multinationals'; and there is a big difference between American and Japanese multinationals in this respect.

Regarding the access of NIC or Korean multinationals, one basically has to assume the goodwill of European research centres. These multinationals are still technologically backward and may not therefore be regarded as strong competitors; so for the time being NIC multinationals can be sure of European multinationals being willing to cooperate.

Notes

1. cf. Ludvigsen Associates Ltd. 'Report to the Commission of the European Communities. The EC 92 Automobile Sector, March 1988'. *Panorama of EC 1989*. Commission of the European Communities, Brussels. 1988.
2. cf. 'Structural Adjustment in the Automobile Industry'. *STI Review*, OECD, No. 3, 1988. p.7ff.
3. cf. Hess Josef, 'Autoindustrie. Die Japaner im offenen Schlagabtausch gekontert'. *Handelsblatt*, 29/30, Dec. 1989.
4. cf. Hasegawa, Hirokazu. 'Automobile Industry Review — Competition heating up in the US Auto Market'. *Nomura Analyst Report*, Sept. 1989, p.1–65.

5. Wildemann, H. *Die deutsche Automobilindustrie — Einblick in die Zukunft,* Frankfurt 1988, p.9.
6. *Manager Magazin.* Several monthly issues.
7. Exim Bank. *Kaigai Toshi Kenkyushuho.* Several issues.
8. 'Verbindung mit Gefühl'. *High Tech,* 7/1989. p.94ff.
9. *Official Economic Promotion Location,* Baseweiler. 1989.
10. 'Japans neue Offensive', *High Tech,* 9/1989, p.49ff.
11. Thus, Mitsubishi Heavy Industries Co. has sent a scientist to Prof. Spur at the Berliner Doppelinstitut (Berlin Double-Institute).
12. The access of foreign companies to technology parks in Germany has not been possible everywhere. Only France, England and Sweden (Lund/Idéon) have allowed restricted access of foreigners. In Germany it is also very difficult. Mitsubishi, for example, has only been allowed to establish an information bureau in the Berliner Innovations- und Gründerzentrum (BIG) (Berlin Innovation and Founding Centre), represented by a German staff member.
13. The magazine *Auto, Motor and Sport* has compared BMW, Mercedes and Lexus, concluding that Lexus showed the worst results (cf. *Auto, Motor und Sport,* No. 17, Aug. 1989, p.24ff.).
14. Diez, W. 'Vertikale Diffusion: Zur Ausbreitung technischer Neuerungen auf dem deutschen Automobilmarkt'. *ifo-Schnelldienst* 29/88. p.20ff.
15. The information on the research and development centres of the Japanese automobile industry in Europe is mainly based on the study of R. Schlunze. *Forschungs- und Entwicklungstätigkeiten japanischer Automobilhersteller in Europa* (1989), conducted on my commission.
16. Park, S. J. *Eine Enquete über die koreanischen Unternehmen in der EG,* Berlin 1989 (unpublished study).
17. *Der Spiegel,* No. 45, 6 Nov., 1989. p.182 (translated from the German).

2 Euro-Japanese co-operation in Information Technology

HELLMUT SCHÜTTE
INSEAD

Background and framework

(i) Agreement and objective

At the end of September 1987, the author was entrusted by the Japanese Government, represented by the Japanese Delegation to the OECD, to carry out a study of 'European-Japanese Co-operation in Information Technology'. The project attempts to collect data on industrial co-operation between Japanese and European firms and to analyse these data with regard to the benefits expected to be derived from, or already brought to the partners and their countries of origin

The study's objective is to contribute to the better understanding of the workings and the constraints of international co-operation in a field which is of utmost importance to both Japan and Europe. It should also give an up-to-date description and analysis of the dynamics of Euro-Japanese co-operation in information technology which are rapidly developing, and as such difficult to follow by outsiders.

This article represents a condensed version of a report submitted in February 1989.

(ii) Definitions and methodology

According to our definition, information technology consists of the computer and office automation, the electronic component and the communication sectors, and comprises the development, production and marketing of related products and services.

Consumer electronics, as well as factory automation, although technologically closely linked to the IT-sector, are excluded, as is the application of information technology for military purposes.

Data collection has been done based on a search through material available in both academic and journalistic publications on the topic. It has been supplemented by interviews with a number of company representatives and government officials both in Europe and Japan.

Since official statements and press reports do not necessarily disclose the real intentions of the parties concerned, interviews with company and government officials were seen as important and have, in general, revealed information not publicly available, and of great relevance.

During the period from September 1987 to January 1989, the author has been in direct or indirect contact with almost all major players in Europe and Japan in the field of information technology.

International co-operation

(i)   Changes in international business: the stage

Up to a few years ago, discussions in the field of international business mainly focused on the multi- or trans-national companies. With these forms competing either among each other on a global scale, or with regional and local firms in limited areas, there was concern about their growing power in particular vis-à-vis national governments. These political bodies felt restricted in their sphere of influence by sovereignty, while multinational firms could easily move their resources across borders.

Within the very large firms, issues of fostering innovation and entrepreneurship, while keeping control and internal coherence, dominate the agenda of top management. Co-operative agreements were seen as second best solutions, often required by governments, especially in developing countries.

This has recently changed. Even very large and diversified companies realise that in co-operating with other firms, risks can be minimised, costs reduced, new markets or segments entered, or, in more general terms, revenues can be enhanced. Medium-sized and small firms are following their lead. Negotiated co-operative agreements across borders have thus grown almost explosively over the last decade both in number and importance. Today the leading global firms in several industries find themselves involved in a number of coalitions with different partners, and consider themselves members of an ever-changing network of international relationships.

Co-operative agreements are not limited to the classical joint venture in which two or more partners invest equity to achieve a common goal in a separate legal entity. Co-operative agreements comprise all efforts of independent partners to work with each other over a long period. It therefore includes everything beyond spot transactions i.e. buying and selling without further commitment, and up to mergers and acquisitions, where independent firms evolve into unified organisations. Joint research projects, OEM (Original Equipment Manufacturer) arrangements and distribution agreements thereby fall into this category.

A clear distinction between co-operative agreements and 'deals' for short-term gain does not exist, as it depends on the willingness of the partners to actually work together. A similar argument can be used regarding the importance of such agreements for the partners. There is an obvious difference between a long-term supplier-buyer relationship for nuts and bolts or paper-clips, and an alliance which influences the overall competitiveness of one or all of the partners involved. Such latter agreements are referred to as strategic alliances and are the focus of this report.

Since co-operative agreements are not bound to any legal form, cover a wide variety of projects, and often do not identify the real intent of the partners, reliable statistics do not and cannot exist.

Moreover, there is a problem of definitions. For the Japanese, 'co-operation', especially in the context of 'industrial co-operation', also includes 100 per cent foreign-owned investment, seemingly because it links the economies of different nations.[1] In this report we do not follow this wider definition.

Since, in many cases, the partners in a co-operative agreement are in the same business, competition and co-operation exist side by side. This competitive co-operation makes the management of joint efforts extremely difficult. To succeed in a joint undertaking, the partners need to share knowledge. At the same time, they have to protect their knowledge in order not to jeopardize their competitive position.

Figure 1 below shows competition and co-operation as alternative modes in business. If, however, the only objective of the individual firm is to win over other firms, then co-operation is only a derivative of competition and, as such, limited.

	Business	Government
Competition	Improve quality/service Increase scale Lower costs etc	Sponsor national R&D Protectionism
Co-operation	Joint research Joint manufacturing Joint marketing	

Figure 1

(ii)   Developments in information technology: the game

Information technology is one of the three core technologies having a sig-

24

nificant impact on the world until the end of this millennium; the other two being biotechnology and new material science.

Military applications make information technology a key strategic resource for governments which also represent major customers for the industry and, at the same time, set the rules through a number of regulations, particularly in the area of communications.

The industry has produced some very large firms such as IBM in computers, and AT&T and NTT in communications, but also many innovative firms which rose from garage-type operations into sizeable companies within a very short space of time. All of them are facing a rapid rate of change, decreasing product life cycles, rising R&D expenses, a proliferation of converging technologies, products and services, and increasing globalisation of their businesses.

These factors, one may argue, make international co-operation among the players not only an option, but a must. From the point of view of the industry we would see the following reasons for going into co-operative agreements[2]:–

(1) Risk reduction
         Failure in R&D
         Being too slow/too late

(2) Economies of scale/rationalisation
         Production in country with comparative advantage
         Lower costs from higher volume
         Concentration on key products/services

(3) Fostering technological competences
         Technological synergies
         Specialisation and complementation
            (horizontal co-operation)
         Subcontracting (vertical integration)
         Access to public research

(4) Overcoming and building market barriers
         Utilizing complementary marketing networks
         Offering complete product ranges/systems
         Overcoming investment/trade/procurement barriers
         Co-opting potential competitors

Obviously, the reasons for co-operation are manifold and overlapping. As the market demands increasingly complete solutions to computing/communications problems, competitors find it increasingly difficult to be both horizontally integrated (with a broad product/service range) and vertically integrated (from R&D to marketing worldwide, from key components to application software).

In order to connect computers with each other, communications systems and equipment are needed. In order to function, communication systems need computing power to facilitate switching. Both sectors rely on electronic components such as semiconductors and microprocessors as major accelerators in their development. The underlying convergence of technologies leads to a convergence of products which in turn leads to a convergence of those companies who aspire to offering 'information technology solutions' rather than products and services of limited value. Further growth of the large firms may be one answer to this trend; mergers or acquisitions are other solutions. Co-operation within the industry is an alternative for the information technology industry.

(iii)   Europe, Japan and the USA: the players

All competitors, even international ones, are shaped and influenced in their strategies by their home country. No firm can yet claim to be truly global and thus to be independent from a national culture or national government.

The major European firms in information technology have long enjoyed government protection and preferential treatment for procurement purchasing. This has produced national champions which suffer in the broader international arena from the fragmented market in Europe, and thus the lack of economies of scale. The over-regulation in some countries has slowed innovation, which in turn has led the companies to lobby against too rapid technological changes from which their faster competitors could benefit. However, strength in some niche markets and in software has remained and a revival of the industry is in the making in line with the European Commission's programme for Europe 1992.

Japan's leading firms were not known internationally when their European and US competitors were already globally represented in the 1950s and 1960s. Their entry came along with the change of the industry from electro-mechanical technologies to electronics. As such they are 'latecomers' in the establishment, admired for their achievements, especially in production technology, and feared for their growth momentum and determination. Fostered by an industrial policy which called for consensus, collaboration, and at the same time competition, the new rules of inter-firm co-operation are not new to them. Particularly vertical integration is carried out through a sophisticated, co-operative sub-contracting system, in contrast with European and American firms who rely primarily in their own resources.

This wealth of experience in managing relationships is exclusively derived from the Japanese environment and internationally transferable only to a limited extent. Even after several years of experience abroad, the Japanese firms still cannot match the expertise of their foreign competitors in dealing with the international business environment.[3] The track record of Japanese firms in computers and telecommunications, in contrast with mass-produced components, is also less impressive. While this may be due to protectionistic policies in telecommunications, in the computer field the underestimation of software led some years ago to some of the very few Japanese international market failures, especially in personal computers.

A similar cooperative spirit among firms or between firms and the government cannot be found in the USA, except in the defence area. This important segment has provided US firms with massive research funds and contracts. Otherwise competition is tough, resulting in high performance fluctuations of firms over time, and quick changes in market shares among competitors. Winning and losing seem to be close to one another in the US, as are high profit and high losses. Mergers, acquisitions, bankruptcies, meteoric rises — all these are the consequences of a generally volatile market in which customer loyalty is less known than in Japan or Europe.

While the economic power of the USA has relatively declined over the last two to three decades, this may not necessarily apply to the information technology sector. The largest and the most profitable IT companies are still American companies, who are market leaders in the US and in many other countries, where they successfully compete with national champions. Only Japan represents an exception, but even here IBM achieved sales of more than ¥1 trillion in 1987 and a profit of ¥170 billion.

Their heavy investments abroad and their local manufacturing in many countries make them rely less on exports from the USA. Thus, the judgement of the strength of the American IT sector from trade statistics alone may be misleading.

Undeniable, however, is the decline of US competitiveness in mass-produced components which has led to some degree of dependence on Japanese supplies even in defence-related industries. The controversial semiconductor pact between Japan and the USA demonstrates the complexities of international government agreements.

Together, Europe, Japan and the USA form the 'Triad Powers' in which the bulk of purchasing power of the world is accumulated. While competition is increasingly global in industries such as information technology, the closest competitors are still perceived as coming from the same country/ area. This means that American firms consider other American firms as their main rivals, European firms other European firms, and Japanese firms see other Japanese firms as their most serious competitors. In order to succeed against one another globally, competitors have to be strongly represented, not only on their "home turf", but also in the other parts of the triad.[4] Should the resources for this undertaking not be sufficient, alliances with other firms from other parts of the triad are a viable option. This explains why cooperative agreements are not only concluded with partners close-by, although geographical proximity and cultural similarity may facilitate communication and thus increase the probability for success. The change from local or regional competition to a global scenario in the information technology industry could be called 'geographical convergence of the market'. It leads probably more to market-driven cooperation, while technological convergence leads primarily to technology-driven cooperation.

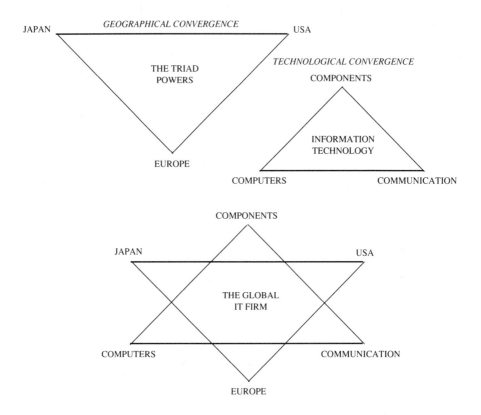

Figure 2

Firms which have taken into account both trends and become globally spread and technologically integrated firms at the same time, do not yet exist. Through cooperation, some major players are moving in the direction of becoming global IT alliances, such as Olivetti-AT&T-Toshiba and Bull-Honeywell-NEC.

Euro-Japanese cooperative ventures

(i) Characteristics of the agreements

Our research has identified 45 cooperative agreements between Japanese and European information technology firms which have been active or newly concluded over the last 3 to 4 years. They span the range from licencing to OEM deals to joint ventures and involve all of the major Japanese and European companies. They are multi-product and international in scope, or local and uni-product, and are transacted on a pan-company basis or only on behalf of a single division.

– Sectors

Cooperative activity is most pronounced in the components, computers and, to a lesser extent, the telecommunications sectors. There are a scattering of agreements involving the major automobile producers in the robotics and factory automation area, and a few examples of agreements with software producers, although neither of these two sectors is a focal point of cooperative activity at present.

– Products

Agreements have concentrated on mainframe computers, integrated circuits and facsimile machines.

It is interesting to note that the focal product areas are the ones in which Japanese companies have achieved a strong degree of competitiveness, if not superiority, in the marketplace. This applies to a lesser degree to mainframe computers, although the Japanese strength in computer hardware cannot be denied. Agreements involving these products are frequently marketing or OEM agreements which help the Japanese firms sell their products in Europe and/or allow European producers to complete their product line(s).

Some cooperative agreements span two or three sectors and are created to develop or market a hybrid product. A hybrid product would be one which combines the technologies from two separate sectors, such as telecommunications and components.

– Companies

Ventures between two small or even two medium-sized companies are rare, perhaps because of the limited international outlook and experience of those firms. The majority of agreements of any importance have been concluded between the largest and most important producers in the industry. The second most prevalent grouping is between a major world competitor and a small/medium-sized national company which is specialised in a certain skill area or product, and has gained a degree of recognition in those areas.

– Size

Looked at as a whole, the vast majority of Euro-Japanese cooperative agreements are rather small in scale, with low volumes or covering one national market, and/or are limited to a single product or product group. There are very few attempts being made either to cooperate globally or to develop complementary product strategies which avoid head-on competition between the two partners in various world markets. The NEC/Bull arrangement, a potentially global collaboration, may develop into one of the few exceptions.

– *Scope*

Many cooperative ventures start out as short-term purchasing or marketing agreements whose life-span is eventually determined by the quality of the relationship over time, as well as by external factors which make it more or less desirable for two companies to continue to cooperate. A straightforward licencing agreement, such as that between ICL and Fujitsu in 1981, can set the stage for a longer term relationship which is fairly extensive and mutually advantageous for both.

One factor adversely influencing the continuity of many cooperative agreements is the fact that most involve a single product or product group. The present pace of technological change is resulting in rapid product obsolescence. Once the technology or the product is obsolete, then the 'raison d'être' of the cooperation can be brought into question. A new agreement on a new range of products must be negotiated which may or may not include a technology which the two companies wish to share.

(ii) Categories

Viewed as a whole, the cooperative ventures which this study has identified fall into one of four categories. First, there are those agreements which concern the Japanese marketplace and involve joint development, production, marketing or distribution in or for that market. Second, there are similar agreements in or for Europe. Third, cooperations are listed which deal with transfer technology, and, lastly, there are those agreements which are broadbased, potentially global in scope and/or cooperative on a corporate-wide basis.

a. Agreements for Japan

Japanese	European
Y-E Data	Olivetti
Matsushita	Philips
Kyocera	Philips
Toppan Printing	Philips
Fuji	Siemens
Canon	Siemens
Marubeni	Siemens
NMB Semi-conductors	Thorn EMI/INMOS

Mitsui	ESS
Denki Kagaku Kogyo	Air Liquide
Sanyo	Acorn
Mitsui	Sinclair Research

There are twelve cooperative agreements that fall into this category. European firms enter such agreements with Japanese firms with one of two objectives in mind: either, it is considered to be an easy way to break into the reputably difficult Japanese market, or the company intends to actively profit from Japanese manufacturing expertise and efficiency.

In the first case, by tying up with a well established Japanese company, a European firm can benefit from the existing contacts and sales support of their Japanese partner, and avoid the large investment required for the establishment of an independent operation. The importance of long-lasting buyer-seller relationships in Japan cements the European firm to the Japanese partner and makes any strategic or structural changes of this kind very difficult.

The Japanese firm enters these kinds of cooperative ventures and benefits from them as it is able to offer its customers a greater variety of products and perhaps a different technology than that which is presently available on the market. Such an arrangement may also permit marketing expenses to be spread over a larger range of products.

In the event that two companies decide to pursue a cooperative venture in Japan over the long term, it can form the basis for a broader and technologically cooperative relationship. Such has been the case of Philips and Matsushita. The Matsushita/Philips agreement is one of the oldest which is still very active and cooperative in both directions.

A second type of cooperative agreement, for manufacturing in Japan, takes advantage of Japan's recently acquired manufacturing expertise, due to very large economies of scale and high productivity in production processes which require a large number of manufacturing steps. Both of these criteria apply to memory chips and consumer electronics.

As a rule, products produced to order in Japan for European firms do not find their way into the Japanese market, but are exported and incorporated into the European companies' final products. The borderline between such agreements and OEM sales of Japanese products by European firms in the European market is fine. OEM agreements mainly cover standardised products sold by the Japanese partner in other markets.

b. Agreements for Europe

Japanese	*European*
Seiko	Olivetti
Kyocera	Olivetti
Hitachi	Olivetti

Hitachi	BASF
Hitachi	Comparex
Sony	Logitek
Canon	Ferranti
Canon	Plessey
Canon	Siemens
Toshiba	Siemens
Toshiba	Telic-Alcatel
Toshiba	Rhone Poulenc
NEC	GEC/Marooni
Fujitsu	Swedish Telecom Admin.
Aster Intl.	Micro Peripherals
Matsushita	Quick-Rotan
Matsushita	Nixdorf
OKI Electric	SGS-Thomson

In one way, the same rationale which is used to explain Euro-Japanese cooperative ventures in Japan can be used to explain Euro-Japanese ventures in Europe. For the Japanese firms, they represent a less expensive, faster and easier way of entering the European market. There are, however, many more agreements for the European market, and for every agreement being signed for Japan, there are two being signed for Europe.

First of all, this is due to the fact that the Japanese are more substantially committed to the European market than the Europeans to the Japanese market.

Secondly, the fragmented European market remains a difficult one to conquer for outsiders facing established and strong national firms which enjoy government support. A cooperative agreement with such a firm can overcome barriers and convert a potential member of the anti-Japanese lobby into a Japanese supporter. This applies not only to marketing ventures, but also to assembly/manufacturing operations which have encountered increasing criticism for appearing to be disguised imports and have been labelled "screwdriver" plants.

Lastly, when examining European-based cooperative ventures, one finds that European companies enter such agreements hoping to have access to Japanese technology or to their high quality products. This is generally not the reason given by Japanese firms for entering a cooperative venture either in Europe or in Japan. The Japanese, who have greater respect for and interest in American technology, enter a cooperative agreement in Europe quite simply to have access to the European market. For the Europeans, a production plant in France for the manufacture of the newest model of facsimile machines brings with it not only the promise of higher sales and profits, but also that of technology transfers.

There are basically three types of agreements currently being reached

32

between Japanese and European firms in Europe. The first is a marketing or distribution agreement, the second is a manufacturing or licensing agreement, and the third is an OEM deal. For the most part, they are all initially rather small in scope and have limited specified time frames, unless they are already part of an overall relationship which has been established between two firms.

As most of the Japanese already have established networks in Europe, marketing and distribution agreements with other European firms are either small — thus not addressed by this report — or are concentrated on only one or two national markets.

The second group, manufacturing and licencing agreements, is on the rise in a response to stiffer local content regulations. They involve manufacturing or manufacturing together with distribution. The Rhone-Poulenc/Toshiba arrangement is an illustrative example. It is in the form of a joint venture for the production of Toshiba's plain paper copiers in France and for the sale of that and related office automation equipment into France.

Such an agreement evidences little true cooperative activity between the two firms and is, rather, a way for Toshiba to avoid protectionist policies and comply with local content regulations.

The third group, OEM agreements, allows for the incorporation of Japanese products into European companies' product lines and for these products' eventual sale in Europe. Such agreements can cover a whole product or any one of a number of components of that product. As such, the borderline between a company with which one has an OEM agreemcnt and with which one has a supplier agreement is rather thin. Even if products of that nature are modified for the European partners, it is the marketing side of the added value chain which is important for the OEM agreement and not so much the origin of the product.

All of the OEM agreements in our list involve computers or computer peripherals or some parts thereof. In the case of Olivetti/Kyocera, OEM sales cover small-sized computers; BASF/Hitachi, high-end memory tape units, and Hitachi/Comparex, mainframes. The present popularity of OEM agreements within the computer sector is not all that surprising, as it is a sector in which completed product lines are rapidly gaining importance. A mainframe producer cannot easily provide, overnight, a complete range of related products and thus buys what it needs from other, often foreign, producers, in order to keep clients and to maximize use of its sales and distribution network.

The publicly announced OEM deals are probably only a portion of the total number of agreements reached between Japanese and European firms. In an industry which feels increasing pressure for technological renewal and advancement, the supply of 'standard' products may not merit the word 'cooperation', even if contracts cover extended periods or represent a major reason for the purchasing company's competitiveness. There are also companies which are not anxious to admit that a certain portion of one of their major product lines is actually being produced by another company, either for reasons of company image or national pride.

While initially OEM agreements may have met short-term objectives, they also have the potential for serving as a basis for the continuation or expansion of the firms' relationship over the long term. With a successful OEM agreement in place, there is little motivation for either party to duplicate the efforts of the alliance partner; both firms are free to explore and expand operations in other areas. In turn, a success relationship fosters its own expansion and can lead partners to cooperate in not just one or two, but in many aspects over time.

c. Technology transfer

Japanese	*European*
Toshiba	Siemens
Toshiba	Alsthom
Fuji Electric	Thomson
Hitachi	Lucas Ind.
Mitsui	Intelligent Terminals

Apart from joint development projects, technology can be shared by transferring it from one firm to another. Contrary to cooperative agreements which are largely long-term, this process normally takes place during a limited span of time. The partnership between firms is, thus, transient in nature, except if the transfer of technology is part of a broader cooperative agreement called strategic alliance (see below).

The basis for the transfer is the sale of technology. As this can normally not be done by handing over blueprints, it requires the cooperation of scientists and engineers from both partners in joint meetings and training sessions, joint setting up of facilities and launching of test runs etc. During these undertakings, the actual flow of know-how takes place.

Technology transfer agreements are not always reported, appear in no trade or investment statistics, and rarely attract as much attention as the agreement between Toshiba and Siemens over the megabit chip. Most of those listed above represent the flow of technology from Japan to Europe such as in the field of transistor modules from Fuji Electronics to Thomson, and deal with production rather than product technology. The agreement between the British company Intelligent Terminals and Mitsui is an exception as it comprises the transfer of software technology for structuring artificial intelligence systems from Europe to Japan.

d. Strategic alliances

Japanese	*European*
Canon	Olivetti

Toshiba	Olivetti
Fujitsu	ICL
Fujitsu	Telefonica
Fujitsu/Fuji	Siemens
NEC	Bull

This group of agreements represents the core of broad-based accords which are truly cooperative and long-term in nature and approach. They involve the active participation of both companies in some step of the development/production/sales process and most often a sharing of technological information. The agreements are negotiated and supported by the top management levels of the companies and can encompass the activities of several divisions. The strategy behind them is a long term one with at least some emphasis on the global coordination of operations and markets.

The possibilities for the integration of the two companies' technologies often leads to a decision to develop a new group of products based on the expertise which the two firms have in the technologies involved. However, such forms of cooperation do not exclude the simultaneous pursuit of other activities such as OEM or licencing arrangements. In a well-developed relationship, the two companies are likely to have a number of joint development projects, involving two or more divisions, in addition to a series of supply and/or licencing agreements.

The dividing line between true strategic alliances and other agreements seems to be determined by the willingness of firms to cooperate in new technologies and, in some cases, on a multi-national basis. Under a number of different cooperative agreements, a company may be willing to share with another a technology which is known and already produced by a variety of companies; however, this same firm may not be willing to share, or cooperate in the development of, a brand new, highly competitive technology unless such a cooperation is part of a strategic alliance relationship. Similarly, a firm may have a joint operation with another for a particular national market, be it the Japanese, Malaysian or Norwegian; yet, these same two firms may never consider cooperating on a global basis and their operations may never pass the borders of a single country, unless the firms are strategic alliance partners.

Most of the companies listed above have important agreements with more than one company. This is not unusual and largely the norm. Corporate management takes the decision to enter into cooperative agreements as an alternative to or complementary mode of expanding the operations on its own. In implementing such a strategy, it may cooperate with one other firm in various fields, but it may also tie up with a number of different firms in different fields at the same time. Often we witness a major strategic alliance between two firms being accompanied by a host of other, less important, cooperative agreements with other firms. However, some firms such as

Olivetti, Fujitsu and Canon have been able to develop major alliances with a deep level of cooperation simultaneously with several partners.

Canon is a good case in point. Canon is in the process of securing its position in global markets and in a broad range of technologies. It has chosen to do so by entering into a number of strategic alliances with firms which have a level of expertise in areas where Canon is weak. By combining Canon's own strengths in the photocopying area of the office automation sector together with European and American companies' expertise in other areas of the same sector, Canon hopes to eventually carve a place for itself in the highly integrated office automation market of the future. At the same time, these alliances are providing Canon special access to national markets where import regulations are formidable or risk to be formidable in the near future. The company is thus using strategic alliances and cooperative ventures as one way of assuring the firm's future growth and expansion.

Quantitative analysis

All of the agreements discussed above represent for the participating firm the contribution of one or many resources at the firm's disposal. The type of contribution made to the agreement is, simultaneously, a reflection of its partners' wants and needs, and of its own expertise in a certain skill area or its comparative advantages from being from a certain nation or having successfully penetrated a certain market. With this in mind, we have classified all of the agreements according to the contribution each party is making to the cooperation. We have chosen as contributions technology, manufacturing (or the product itself), and marketing or distribution capabilities. Where none of these resources is supplied or exchanged, financial compensation is paid in lieu and listed separately. Each number in Figure 3 below represents a contribution by the partners in one area. Multi-faceted relationships have more than one mark. For example, in the Kyocera/Philips agreement, both firms are contributing technological knowledge (one mark in the Tech/Tech box), the firms are jointly manufacturing the product (a second mark in Manu./Manu. box), but the products are only being sold in Japan by Kyocera, thus a third mark in the Japanese Dist., Marketing/European Financial Compensation box.

The strategic alliances identified in list *d* above, all fall in the middle of Figure 3 with predominantly joint technological development, joint manufacturing and joint marketing or distribution (boxes 1, 6, 11).

The large number of agreements which involve joint technological development or exchange is noteworthy. While the majority fall under the umbrella of a strategic alliance, the remaining are agreements between Japanese and Europeans to jointly develop a particular technology or product. There

36

are more than a few of these types of agreements. This supports the general hypothesis that the exchange of technological information is a major motivation for cooperative agreements.

European Companies Japanese Companies	Technology	Production/ Manufacturing	Marketing/ Distribution	Financial Compensation
Technology	(1) 16	(2)	(3)	(4) 5
Production/ Manufacturing	(5) 1	(6) 12	(7) 15	(8) 1
Marketing/ Distribution	(9)	(10) 7	(11) 9	(12) 1
Financial Compensation	(13) 3	(14)	(15) 1	(16)

Figure 3   Contribution of partners to cooperation

The relatively small number of agreements for the Japanese market (box 10), in which the Europeans provide the products or the manufacturing expertise and the Japanese the marketing or distribution expertise, can in part be explained by the fact that a number of such agreements are structured as joint ventures, and thus, in our chart, they appear under joint production and joint distribution/sales. Otherwise, we can comment that the rationale for their creation lies in the closed nature of the Japanese market which makes it more interesting for a European firm to enter this market under the auspices of a marketing/distribution agreement with a Japanese firm.

Having said that, it must be pointed out that there are many agreements which combine only European marketing capabilities and Japanese manufacturing expertise (box 7); their number far outweighs the number of cooperative technological exchange agreements (those not covered by a strategic alliance). They are principally the OEM or OEM-type arrangements discussed in section b. on page 31 above. Their relative abundance, in comparison with similar OEM or distribution agreements for the Japanese market, is certainly a distortion. The Japanese, finding it difficult to sell directly into Europe, have entered into cooperative marketing/distribution/OEM agreements which are at least for the time being more effective, and more favourably viewed by government authorities than their own European-based sales networks. On the chart, when we take away the multiple markings for some of the strategic alliances, the resulting distortion in favour of box 7 — Japanese manufacturing and European marketing — is even more pronounced. This has been done in Figure 4 below.

European Companies / Japanese Companies	Technology	Production/ Manufacturing	Marketing/ Distribution	Financial Compensation
Technology	(1) 6	(2)	(3) 1	(4) 5
Production/ Manufacturing	(5) 1	(6) 6	(7) 15	(8)
Marketing/ Distribution	(9)	(10) 6	(11) 5	(12) 1
Financial Compensation	(13) 3	(14)	(15)	(16)

Figure 4   Principal contribution of partners to cooperation

All in all, these charts support the comments made in (ii) above. There are four basic groups of agreements: those relying on European marketing expertise and Japanese manufacturing expertise, mostly for the European market; those designed to allow Europeans to sell in the Japanese market; those through which technology is transferred; and those agreements which are part of a strategic alliance agreement. The two first groups of agreements are entered into in order to profit from another firm's expertise in a certain skill area or market. They are particularly valuable when the skill area or market is one which would require considerable investment to master and which would not necessarily generate the desired return to the inexperienced firm. In other words, the cooperative agreement serves as a convenient expedient in the normal course of business affairs. Transfer of technology agreements are of a transient nature.

Strategic alliances are different. Those which we have identified in this report, in contrast to OEM, marketing, manufacturing or licencing agreements, cover the full range of joint technological development, joint manufacturing and joint marketing and distribution. More importantly, they are the result of a deliberate policy of the participating firm of growth or globalisation through strategic alliances. Of all of the agreements discussed in this paper, it is this last group of Euro-Japanese agreements that truly merits the name of strategic alliance. They are broad-based and technologically cooperative. They are at least potentially global and they are long-term.

Experiences and perceptions

International agreements: a comparison

(i) Statistical indications
By examining available statistics on cooperative agreements we can see that there are far fewer cooperative agreements between European and Japanese firms than between either of these two parties and the Americans. Information from FOR, a database of agreements in information technology created by Montedison, shows that there were 81 agreements contracted between Japanese and European firms over the period 1982–86, versus 128 American/Japanese agreements and 253 EEC/US agreements. Similar surveys come to the same result.[5]

Moreover, while there is spectacular growth today in inter-European agreements and an increase in such general agreements of more than seven times between 1983 and 1986,[6] the growth in the number of Japanese/European agreements is negligible. It is certain that the increase in inter-European agreements has been fuelled by the EC programmes ESPRIT and RACE and by the approach of 1992 and European union, yet, this does not necessarily explain the lack of cooperative venture activity between Europe and Japan. It cannot be attributed to a lack of interest in foreign partner ventures, because the number of international cooperative agreements as a whole has risen during this period and, in particular, the number of US-European agreements has risen from 32 (1983) to 49 (1986). Nor does the lack of growth appear to be the result of a public manifestation of anti-Japanese sentiment, along the lines of the "buy US" campaign in the United States.

The question therefore is, what motivates a company to enter into an agreement with one company rather than another. More specifically, why is it that Japanese and European firms more often choose to enter into agreements with an American firm rather than with a European or Japanese firm, respectively?

Technological expertise

(ii) Partner selection
In selecting a partner for a cooperative venture, firms have to identify the strengths of those who are potential candidates for an alliance. In terms of technological expertise, American companies' strength in innovation makes these firms attractive partners for cooperative alliances both to Japanese and Europeans.

The Japanese, for all their expertise in product perfection and in manufacturing, continue to lag in breakthrough technologies and are keen to link up with partners in the development of the latest technology. Being large firms themselves, they suffer from well-established bureaucracies which slow them down in an industry which is fast-moving and constantly changing. Smaller American firms, on the other hand, suffer from a lack of manufacturing and marketing resources, but provide an environment in which innovation flourishes.

A cooperative agreement between the two firms, if carefully managed, can plug the small firm into the large resources of the bigger partner and, thus, provide benefits for both. In such a case, the smaller firm becomes a "sub-innovator" similar to a sub-contractor in other industries but European small firms are less prepared to take over such a role. They shy away from agreements with the Japanese and seem to be reluctant to share their technology with them.

Vice versa, the Japanese do not demonstrate enthusiasm for European technological know-how either and have not pursued agreements with small European firms. Present agreements with large European firms do not seem to have been contracted in order to access their technology but rather their marketing networks.

As for the Europeans, they have recently become aware of their weaknesses in the R&D area and are striving to regain earlier strengths. Cooperative agreements with the Americans are seen as an excellent way of initiating this process, as the technologies which are transferred can rapidly put them on an equal footing vis-à-vis the rest of the industry.

Nowhere documented, but well understood, is that the Europeans perceive the Japanese as being less willing to share information or resources with alliance partners than the Americans. The Japanese are takers or absorbers of information whereas the Americans are sharers or just plain talkative.

The Americans themselves are also anxious to gain access to new technologies and appear ready to try a number of sources. On an individual basis, European firms are often viable candidates for cooperative agreements, often because of their expertise in a particular area.

Recently, Americans' respect for Japanese technology has risen. The highly publicised "Japanese threat" in the US has probably served to fuel Americans' interest in the Japanese because it has focused public attention on the extremely viable technological challenge that Japan is posing. This same Japanese challenge is less perceived by European firms operating in fragmented and more protected markets.

Manufacturing expertise

The Japanese are today leading in manufacturing techniques and efficiency. For this reason, both the Americans and the Europeans are interested in learning more about Japanese manufacturing methods. The forming of cooperative agreements is one way of doing so — the Americans view such agreements as an excellent way of learning; the Europeans are more reluctant.

Instead, the Europeans are studying Japanese methods at arm's length. In the interim, the Europeans are "farming out" production to the Japanese in areas where European industry is uncompetitive. A strategic alliance for the purpose of learning about Japanese manufacturing methods is perhaps a last alternative and not a very appealing one. The Europeans are not so hungry for manufacturing knowledge that they are willing to share either market access or technological knowledge in return.

The Americans view Japanese manufacturing expertise with much more probing interest. It represents the first time in decades that a nation has bypassed American technological superiority on a grand scale. Perhaps this fact alone explains the near obsessive interest which many Americans have in this topic today.

There are volumes and volumes on the US market on the Japanese success story, examining their methods from every angle. In addition, there are Japan tours for manufacturing executives; exchange programmes whereby American firms receive Japanese employees, and Japanese firms welcome American employees; or consultancy projects, such as in the steel industry, through which Japanese manufacturing expertise is transferred to the United States.

Last, but by no means least, cooperative ventures and strategic alliances have been formed in line with the proverb, "If you can't beat them, join them". Unable to outmanufacture the Japanese, the Americans are now joining with the Japanese in order to learn directly from them in a cooperative environment. The NUMMI project of GM and Toyota is a good example of such a venture. The Americans are most anxious to learn what the Japanese have to teach them and are willing to exchange technological experience or market access for that information.

Market access

The third major reason for which a company chooses to enter into a cooperative agreement with another is to have access to new markets. These can consist of new market segments in an existing national market and/or of additional national markets, normally represented by the partner's home market or market strongholds. For the partner who receives products for sale in new markets, the agreement represents a horizontal integration in the sense that it enables it to offer a broader product line.

Both the Europeans and the Japanese are attracted by the American market. It is the world's largest borderless market and is homogeneous in nature. There is also a perception that this market is in excellent economic health and will continue to grow for some years to come.

Some of the same could be said for the Japanese market and, indeed, many foreign firms have entered into cooperative agreements in order to have access to the Japanese market. Yet, when compared with the American market, the Japanese market is less appealing to most Europeans, despite the fact that in terms of economic buying power, Japan is no longer behind the US and is ahead of many European countries in terms of GNP per capita. Part of this can be explained by the problems encountered by Western firms in the area of information technology in dealing with the Japanese language, and more specifically with the switch to the Japanese writing of Katakana and Hiragana and its final conversion into Kanji. This requires major efforts in software and hardware development and represents a formidable entry barrier surmountable only by fully committed firms.

The European market is attractive in size, but fragmented. In the information technology sector, the direct and indirect influence of national governments on purchasing decisions is strong, at least stronger than in the US. This requires a differentiated marketing strategy for each market, a difficult task for outsiders to master within a limited time. So far, Japanese subsidiaries in Europe have found it difficult to sell their own products under their own brand names, through their own distribution channels. Cooperative agreements have proven to offer a good solution to these structural barriers, particularly OEM agreements.

The Americans are also attracted by Europe, perhaps more so than the Japanese. They are looking to 1992 and the enhanced possibilities for American products in a standardised, unified European market. Markets in which American firms are not active today, can be accessed through already existing nationally-based US subsidiaries.

Asymmetries in partnerships

(i) Competitive cooperation
It was briefly stated above that international cooperative agreements are often concluded between competitors, a fact which renders the successful negotiation and management of such competitive cooperations, for both or all partners, extremely difficult.

Observations of alliances between competitors have so far shown that the incongruity of objectives of the partners, differences in competences contributed to the partnership, and the diverse ability to learn from another are important factors leading to failure.[7] Failure in this respect is defined as the premature break-up of the partnership, and/or the emergence of one partner as a clear winner over the other.

From this, one can conclude that competitive cooperation should ideally be based on very similar objectives, competences, and learning abilities. Such a situation, however, does not and can not exist. Competitors operate in different environments, and, thus, have their own individual strategic logic. They have different historical backgrounds, different strengths and weaknesses, and different corporate cultures. Even if all these characteristics could be the same at the time of the initial agreement, they would change over time and move in different directions.

Differences are, as such, not problematic. In fact, if partners contributed precisely the same resources and competences, cooperation would, at best, produce scale effects. Synergies, on the other hand, require complementary competences which are therefore much more attractive as a starting point of cooperation. It is only when differences are considerable and structural, i.e. not related to a passing phenomenon, that they threaten the success of a partnership. The threat may come from one partner benefiting more from the joint undertaking than the other, or from a shift of negotiating power from one partner to the other.

Considerable and structural differences between partners which determine the outcome of a cooperative agreement we call asymmetries. Our research and discussions with executives in the IT sector have shown the existence of a number of asymmetries between European and Japanese firms which are either explicit, implicit or based on different management systems.

Explicit asymmetries

(ii) Asymmetries
When partners in an alliance openly acknowledge that they are making a different kind of contribution to their undertakings or have a different status or obligations in the venture, explicit asymmetries come into being. In the Euro-Japanese projects in the IT industry, such asymmetries are apparent when the Japanese partners are provided with access to the European market, while the European partner secures supplies from Japan on a long-term basis. Access to the Japanese market is seldom given, or is not demanded in exchange. The European partner benefits from cost savings or the broadening of its product range, while the Japanese partner expands its foreign markets without transferring manufacturing activities abroad. This enables it to accumulate manufacturing experience, a process which generally leads to lower production costs and a strengthening of the overall competitive

position of the Japanese partner. The European partner, on the other hand, works on the last parts of the value added chain, i.e. marketing and sales, and eventually on system integration for the specific product or product range. It is doubtful that this activity can fertilise other parts of the firm in such a way that the partner's overall competitive position is strengthened.

Even if such cross-fertilisation is achieved, the long-term benefits for the European partner from selling Japanese equipment are questionable. If it is very successful in penetrating the market, the Japanese partner will sooner or later decide to go it alone and set up a distribution network based on the reputation gained with the help of the European partner. Such a development is neither new, surprising nor unique to Europe or Japan. It touches on the very nature of distribution agreements between firms and does not merit the comparison with the Trojan horse so often depicted by Western politicians and writers.[8]

The more products that are sold under direct or indirect OEM agreements in such scenarios, the more feasible it becomes to switch to own marketing strategies under one's own name, and the less the Japanese producer depends on his European distributor. On the other hand, by gaining more manufacturing expertise, the Japanese partner will not only be able to reduce his cost and improve the quality, but will be increasingly capable of developing related new products which attract the European partner to purchase even more from Japan. It will thus transfer more manufacturing activity to Japan and become even more dependent on the Japanese supplier. This expanding asymmetry, called "an extended dance of death"[9] is inherent in all market based cooperative agreements aimed at the European market. It provides an in-built threat to the European partners in all of those alliances and, as such, a risk in the relationship between Europe and Japan.

K. Ohmae's concept of the 'Triad Powers' requires future global competitors to be present in Japan, Europe and the USA. In obtaining access to Europe and the US without getting access to the Japanese market even through alliances, European and American competitors are reduced to regional players, with the only global players being the Japanese. Such a development may not be inevitable. European firms, however, have not been successful in demanding reciprocity, a term now frequently used in trade talks and reflecting today's perceived need to obtain market access through political pressure rather than, or in addition to, negotiations at company level.

Implicit asymmetries

Implicit asymmetries are not written into cooperative agreements, but provide the motivation for the firms to associate. They are based on the firms' strategic intent or vision, and are rarely openly spelled out. Even if an interpretation appears to be easy, due to an obvious strategic intent, the existence of a "hidden agenda" cannot be ruled out. As interviews show, the purpose of strategic alliances is differently assessed by the partner firms concerned, and even by individual managers working together for either one or the other firm.

The explicit asymmetries of market access versus manufacturing expertise described above have led to the assumption that Japanese partners use cooperative agreements as a way to expand and to reach global leadership, while European partners see them as a rescue anchor to stem decline.[10]

Such an interpretation seems justified since, in most markets, Japanese firms are fast growing latecomers who are taking market share from long-established moderately growing or stagnating European (or American) competitors. The example most frequently cited in this context is that of the alliance between British Leyland/Rover and Honda.

European executives in information technology, however, do not agree to the existence of such implicit asymmetry. While acknowledging the shift of key manufacturing activities to Japan and their own role as market access providers, they consider software and system integration the key to their customers and do not mind their Japanese partners producing the hardware. The apparent weakness of the Japanese firms, at least abroad, in software, and the increase of software expenses versus hardware in total IT costs reassures them of not being "hollowed-out" by their Japanese partners. In arguing this way, they assume that the Japanese will not be able to overcome their software problems in the foreseeable future and, thus, will not be able to erode their European customer base. Different business cultures and language difficulties are cited in support of this view.

It is probably for this last reason that Europeans do not feel misused by their Japanese partners as proxies in the global battle with IBM. Such an allegation can easily be put forward by believers in the "Japan Inc." concept who can point out that all major European computer firms are tied to Japanese partners and face IBM as their most important competitor, in their national markets. With an overall market share of 50 per cent in Europe, IBM has no need to cooperate with European companies, either in the hardware, or in the software area. The European firms, on the other hand, believe in their marketing strength and their software competences. They look for partners in need of or depending on those strengths and providing other expertise such as in manufacturing. Following this logic, Euro-Japanese alliance should provide an ideal "strategic fit".

Two questions, however, remain for the future. One is the impact of the wider usage of standardised software systems such as UNIX on the industry, which so far has extensively used firm-specific software as a way of differentiation and as entry barriers for competitors into the territory of existing customers. Even a partial lowering of these entry barriers may re-emphasize the value of hardware as the most important competitive weapon. Secondly, the importance of chip technology for both the computer and the telecommunication sector must be considered with regard to the continuing trend towards higher integration, to the opportunities to transfer software on to chips, and to compensate for software weaknesses with greater hardware power.

Managerial asymmetries

Managerial attitudes, systems or cultures are formed by the environment in which an organisation operates as well as by individuals or groups. They are implicit, and influence managers' decisions substantially, often unconsciously. If one looks at firms in groups such as the Japanese IT firms and the European IT firms, the influence of individuals can be neglected and the impact of national culture on managerial behaviour can be studied.

Much has been written on Japanese management, and despite many contradictions and exceptions to the rule, there is an acknowledgement of certain differences in managerial culture between Japan and the West, the latter often mistakenly identified as American management. A European managerial culture as such does not exist, as the behaviour of managers differs significantly from country to country, or at least between those from the Northern and the Latin countries.

The assessment of managerial asymmetries between Europe and Japan therefore cannot be very specific and must contain generalisations, but it may nevertheless provide us with valuable insights into the "inner workings" of Euro-Japanese strategic alliances.

One of the striking features of Japanese management is the role of information as a strategic resource. It puts emphasis on collecting, diffusing and analysing information systematically. Information in Japan is shared internally and is a property of the organization. Information in European firms is often obtained by chance, not diffused, and used to strengthen the position of the individual. Related to this is the inherent Japanese urge to learn continuously from others which has no equivalent either in the US or in Europe.

Both aspects are vital for cooperative undertakings between European and Japanese firms. If in an alliance, new knowledge is emerging or existing knowledge made available to the partners, and only the Japanese side is interested in collecting and diffusing it, the benefit for this partner will invariably be much greater.

This process is aggravated by the fact that Japanese firms have not much hesitation to adapt foreign know-how, while in European firms the "not invented here" syndrome often leads to the rejection of new ideas from the outside and, as a consequence, to unnecessary delays and/or development costs.

This asymmetry in fertilising or leveraging other activities of the firms provides the partners in an alliance with very different benefits and can lead

— over the life of a joint undertaking — to significant shifts in competitive position, even if the direct benefits from the alliance are equally divided between the partners.

The long-term approach to business is another characteristic of the Japanese firm, often contrasted with the short-term outlook of Western firms geared towards quarterly or yearly results. This is an area where European firms certainly differ from American ones, and are to some extent, more similar to their Japanese partners. Asymmetries exist nevertheless. Constant organisational learning in the Japanese firms combined with a strong strategic intent to expand globally have resulted in an endless process of new product developments, matched by the European partners neither in volume, depth nor speed. It is especially the latter aspect which seems to be important in the fast changing information technology sector which requires from competitors today economies of scale, of scope, and of speed.

(iii) Management and perceptions
Marketing/manufacturing-based strategic alliances between European and Japanese IT firms show a greater degree of asymmetry mainly due to explicit arrangements. This would argue in favour of joint R&D-based cooperative agreements.

These joint undertakings, however, tend to create more problems in defining common ground and destination than the other ones. New developments by definition lead into uncharted waters. The targeted output is difficult to specify, as is the required input of resources and time.

Projects of this nature are ambiguous, and require constant adjustment to meet the needs of the partners and the task, as well as to the changing environment. The Japanese are known to be able to cope well with uncertainty and to react with flexibility. Not all European firms have this capacity.

The management of alliances requires full attention and the will for constant bargaining and re-bargaining with one's partner. Under these circumstances, excellent managers are needed on both sides to steer the partnership through the complexities of inherent instability.

The outcome of a cooperative agreement may be judged by comparing costs and benefits, but can rarely be accurately measured due to the multifaceted character of the projects. Perceptions of the outcome therefore vary from person to person, especially when taking into account the effects of organisational learning and the leveraging of benefits through the organisations of the respective partners. This is naturally a subjective process, made more difficult by the fact that benefits may not only be perceived in absolute but also in relative terms, i.e. in comparing one's own benefits with those obtained by the partner.[11]

European managers interviewed somehow admit that their Japanese partners benefit more from cooperative ventures than their own firms. Reasons given are mostly emotional and range from accusations of unfair practices by their Japanese partners to the admittance of their own failure in managing these complex relationships. The latter perception is more frequently found among managers directly involved in partnerships with Japanese firms. The Japanese managers who were interviewed were less open in their judgement, but showed general disappointment and tended to belittle the competences of the European partners.

This provides a dangerous breeding ground for using outside pressures and unfair practices to strengthen the bargaining power within the partnership.

Notes

1. Turner, L. 'Industrial Collaboration with Japan'. *Euro-Asia Business Review*. INSEAD, Fontainebleau. July 1987. pp.11-26.
2. Contractor, F. J. and Lorange, P. 'Why should firms cooperate? The Strategy and Economic Basis for Cooperative Ventures'. *Cooperative Strategies in International Business*. Lexington Books, New York. 1988. pp.3-28.
3. Ohmae, K. 'Companies without Countries'. *McKinsey Quarterly*. No. 3. 1987.
4. Ohmae, K. *Triad Power*. Free Press, New York. 1985.
5. FOR. 'Joint Ventures and Inter-Company Agreements: an Introduction to a Comparative Survey in High Technology Sectors'. Presented at 1986 Lucca (Italy) conference on Technical Cooperation and International Competitiveness. See also: Reseau. *Draft Report for the Industry Committee*. OECD.
6. 'Keeping Europe on the IT Map'. *Financial Times*, London. 18 May 1988.
7. Doz, Y., Hamel. G. and Prahalad, C. K. 'Strategic Partnerships: Success or Surrender? The Challenge of Competitive Collaboration'. Revised AIB conference paper. 1986/7.
8. Reich, R. B. and Mankin, D. D. 'Joint ventures with Japan give away our future'. *Harvard Business Review*. March-April 1986.
   James, B. G. *Trojan Horse. The Ultimate Challenge to Western Industry*. Mercury, London. 1989.
9. Reich, R. B. and Mankin, D. D. op.cit. p.85.
10. Doz, Y. et al. op.cit.
11. Doz, Y. and Shuen, A. 'From Intent to Outcome: a Process Framework of Partnerships'. INSEAD, Fontainebleau. Working Paper No. 88/46.

3 Internationalisation strategies of German firms: three industries in the Ruhr region

GÜNTER HEIDUK
DUISBURG UNIVERSITY

Stages of internationalisation

The internationalisation of companies is brought about by wishing to take advantage of the competitive opportunities in foreign markets. To achieve this, the following are the most important prerequisites needed:–

(i)   the framework of conditions must be such as to allow access to foreign markets.
(ii) there must be a potential for competing with companies in other countries.

Because of the immense complexity of competitive market processes it is not possible to list all of the activities companies should engage in, in order to gain competitive advantages in international trade. But fundamentally, it is true to say that all of the activities companies engage in are potentially suited for achieving this end. To name but a few of these activities: information, skills in buying and producing, in selling, in financing and in management (planning, organisation, company strategy) — all these can decide whether a company is successful in foreign markets or not,[1] though in the final analysis it is market conditions themselves that will determine which company characteristics best fit in with taking advantage of a competitive situation.

Taking account of the framework of conditions, which differs sharply from one country to another, it is unlikely that a company can within a given period and at any one time take advantage of all the differing com-

49

petitive situations prevailing in the various countries. This would also explain the different periods of time needed by companies to adjust to particular markets. In analysing empirical models, science tries to ascertain how best to achieve an optimum advantage of international markets by applying criteria such as the employment of trade, direct investment, or licences. It would be short-sighted to make decisions on such matters from a purely cost-orientated point of view, as factors of quality, like non-tariff barriers, for example, are steadily gaining influence. This last point seems also to have been the reason why companies have since the beginning of the 1980s increasingly turned to finding "new" forms of foreign cooperation.

In recent years, reference has been made in the relevant literature to the way in which the focus of internationalisation strategies has been shifting. It is obvious, too, that since the beginning of the 1980s there has been an increase in the creation of new forms of foreign cooperation, though it is difficult to give exact figures. This is unfortunate, because it means that as yet there is no empirical basis for working out a theory of internationalisation. However, the quite significant expansion in the companies' scope for activity in international markets is making it necessary to design models based on empirical analysis.

Very roughly, the changes in the emphasis on foreign economic transactions over the years can be summarised as follows:

- Export phase (1945–approx. 1965).
- Multinationalisation of companies, especially through direct investment (1965–beginning of the 1980s).
- "New" forms of internationalisation (since the beginning of the 1980s).

The export phase was shaped by the following two developments:

(i) To start off, "classical" inter-sectoral, international trade between the industrial and the developing countries increased. Then, growth was impeded by, among other things, savings in the employment of raw materials and agricultural protectionism in the industrial countries, and a shortage of purchasing power and foreign exchange, as well as import subsidy policies, in the developing countries.

(ii) As a result of their increasing industrial capacity and their potential demand for raw materials, the industrial countries then proceeded in a sort of valve effect to make use of the markets of other industrial countries. A very important consequence of this expanding intra-industrial trade between the industrial countries was the pressure, though hardly noticeable at the time, for structures to be brought into line with this development, as in the following quotation:–

The main strategies of internationally active (export) firms are, on the one hand, specialisation, and on the other hand, product differentiation carried out within the framework of monopolist and oligarchic market forms, thus simultaneously making possible innovative processes and mass production without having to engage in far-reaching decisions about new locations. There are consequently no problem-laden transfers of production or regional deindustrialising processes involved.[2]

The high growth dynamism engendered as a result of a coincidental meeting of factors pointing in the same direction, as for example, the reduction of customs duty within the GATT framework, has meant a mobilisation of advantages in location and has created and strengthened a relatively simple pattern of international trade. The more industries became caught in the maelstrom of export-led growth, the less it was necessary for companies to be active. This did not only apply to large companies, but it included small and medium-sized enterprises as well.

The direct-investment phase was not least the result of

– increased efforts to tap and secure inexpensive foreign resources (raw materials, labour)
– pressure to fit in after the abolition of fixed exchange rates in 1973
– the jumping of trade barriers which a number of industrial countries had erected after the first oil crisis

Since the middle of the 1970s European companies in particular have increasingly used multinationalisation as a vehicle towards creating and securing advantage in international competition. Factors that had previously determined the way in which specific countries had acted to remain internationally competitive lost some of their importance and so did whole ranges of industries. The processes of international competition are increasingly determined by quite complex company strategies, including the variability of location.

At the beginning of the 1980s this development came under the influence of

– the second oil crisis and its consequences
– a reduction in marginal productivity, or rather an increase in total cost in the development of new locations
– a rapid decrease in favoured positions because of innovations in the information-, communication- and transport systems
– the financial bottlenecks which many companies faced
– problems in connection with the strong growth of international indebtedness (non-tariff barriers, restrictive investment conditions, foreign exchange controls)
– aggressive industrialising policies practiced by some of the new industrialising countries on the one hand, and defensive industrial preservation policies in some of the developed countries on the other

Much points in the direction that, in this latest phase of international structural change, the criterion deciding success or failure covers a complex range of factors, from hardware and software components to a company-specific know-how core, in association with a consequential pursuit of utilizing to the maximum the options offered by the world economy as a whole.

In contrast to the age of classical interdependence, when product differentiation and export specialisation were as a rule the dominant features of company strategy, and in contrast to the multinational stage, when company expansion and control were considered of more importance than direct investments, today the possibilities of developing company-specific core skills along with their international utilisation and deployment are far more varied, more complex and more difficult. Complementary to or as a subsidy for the investment orientation of the traditional direct investments practised by the multinational companies, the aims of the 'new forms' of internationalisation again increasingly include contract-based cooperation types, such as joint ventures, turnkey and equipment sales, licence- and franchising contracts, management contracts and international sub-contracting. They also reflect the tendency of wishing to do away with production transfers in the narrow sense and to internationalise practically all of a company's operations instead. Together with the new technological processes which make it possible to combine flexibility and automation in such a way as not to hinder mass production, 'learning curves' and product cycles restrict the scope of action — as has previously been the case — such multi-dimensionality of international utilisation will also mean that the multinational companies and the small and medium-sized firms will draw closer together.[3]

The end of the 1980s seems to be heading towards a considerable intensification of foreign economic relations between East and West owing to the liberalising and opening policies in Eastern Europe, which to begin with will surely be reflected in the increased use of new forms of cooperation.[4]

Finally, the abolition of trade barriers in the Common Market envisaged at the end of 1992, will no doubt have a positive influence on the tendency for Common Market companies to increasingly make use of foreign cooperation. An investigation by the research institute Ifo questioning 1,400 companies in the whole of the Federal Republic of Germany about their plans and preparations for 1992, showed that the companies in adjusting their production strategies were much more frequently prepared to cooperate with foreign companies than to transfer their production totally abroad, or to increase their production capacity at home. In opening up the envisaged new European markets, companies are hoping — and above all those with less than 50 employees — to make use of the cooperating partner's marketing system in the particular foreign country concerned.[5]

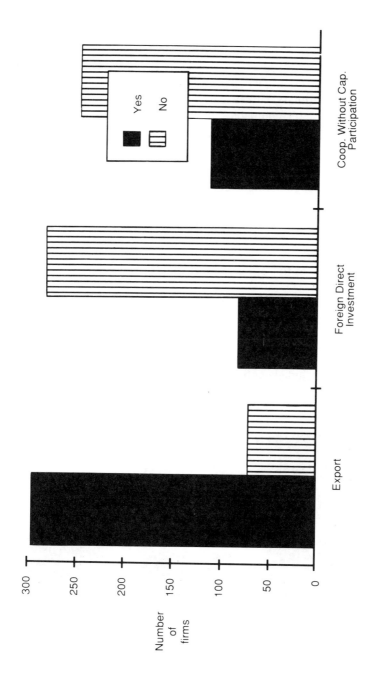

Figure 1   How firms make use of internationalisation

Fundamental data underlining the empirical study

The aim of the empirical study was to comprehensively list the development and present level of foreign economic activity engaged in by the various companies. To achieve this, it was necessar to interpret the term 'internationalisation' quite broadly, in order to include all possible types of cross-border company activity, whether it be a first-time or follow-up venture.

This was a primary survey carried out by written questionaire in two stages covering 803 companies in the Ruhr industrial region from May 1988 to January 1989. The following were surveyed:–

– Chemical industry
– Electrical engineering
– Mechanical engineering

At the first/(second) stage of the survey, the response rate was 45.7 per cent (43.1 per cent of answers at the first stage).

Extent and type of foreign economic activity

(i) Forms of internationalisation

Of the companies which responded, 81.5 per cent are active abroad. Although export is the dominant form of internationalisation (81.2 per cent), at least 22.6 per cent of companies had engaged in direct investment, while as many as 30.2 per cent had concluded cooperative agreements without a capital share.

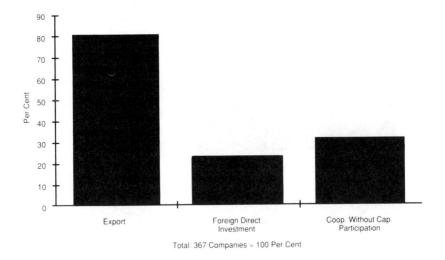

Total: 367 Companies = 100 Per Cent

Figure 2   Percentage of firms making use of internationalisation

54

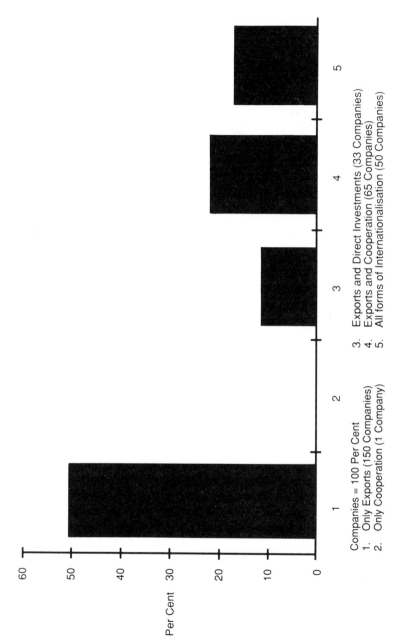

Companies = 100 Per Cent
1. Only Exports (150 Companies)
2. Only Cooperation (1 Company)
3. Exports and Direct Investments (33 Companies)
4. Exports and Cooperation (65 Companies)
5. All forms of Internationalisation (50 Companies)

Figure 3   Diversification of company-level activities

Taking all companies in the Ruhr region as a whole, exports in mechanical engineering stood at 40.8 per cent, in the chemical industry at 39.3 per cent, and in electrical engineering at 18.8 per cent, as shown in Rath's work of 1988.

The following is the result of a detailed analysis of the various forms of internationalisation studied:–

Rank	Forms of internationalisation	Number of companies
1	Exports	298
2	Licences	80
3	100%-owned subsidiaries	62
4	Co-Production	28
5	a) Managerial and technical advisory contracts	27
	b) Turnkey projects	27
6	a) Majority joint ventures	22
	b) Minority joint ventures	22
7	Sub-contracting	19
8	50%-owned joint ventures	17
9	Other forms of cooperation	13

Approximately one third of the companies which responded had made use of the new forms of foreign cooperation, though as a rule several forms of foreign cooperation, though as a rule several forms were being used simultaneously. With almost 90 per cent, cooperation without a special share is dominant, while only about 35 per cent of the companies had concluded joint venture agreements.

The special role being played by licences is illustrated by the fact that they are issued in connection with other foreign activities. Thus, licences are issued to joint ventures or are brought in as a form of share in a business. The survey confirms the trends roughly sketched out at the beginning with regard to the changes in international strategies: in the majority of companies, export-related activities have existed for well over 20 years, while wholly-owned subsidiaries were mainly founded during the 1970s; since that time also, forms of cooperation without a capital share have been on the increase.

(ii) Regional spread of foreign economic activity

Foreign economic activity in the various countries and regions is divided as follows:–

– It is in the industrial countries where the emphasis on foreign economic activity is concentrated. Almost 100 per cent of all of the firms engaged in foreign trade abroad are to be found in this category, with 40 per cent active in Eastern Europe and 40 per cent in the newly industrialising countries (NICs), while developing countries only account for about 30 per cent of contacts

- The companies active in these various countries and regions almost without exception choose exports as their main strategy. When other forms of internationalisation are chosen, these are found most frequently in other industrial countries rather than in Eastern Europe or the NICs and developing countries

- Internationalisation strategies and foreign activities chosen by Western companies vary according to country and region. There is no such thing as a comprehensive internationalisation strategy for developing countries or for countries within the Eastern bloc.

The form of internationalisation most frequently found in all the countries and regions involved is a combined use of exports and cooperation, though in Eastern Europe and the developing countries this combination is of more importance than in the industrial or the newly industrialising countries.

(iii) Industry-specific exceptions

Even though the three industries concerned showed slight differences in the intensity of their foreign engagement, generally speaking, the profile of their internationalisation did not diverge significantly. Electrical engineering, as compared to the other two, has the weakest internationalisation profile, but in all three industries exporting as the only form of foreign activity is encountered most frequently. Exports and cooperation each occupy second place in the ranking of foreign activity. In each of the three industries at least two thirds of the companies are active in other industrial countries. It is remarkable though, that it is mechanical engineering which has the largest spread of foreign activity, both in regional as well as in factual terms. Finally, it could be shown that in their foreign engagements companies as a rule stuck to their original line of business. Only investments and cooperation concluded with the trading and marketing sector reach a share of approximately 16 per cent or 19 per cent respectively of the particular form of internationalisation.

(iv) Correlation between company size and internationalisation

There is a significant correlation between the size of a company and its foreign engagement. Small and medium-sized companies (SMCs) are usually far less active in foreign countries, and it emerged that their activities are more often limited to exports as the only form of internationalisation.

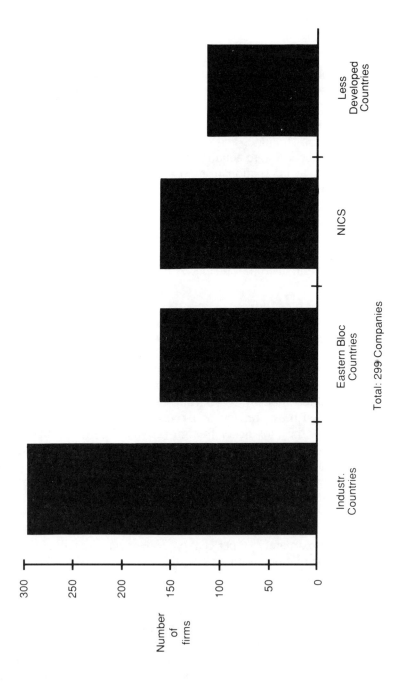

Figure 4 Regional structure of foreign involvement

Total: 299 Companies

Number of firms

300 — 250 — 200 — 150 — 100 — 50 — 0

Industr. Countries   Eastern Bloc Countries   NICS   Less Developed Countries

On average their rate of exports is smaller than that of large companies. And as far as founding 100%-owned subsidiaries and majority joint ventures was concerned, SMCs occupy a relatively weak position.

The foreign engagement of small and medium-sized companies is largely concentrated on industrial countries. Only a small percentage of SMCs are engaged in developing countries.

(v) Experience in foreign trade and internationalisation profile

The way internationalisation is conducted is obviously influenced by experience in foreign trade. Experience is measured, on the one hand, by the rate of exports and, on the other hand, by the number of years a company has been engaged in export activity (average 1985–1987).

It became apparent that the rate of exports is higher the longer a company has been engaged in exports. A rate of over 30 per cent is reached by companies exporting for at least eleven years.

The higher the volume of exports, the more other forms of internationalisation are also used. Cooperation without a capital share is realised already after an export activity of 0–5 years, while 100%-owned subsidiaries are founded after 6–10 years in foreign economic activity. Joint ventures, however, are only founded after 11–15 years of experience in foreign trade.

(vi) Future steps towards internationalisation

The following developments can be observed:–

– Companies already active in foreign trade abroad are determined to intensify their engagement

– Companies that have so far only concentrated on the home market do not as a rule intend to change their strategy

– Companies solely engaged in exporting either wished to limit their foreign activities or to start concentrating on contract-based cooperation

– The direct investment picture is equally diversified. While the founding of 100%-owned subsidiaries will quite likely decrease in the future, new joint ventures are being planned

– SMCs especially would find cooperation without a capital share a worthwhile objective, setting great store by the signing of licencing agreements

– The wish to intensify cooperation with foreign companies is concentrated in Common Market countries, thus indicating how adjustment to the abolition of trade barriers and frontiers in the Common Market by January 1, 1993, is influencing company strategy

– It can be presumed that some companies will replace the traditional

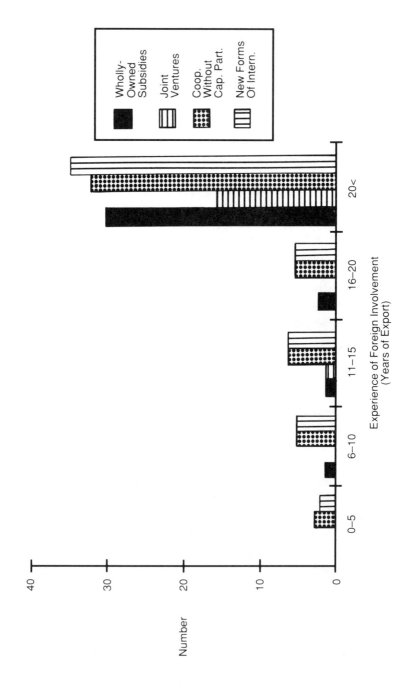

Figure 5   Correlation between foreign trade experience and internationalisation

forms of foreign engagement with joint ventures and/or forms of cooperation without a capital share

Motives for utilizing the new forms of company cooperation

Motive analysis shows that securing and opening up foreign markets is the dominant motive for initiating and founding foreign cooperative agreements. This is also confirmed by the kinds of goods produced within a given cooperative project. The supply of the local markets with goods from such a project as being complementary to or a subsidy for goods exported directly from the Ruhrgebiet itself is seen as being of more importance than supplying third country markets or the German market. In addition to marketing motives, it is furthermore the use of (non-technological) knowledge and the ability of the local partner in the country of cooperation, and commercial utilisation in a foreign country of one's own technologies, which are considered important when concluding foreign cooperative agreements.

The international application of any other (non-technological) knowledge and abilities by Ruhrgebiet companies proved to be a relatively insignificant point in the motive analysis. To make use of the foreign partner's technological know-how is of importance only to SMCs. Likewise, to think that foreign cooperation is founded on a defensive reaction to existing limitations on trade and restrictive investment policies is, on the whole, of little significance. However, for SMCs and for companies which have concluded cooperation agreements outside the industrial countries, new forms of company cooperation do serve as a way of getting round trade and investment restrictions. Viewed as a whole, though, the motive structure for all three company categories studied does not show any great deviation. There is, however, no definite proof of a connection between the motives for cooperation and the regional orientation of a company's foreign engagement.

Company-specific advantages in international competition

The analysis dealing with company-specific advantages tried to cover all those factors pointing towards the existence of, or possible potential for, specific built-in advantages in international competition. In addition to being able to produce a wide variety of goods and having a high level of technological know-how in the area of product as well as production technology — the existence of which can be deduced from other details in the questionnaire — factors, such as product quality, reliability of supply and service were above all considered by companies to be strong points in their favour.

Although in actual fact the level of 'points in favour' in any of the

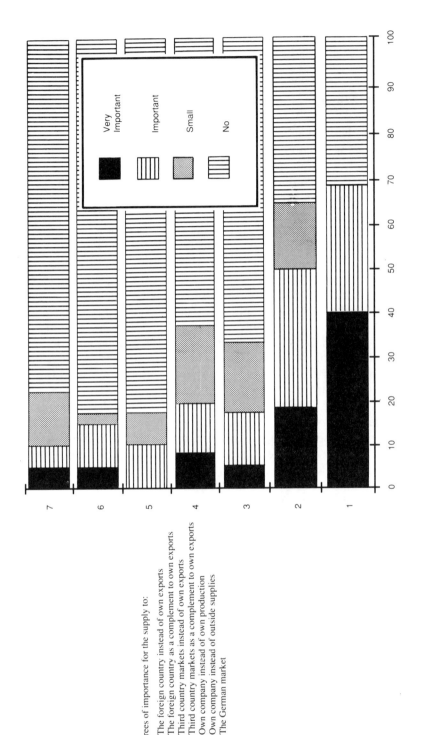

Degrees of importance for the supply to:

1. The foreign country instead of own exports
2. The foreign country as a complement to own exports
3. Third country markets instead of own exports
4. Third country markets as a complement to own exports
5. Own company instead of own production
6. Own company instead of outside supplies
7. The German market

Figure 6   Market orientation of foreign cooperation

particular factors increases with the size of the company, the ranking of company-specific advantages remains to a large extent unchanged. Companies having wholly-owned subsidiaries generally reach a higher level of points in favour than do companies with joint ventures and forms of foreign cooperation without capital share; while still being in a comparatively advantageous position vis-à-vis firms solely engaged in exports. This is shown by a cross-tabulation of the corresponding variables.

As expected, in the opinion of big companies, their particular company-specific economies of scale are a strong point in their favour. The SMCs thought economies of scale were of much less importance as far as their own competitiveness was concerned. The differences in assessing the question of technology were also significant: since about 90 per cent of big companies, one third of small firms and two thirds of medium-sized enterprises considered a lead in technology to be a company-specific advantage. SMCs, on the other hand, considered the ability to adjust to changes in market conditions to be a real advantage, while big companies did not value this factor very highly.

Advantages and disadvantages of the new forms of cooperation

Companies will only conclude cooperative agreements with foreign partners if net advantages are to be gained. According to the companies surveyed, without taking into account their actual level of internationalisation, it is the local partner's knowledge of the market which above all makes foreign cooperation attractive. Also the fact that dealings with local authorities were made easier was often mentioned as a point in favour of foreign cooperation. Interestingly though, companies with no experience of foreign cooperation evaluated the advantages more highly than did companies which had already concluded cooperative agreements. While aware of the advantages, companies also mentioned what they considered to be disadvantages of the new forms of company cooperation; namely the limitations put on supervision and decision-making processes, as well as the need to show consideration for the interests of the partner.

Insufficient means of supervision are seen to be strongly correlated with another disadvantage, namely the risk of losing company-specific know-how. As was the case with the advantages, companies having no cooperative agreements mentioned what they viewed as disadvantages more frequently than did companies which had experience of foreign cooperative activity.

Despite the fact that limited supervision was generally viewed as a disadvantage of foreign cooperation, further analysis showed that even companies having no capital share in these new forms of company cooperation nevertheless quite often have a sufficient measure of supervision. Accord-

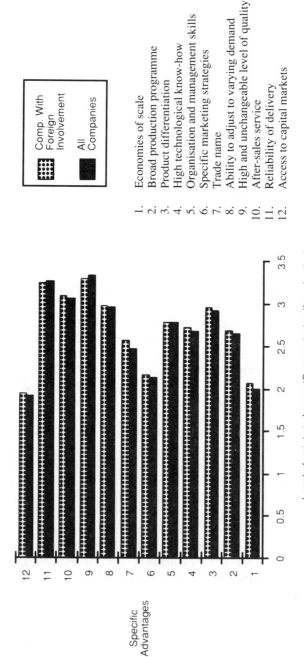

Figure 7 Potential company-specific advantages

Legend:

- Comp. With Foreign Involvement
- All Companies

Specific Advantages

Level of points in favour (Companies' self-evaluation)

1. Economies of scale
2. Broad production programme
3. Product differentiation
4. High technological know-how
5. Organisation and management skills
6. Specific marketing strategies
7. Trade name
8. Ability to adjust to varying demand
9. High and unchangeable level of quality
10. After-sales service
11. Reliability of delivery
12. Access to capital markets

ing to the companies surveyed, supervision is not only exercised through the holding of capital — even though companies having majority joint ventures more often have total or at least a sufficient amount of supervision than do companies having minority joint ventures or forms of cooperation without a capital share — but supervision can also be effected by the way in which the particular cooperative agreement is worked out, and by filling key positions in the companies concerned with own personnel.

Furthermore, the analysis focused on how far foreign cooperative agreements involved know-how transfer to the foreign partner and how up-to-date the technology passed on actually was. It transpired that within the framework of cooperation most companies pass on either product- or production technology or other technological know-how. Since, in the majority of cases, the same goods are produced and the same production processes are used as in the Ruhrgebiet itself, and since the companies concerned evaluated both the level as well as the speed of developing their product- and production technologies to be quite high, it is not true to say that the new forms of company cooperation only involve the transfer of out-of-date and mature technologies. Although this has quite often been claimed in the literature, supported in part by empirical research, the data collected for the Ruhrgebiet do not bear out this hypothesis.

There arises the question, however, of whether it is sensible to transfer the most modern technologies to countries having a low level of development in this field. The analysis dealing with the problems in connection with foreign cooperation quite clearly shows that approximately one quarter of companies cooperating with other firms abroad found the partner's inability to adapt the transferred technologies to the required needs a real obstacle. And as far as cooperation with partners outside the industrial countries was concerned the percentage was even higher. The higher the level of technology transferred, and the lower the level of technology in the country of cooperation, the more there is a need for a simultaneous transfer of personnel. But it is the shortage of qualified German personnel to be assigned abroad which has shown itself to be the most serious problem for companies cooperating with foreign forms.

The second most frequently found problem regarding companies' involvement with new forms of company cooperation is a deficiency in information, while problems of financing are of minor importance.

Regarding problems in the host country, language difficulties and difficulties in dealing with local authorities feature prominently. Conditions imposed regarding 'local content' are not of major importance, according to the survey, but they are increasingly an obstacle to cooperation for companies undertaking turnkey projects abroad. Here, the quality of labour and of local product content often leave much to be desired and are two of the most serious problems in overseas cooperation. Generally speaking, these kinds of obstacles generate problems on both sides.

Because working relations in foreign joint ventures reach high levels of intensity, most companies with this type of foreign engagement experience problems more frequently than companies engaged in cooperation without a capital share. In fact the German joint venture partner complained more often about not being able to find a suitable partner than did the other groups. When analysing the problems and their frequency according to the region and location of cooperation, it was found that companies cooperating with partners outside the industrial nations mentioned these problems more often than those cooperating within the industrial countries.

A number of companies had not been able to realise cooperative projects they had planned because of internal obstacles or because of problems abroad. Regarding internal problems, a shortage of qualified personnel for employment abroad was once again the reason for abandoning overseas engagements; reinforcing the point that foreign cooperation is only possible if there is a suitable partner in the country in question. Comparing the firms having experience in cooperation with those having none, the latter contained a much higher proportion of firms that thought the absence of a suitable partner would be a real problem for companies cooperating internationally.

Some conclusions

(i) Internationalisation strategies should be developed by analysing companies' core abilities and advantages, including the way in which these should best be utilised for foreign business

(ii) Experience has shown that company-specific core abilities are not distributed evenly over all areas of operation

(iii) By analysing the factors which have made a finished product competitive in the export market, it would be possible to put together a quality table listing company-specific core abilities

(iv) The particular competitive factors could then be made use of by assigning an optimum of suitable instruments to them

(v) By taking account of the framework of conditions varying from country to country, it would then be possible to develop internationalisation strategies containing a bundle of company- and country-specific proposals and measures

(vi) It seems that foreign cooperation is best suited to exploiting to the maximum the complex area of company-internal and company-external factors having an influence on international competitiveness

(vii) Since in the competitive process these factors are constantly changing, internationalisation strategies, too, are subject to change. To limit the duration of cooperative agreements is therefore of great importance

(viii) Cooperation can, by mobilising company-specific core abilities, open up the internationalisation potential of small and medium-sized companies in a much more diversified way than would as a rule be the case with exports or direct investments

(ix) The putting together of a company-specific mixture and the feasibility of applying it to the various alternatives in choosing particular forms of internationalisation is an open field for the development of theory

(x) The search for the most suitable cooperative partner is the central practical problem in expounding such a theory of internationalisation.

Notes

1. Borner, Silvio. 'Drei Grundperspektiven zur Interpretation des weltwirtschaftlichen Strukturwandels'. *Aussenwirtschaft*, 39. Jg. (1984). pp.219–41, here p.221.
2. Ibid. pp.230–1.
3. Heiduk, G., Kadyke, H. and Rath, H. 'Trade Relations and Industrial Cooperation Between The People's Republic Of Poland And The Federal Republic Of Germany'. *Monografie I Opracowania 297*. Szola Glowna Planowania Statystyki, Warsaw. 1989.
4. Penzkofer, E. T. 'Unternehmensstrategie und europäischer Binnenmarkt'. *Ifo-Schnelldienst*, 42. Jg. (1989), Nr. 11, pp.11–4.
5. Ibid.

4 Technology transfer by German small and medium-sized enterprises to developing countries

B. KUMAR AND H. STEINMANN
BUNDESWEHR UNIVERSITY AND UNIVERSITY OF
ERLANGEN-NUREMBERG

Introduction and method

Using empirical findings, the experience of German small and medium-sized enterprises (SMEs) in carrying out technology transfer to industrialising or developing countries is analysed. Technology transfer is understood as exchange of tangible and non-tangible goods e.g. technological hardware, technical and management know-how, with equity and non-equity forms of international cooperation e.g. direct investments, licencing, management contract etc.

The analysis draws on an empirical study of 13 German SMEs that were identified from several sources e.g. Chambers of Commerce, as having technology transfer agreements with firms in Argentina, Brazil, India, Mexico, Singapore and South Korea as recipient countries. The firms were interviewed by the authors in 1988 on the basis of a questionnaire developed in accordance with the conceptual framework below.

The sample includes a total of 20 cases of technology transfer, since some of the 13 firms had more than one operation in the recipient countries. The case data have been aggregated to present an overall picture. Where variances between individual cases are of importance, for instance according to recipient countries, they are pointed out.

Obviously the sample may not suffice to give results representative of the total of German SMEs engaged in overseas technology transfer operations but, as well as giving a picture of the sample, the results do have the heuristic function of generating hypotheses.

The conceptual framework

During the past years quite a lot of consideration has been given to international technology transfer in the literature. The important features of these studies can be summarised in two ways:– firstly, international technology transfer analysed mainly within the context of the multinational enterprise (MNE); and secondly, in most cases the specific question under consideration is the motivation issue. Recently the focus has been put on technology transfer by SMEs, see especially the UNCTAD research[1], where again firms' motivation has been a predominant issue; being of course the initiating factor and also an aspect which can be given extensive and sound treatment within the existing framework of direct investment theories[2].

Technology transfer is, however, a complex issue consisting of a wider range of problems. These can be put together in a concept consisting of three connected elements described below.

The first element pertains to the corporate characteristics of the suppliers of technology. In our case the focus is on German SMEs, which we define as firms with 500-1000 employees in the parent company; in most cases owned and managed by a family[3].

As shown in several empirical studies, firms of this size have some specific basic strengths and weaknesses vis-à-vis large companies, e.g. limited, but specialised product programmes as strengths, and limited resources and unsystematic decision-making as weaknesses[4]. Besides such factors, SMEs are known for personalised management and conservative risk-bearing behaviour[5].

Related to these basic firm characteristics is a set of derived characteristics pertaining to the international disposition of the company. It has been shown in several studies that items like company products, corporate goals, organisation and so on determine their motivation and potential to get involved in overseas activities[6]. By the same token, Steinmann et al.[3] and Newbould et al.[7] have shown that SMEs' characteristics, like owners' risk attitudes or specialised products, determine motivation to go abroad or choice of type of foreign activity in a specific manner other than that of large MNEs. It is hypothesised, that both the basic and derived characteristics of the technology supplier, in negotiation with the potential recipient, will influence the pattern of technology transfer.

Designing the technology transfer process in the strict sense is the objective of the second element of the concept. This process can be divided into two main phases interconnected with each other. In the first phase, the problem is the fundamental choice of the organisational form or form of involvement of technology transfer. This decision pertains to setting the overall framework within which technology transfer is implemented. Basically it means deciding under the influence of corporate characteristics, such as resources, foreign experience and so on, whether technology transfer will be carried out within equity or non-equity cooperation of the technology supplier in the recipient country. It seems quite plausible that on this property/control issue will depend how the various detailed problems of technology implementation, like choice and method of transferred know-how, terms of agreement etc., will be solved. Technology implementation will then be the focus of attention in the second phase. This is of course also influenced by some relevant corporate characteristics, like international experience etc.

The final element in the concept is the success of technology transfer. Since two parties are involved in the process, success should be defined from the point of view of the supplier as well as the recipient. From the perspective of the former, success is pertinent mainly in terms of managerial goal efficiency; that is to say, how far the initial objectives of the technology transfer project have been achieved e.g. contribution to overall goals like world market share, profits etc.

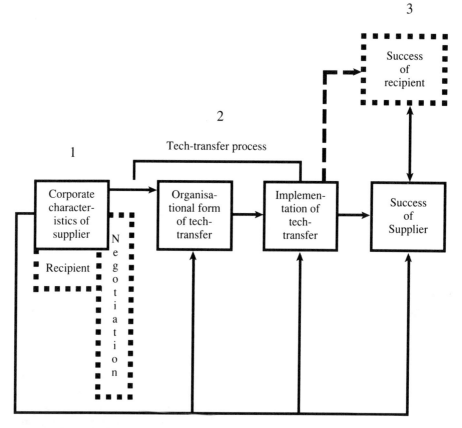

(■ ■ ■ ■) = relationships which will not be analysed

Figure 1   The concept of technology transfer

70

From the point of view of the recipient, two perspectives of success are relevant. Firstly, the attainment of his own objectives in terms of learning to utilise the transferred technology himself and thereby to improve his skill and competitiveness; secondly, the achievement of development goals which were followed in connection with the project, e.g. import substitution, increase of exports, linkage effects etc.

The elements and relationships in the concept are put together in Figure 1 and serve as the basis for the following analysis.

Characteristics of the technology suppliers (sample firms)

Some basic characteristics

Not all firms in our sample complied strictly speaking with our definition of SMEs. As Table 1 shows, all firms were compatible regarding the number of employees, but not all were independent of a group of companies as family-owned companies.

Table 1   Size of the technology suppliers (1988)

Number of employees	Number of firms (N = 13)
50–250	4
251–500	6 (2)
501-750	3 (2)

( ) = firms member of group of companies

Some important characteristics which throw light on the international potential of the examined SMEs are now listed below:–

–   **Branch-wise** distribution of the sample showed a clear concentration of firms in capital goods industries, especially in the metal-working sector, e.g. the machinery industry (6 out of 13) where German products traditionally enjoy international comparative advantage. On the supply side, the firms' markets were considered to be concentrated rather than competitive

–   **Specialisation in market niches**. Out of 13 companies 9 have made-to-order production with high flexibility for customers' individual needs

–   **Level of technology**. All firms considered their technological standards to be somewhat higher than the average domestic and international level

–   **R & D**. The majority of the SMEs examined had relatively high R & D

71

expenditures. Out of the 13 firms, 11 had been able to register their own patents in the past five years
- **Goals and objectives**. Most firms (9 out of 13) in the sample were growth-oriented, with a 5-10 per cent increase in sales volume in the past five years. This level exceeds average growth rates in German industry
- **Size of firms**. Within the range of SMEs examined, firms were on the larger side
- **Export performance**. All companies had export ratios of over 30 per cent of total sales, with five firms having more than 60 per cent

The SMEs in the sample basically belong to the metal-working markets and have a specialised product programme catering for market niches. There is an indication that this competitive advantage is based on R & D, which relative to SMEs in general is quite developed, even though somewhat haphazardly organised. Furthermore, these SME are by and large growth-oriented and can generally rely on export experience when setting up more intensive international operations.

International disposition and orientation

With the above-mentioned corporate background, we can expect the firms in the sample to show some disposition towards more intensive modes of foreign activity than mere exporting, such as different forms of technology transfer.[8] There is also some indication for their international orientation, for instance the duration of international involvement on the basis of technology transfer. More than half of the firms examined had started operations prior to 1975.

International disposition is also demonstrated by the fact that in the majority of responding firms (11 out of 13) and as well as recorded cases (12 out of 20) foreign technology transfer involvements were based on self initiative. In the remaining few cases (2 and 8) proposals from outside e.g. customers, clients etc., were responsible for the step to look abroad. This somewhat defensive attitude in the latter case was justified by the respondents on grounds of lack of information and scarcity of resources.

In line with the general growth objectives of German SMEs in the sample as reported earlier, the main driving force to take the initiative to look abroad in terms of technology transfer were potential growth prospects together with profit expectations (in 9 out of 20 cases). Other motives mentioned in the literature, like defending existing markets, risk diversification, availing of government incentives or of lower production costs abroad, did not play an important role. One can say that the responding German SMEs by and large demonstrated an orientation which can be characterised as 'aggressive' rather than 'defensive'. This disposition is known to facilitate expansion overseas.[6]

Corresponding to this 'aggressive' disposition of the SMEs in their risk-taking behaviour, as demonstrated by two phenomena. Firstly, most firms (8 out of 13) had begun their operations abroad with equity forms of technology transfer. Given the scarce resources of SMEs, one would rather have expected an incremental approach in developing the activity by starting off with less risky non-equity forms and gradually increasing commitment as market knowledge is gained.[9] Apparently, the firms were open-minded and confident enough about international activity in order to risk intensive involvement abroad right away. Many firms had in fact preferred to take the opposite path than what might be expected from the risk standpoint: they began first with equity ventures and continued in the later stages with non-equity forms.

The second observation in this respect is that most firms in the sample (7 out of 13) had begun their first foreign operations in developing countries, rather than in familiar developed countries. Remarkably, those SMEs that did begin first in developed countries were the larger ones in the sample. Apparently, the smaller firms are less risk averse and also somewhat more predisposed or flexible towards activity in developing countries.

These few indicators show that the German SMEs in the sample have by and large an international orientation: an important corporate characteristic that will enable us to explain the technology transfer process.

Organisational forms of technology transfer and their determinants

The first phase of the technology transfer process refers to the choice of form of involvement. Table 2 shows the pattern established among the sample firms: both organisational forms, i.e. non-equity and equity cooperation being equally present (10 each). Only with regard to the recipient country is there an uneven distribution. In the Brazilian sample, firms of equity participation dominate; whereas among the firms engaged in Korea, non-equity firms are in the majority. Most of the equity operations in the sample are in minority joint venture form, with only two firms having wholly-owned subsidiaries in Brazil.

Influencing factors

According to the concept used here, it can be assumed that the choice of the organisational form of technology transfer is influenced by relevant corporate characteristics. The main connection found in the sample is between what we have called the international orientation of the firms and their choice of organisational form, as shown in Table 3.

73

Table 2   Choice of organisational form of technology transfer according to host country (1987)

Form \ Country	Non-equity: Technology agreement only (e.g. licencing) (n = 10)	Equity involvement Minority joint venture	Wholly-owned subsidiaries	Total (N = 20)
Brazil	2	3	2	7
South Korea	5	1	–	6
Mexico	–	2	–	2
India	1	1	–	2
Argentina	2	–	–	2
Singapore	–	1	–	1

Table 3   International motivation and choice of organisational form

Indicator of international orientation: driving force to go abroad	Non-equity forms Wholly joint-owned ventures (no. of cases) (n = 10)	Non-equity forms e.g. licencing, contracts (no. of cases) (n = 10)	Total (N = 20)
Growth and profit prospects	1	2	9
Attractive proposal from outside the firm	–	8	8
Others	1	–	3

Clearly, most of the respondents who were growth-oriented preferred to choose equity forms of technology transfer. Since half of the cases with equity participation in our sample are situated in Brazil, as in Table 2, there is a strong influence of prospects in this particular market on the choice of organisational form. Obviously, the factor of control underlying equity participation is seen as a necessary condition for the achievement of growth goals.

As can further be seen from Table 3, in all eight cases where respondents were initiated to look abroad by outside proposals e.g. by foreign customers, non-equity organisational forms of technology transfer e.g. licencing, were selected. The main factor underlying this connection, according to the respondents, was the relatively low risk attached to this type of involvement. Whenever firms themselves did not take the initiative in scouting abroad, they felt neither able nor keen to go in for high risk strategies.

There also seems to be a relationship between the age of established operations and the choice of organisational form. The older operations are more organised in equity forms; the recent ones as non-equity ventures. This connection is especially to be seen in the context of past industrialisation policies in Brazil and the influx of foreign direct investment to that country on the one hand, and recent Korean economic development and a general shift of preference towards non-equity cooperation among German SMEs on the other.

Apart from the above-mentioned factors, there does not seem to be any evidence in the sample that other corporate characteristics, such as R & D activities, product lines or export sales, had any notable impact on the choice of organisational form of technology transfer.

Implementation of technology transfer

Contents and mechanism

At the beginning of the implementation phase, the relevant issue is what should be transferred within the framework of the organisational form and how. Table 4 shows that in all cases technology in the form of know-how was considered to be the most important resource for transfer. Foreign exchange and capital goods were imparted by SMEs involved in equity transfer; intangible technology was transferred within both equity and non-equity deals.

Table 4   Category of transferred resources

Resources	No. of cases (N = 20)*	
Foreign exchange	3	equity ventures
Capital goods	6	
Technology (intangible know-how etc.)	20	(equity and non-equity ventures)

* Sum greater than N=multiple answers

Looking at the content of transferred (intangible) technology in detail, three main elements are relevant:– Plant design technology (layout, buildings, infrastructure etc.), process know-how (organisation of production lines, planning of material flow, quality control etc.) and product technology (choice of materials, product design, new product know-how etc.). They are shown in Table 5.

Table 5   Nature of know-how transferred, by organisational form

| Elements of know-how | Organisational forms | | | Total (N = 20)* |
	Non-equity: e.g. licencing (No. of cases) (n = 10)	Equity: Joint venture Wholly-owned subsidiary (No. of cases) (n = 10)		
Plant design technology	1	2	2	5
Process technology	6	8	2	16
Product technology	10	8	2	20

* Sum greater than N=multiple answers

A question closely related to technology content is, through which mechanism are the elements under consideration transferred. Here the focus is on the medium of transfer. By far the most important one used by German SMEs in the sample are blueprints, designs and technical assistance (see Table 6). The use of special equipment as the transfer medium in more equity ventures than in non-equity is compatible with the higher capital goods export in the former (see Table 5). The export of 'critical parts' was pertinent only in cases relating to ventures in Brazil (equity) and in Korea (non-equity). In both instances, the main purpose was to upgrade the quality and relaibility of local production.

The findings show that the single most important mechanism is 'technical assistance' (see Table 6) in the form of the training of personnel, training programmes, assistance in assembly etc. This is a clear indication that both the German suppliers and the recipients of technology see personnel transfer, through which human capital endowment can be improved, as the basic element of the transfer process.

The main mode of technical assistance followed was training key employees of the recipient firm. In most cases training was conducted in the suppliers' company in Germany followed by assigning supplier-company expatriates abroad (Table 7). Practice of these modes was rather independent of form of involvement, although joint ventures had a relatively greater tendency to avail of training in the parent-company. Also with respect to size of technology supplier the modes did not vary much except that the larger firms used both methods of training evenly (Table 8).

Table 6   Mechanisms of know-how transfer, by form of involvement

| Elements of know-how | Organisational forms | | | Total (N = 20)* |
	Non-equity: e.g. licencing (No. of cases) (n = 10)	Equity: Joint venture Wholly-owned subsidiary (No. of cases) (n = 10)		
Blueprints/ designs	10	8	2	20
Technical assistance	9	8	2	19
Special equipment	2	4	–	6
Exports of 'critical parts'	4	2	2	8

* Sum greater than N=multiple answers

Table 7   Location of technical training of recipient firms' employees, by form of involvement

| Location | Organisational forms | | | Total (N = 20)* |
	Non-equity: e.g. licencing (No. of cases)	Equity: Joint venture Wholly-owned subsidiary (No. of cases)		
Blueprints/ designs	5	3	2	10
Technical assistance	6	8	2	16

* Sum greater than N=multiple answers

Standardisation and adaptation of transferred technology

Another basic question with which firms are faced while implementing technology transfer overseas is whether technology should be adapted to local conditions or be left standardised according to parent company norms.

Table 8 Location of technical training of recipient firms' employees, by size of technology suppliers

Location	Size: No. of employees			Total (N = 20)*
	Up to 250	250 to 500	500 to 750	
	(No. of cases)			
At the recipients' firm	2	5	3	10
At the parent company	4	9	3	16

* Sum greater than N = multiple answers

Large MNCs have in the past often been criticised in connection with the transfer of inappropriate technology which is capital intensive, too big and highly automated, to name but a few points.[10] On the other hand, SMEs are considered to be more flexible regarding the adaptation of technology required by recipient countries.

To assess the adaptation issue in this study, responding SMEs were asked to compare and evaluate technology installed in the affiliated recipient firms.

The overall general level of installed technology found in host country companies, as well as in the affiliates in the developing countries, was perceived by the responding SMEs in most cases to be obsolete compared to the technology in the home plant (see Table 9). But most responding German SMEs considered that it was adequate and adapted to local requirements. There was no difference in this view with respect to the organisational form of the operations.

Table 9 How modern is technology installed in affiliates?

Organisational form	How modern vis-à-vis home plant				Total (N = 20)
	equal (less than 2 years behind)	2-4 years behind	5-10 years behind	more than 10 years behind	
		(No. of cases)			
Wholly-owned subsidiary	–	1	–	1	2
Joint venture	2	3	3	–	8
Pure licencing	3	4	3	–3	10

78

The technology that was transferred by the German SMEs was considered by most respondents to be modern and similar (standardised) to the home country level. This was the case with the transferred production and factory equipment as well as with products and product design.

In a small number of cases (4 out of 20) where production and factory equipment was considered adapted, three factors were seen as mainly responsible.

First, the size of the production runs in these particular recipient firms was much smaller than in the parent company.

Second, in all four cases equipment was adapted to lower labour costs in the recipient country. This had mainly led to lowering the degree of mechanisation.

Third, in all four cases respondents reported adaptation of equipment according to the greater degree of vertical integration in the foreign affiliates. All the corresponding recipient firms were compelled to produce more components for the end products themselves than was the case in the German parent company. As a consequence, more and different plant equipment had to be installed.

Regarding product and product design, the findings show that in the majority of cases (15 out of 19, 1 missing) similar or even very similar technologies were preferred. In connection with these 15 cases, all respondents borrowed standard technology from the parent company and avoided adaptation as far as possible. The respondents were generally of the opinion that recipients basically wanted original products. In fact in most cases only original products without modifications were considered competitive in local markets.

In the few cases where adaptation was undertaken, it was done because of local materials and components. For instance a manufacturer of brake and clutch-linings was using asbestos in its joint venture in India as lining material. This was quite in line with local practice but very different from Germany, where this material is forbidden by law. Specific demand requirements and climatic conditions were also mentioned as influencing factors for the modification of products and product design.

Interestingly, in all cases where adaptation was reported, made-to-order production prevailed. On the other hand, where product standardisation was practised, the recipient firms catered for the anonymous market. This too is an indication that local markets by and large preferred original product design.

Summarising the results, there is what at first sight might seem to be contradictory practice on the part of German SMEs. On the one hand, the general standard of technology in the recipient firms is perceived in most cases as lagging behind the home level, but is considered adequate according to local conditions. On the other hand, the equipment and products transferred to the recipient firms are not adapted, but rather similar and standardised to parent company norms.

This pattern suggests that German SMEs are not particularly keen and/or able to modify transferred technology to developing countries. At least their behaviour seems to be rather undecisive. Unfortunately, in most cases they also do not seem to get much support from their local partners in solving this problem; who on the contrary generally insist on getting the most modern technology, even though it may not be suited to local conditions.

Success and appraisal of technology transfer operations

As mentioned earlier, the success of technology transfer should be looked at from the point of view of both the technology supplier and the technology recipient. However, due to lack of space and information only the former is assessed here.

From the point of view of the German SMEs, success was measured on the basis of a goal attainment criterion. The findings show that in most cases (11 out of 20) the expectations placed on the respective technology transfer projects by the supplier firms had, in their opinion, either been fully met (6) or even surpassed (5). In five cases the original goals had not been fulfilled, and concerning the remaining four projects respondents could not give reliable opinions because the activities were too recent; but on the whole, the results indicate successful operations.

This opinion is supported by further evidence that in 18 out of 20 cases supplier firms expressed plans either to expand (7) or at least to continue (11) operations in the present manner. Only in two cases was the involvement either planned to be terminated or been partly closed down already due to bad experiences. In the first case, the German SME had complaints about the unfair behaviour of the Korean partner regarding the secrecy of know-how. In the second case, a manufacturer of switchgear cabinets had earlier in 1984 terminated part of his collaboration with his Argentinian partner because of serious problems concerning the amount of the licence fee and its transfer to Germany.

On the other hand, given the choice, supplier firms in seven out of the ten cases of equity participation would rather reinvest profits in their respective foreign projects than repatriate them to the parent company. In fact only in one case did the supplier firm insist on continual repatriation; in the other two cases, the German companies would choose alternating policies. This again shows that by and large respondents were satisfied with their projects in the developing countries.

In several previous studies German SMEs reported the learning effects resulting from foreign activities as one of the important motives for setting up operations abroad.[8] Due to lack of experience, SMEs more than large MNES hope to improve their competitive advantage with the help of feedback from foreign operations. In the sample here, beneficial feedback for the home organisation from the technology transfer projects was reported explicitly in only six out of twenty cases. However, all responding firms agreed that their present involvement abroad gave them valuable experience for entering into new foreign ventures in the future. From this point of view, their present activities could also be considered as fruitful.

Influencing factors

According to various studies of international companies, success factors in international operations can be summarised into three major categories of influencing variables:– (i) characteristics of the foreign operations of the subsidiary; (ii) characteristics of the parent company and finally, (iii) the environmental conditions of the host countries.[11]

In connection with the characteristics of the foreign affiliates, the most important variable in the present study is the organisational form of technology transfer. The influence of this variable must be seen primarily in connection with the property/control paradigm. Equity ventures offer suppliers of technology more possibilities of influencing operations than non-equity projects. On the other hand, the former bind relatively large amounts of resources, perhaps more than SMEs can afford.

Table 10 shows how the choice between equity and non-equity forms relates to the findings on success. It is worth mentioning that, in four out of the five cases where results did not meet expectations, equity participation was the form of involvement. It can be noted that most of the non-equity operations (7 out of 10) can be considered as successful. On the other hand, among the ten cases of equity participation five were unsuccessful, and there was no fully-owned subsidiary among those cases where expectations had been surpassed. All told, it seems that non-equity involvement is the more successful mode of technology transfer in developing countries. Apparently, control connected with equity ventures is either unnecessary for success (or even maybe a hindrance!) or it is possible to exert control in the context of non-equity projects, e.g. via agreements. In any case, an equity presence does not seem to be a *conditio sine qua non* for successful technology transfer.

A major success factor in connection with the corporate characteristics of the parent company are its competitive advantages. Such skills are an important base for internationalisation and the firms in the sample seem to possess quite a lot of potential in this respect.

Table 11 shows the competitive advantages in detail which the firms investigated claimed to possess vis-à-vis their national and international competitors in the recipient countries. 'Better proprietary technology', which is the basic know-how transferred, is of course the most important factor which was equally present in both equity and non-equity forms of involvement. A certain relationship with the success of operations can be seen in the sense that in all but one case where goals were met, better proprietary technology was also found to be present. This result confirms the importance of some specialised know-how for starting and running successful projects abroad. With respect to the other items of competitive advantage, no definite success relationship could be seen.

Table 10   Success from the viewpoint of German SMEs according to organisational form (1987)

Success criteria	Non-equity: e.g. licencing (No. of cases)	Equity:		Total (N = 20)
		Joint venture	Wholly-owned subsidiary	
		(No. of cases)		
Results surpassed goals/expectations	2	3	–	5
Results met goals/ expectations	5	–	1	6
Results didn't meet goals/expectations	1	3	1	5
Too early to judge	2	2	–	4

Table 11   Perceived competitive advantages of German SMEs in the recipient countries, by type of involvement

Competitive advantages (vis-à-vis local competition)	Non-equity: e.g. licencing only (No. of cases)	Equity:		Total (N = 20)*
		Joint venture	Wholly-owned subsidiary	
		(No. of cases)		
Better proprietary technology	6	7	–	13
Better appropriateness of the technology	3	5	–	8
Previous experience in similar projects	3	1	1	5
Better organisation and management	1	4	–	5
International prestige	1	1	2	4
Willingness to adapt technology to local conditions	2	–	1	3

* Sum greater than N=multiple answers

Finally, the influence of conditions in the recipient countries on the success of operations has to be investigated. It can be assumed that most SMEs will find it difficult to cope with environmental influences in developing countries that are very different from the home country; as in the past German SMEs have always shown a preference for establishing operations in countries whose culture and economic dimensions are familiar viz. the European Common Market countries and USA.[12]

Table 12 shows how the success of sample firms is spread according to recipient countries. Although the number of cases is too small to allow statistical analysis, it can be observed that in all five cases where goal expectations were not met, the location of operations was in Latin America. The cases where operations were considered successful were distributed quite evenly throughout the different regions.

Table 12 Success from the viewpoint of German SMEs, according to recipient country (1987)

Success criteria	Brazil	Korea	Mexico	India	Argen-tina	Singa-pore	Total (N = 20)
			(No. of cases)				
Results surpassed goals/expectations	2	1	1	–	–	1	5
Results met goals/ expectations	2	3	–	–	1	–	6
Results didn't meet goals/expectations	3	–	1	–	1	–	5
Too early to judge	–	2	–	2	–	–	4

The types of environmental problems encountered are shown in Table 13. Some interesting findings are that cultural problems were only encountered in forms of involvement where cooperation with local partners existed. Apparently these problems were experienced in connection with conflicts with foreign partners themselves. However, such cultural conflicts do not appear to be so relevant for success as administrative and economic problems in the recipient countries. Here especially the Latin American countries were cited as examples where German SMEs had cumbersome experiences. For instance, problems with import restrictions and economic conditions were reported as negative influences on success only in connection with projects in Brazil and Argentina, and difficulties in connection with infrastructural facilities (e.g. water, electricity supply, telecommunications) were encountered only in (joint venture) operations in Brazil and Mexico. Most of the cases that reported no problems (3 out of 4) were located in

Korea. As all of these four cases apply to non-equity ventures, it can be suggested that these forms of involvement have lesser environmental problems than equity ventures. This also could be an explanation for there being more success among the former projects, as reported elsewhere.

Table 13 Main environmental problems encountered by German SMEs in recipient countries, by type of involvement

Problems	Non-equity: licencing only (no. of cases)	Equity: Joint venture	Equity: Wholly-owned subsidiary	Total (N = 20)
		(No. of cases)		
Mentality/culture	4	3	–	7
Regulations concerning foreign involvement and bureaucracy	2	1	–	3
Import restrictions	–	1	–	2
Infrastructural facilities	–	2	–	2
Socio-political and economic situation	–	–	1	1
No major problems	4	–	–	4

To summarise the findings, it can be concluded that in most cases of technology transfer German supplier firms seem to be quite satisfied with the outcome, with non-equity ventures appearing to provide better conditions for successful operations than equity cooperation. The main factors contributing to success seem to be the competitive advantages of the supplier firms in basic technological know-how. Administrative and infrastructural problems encountered in Latin America seem to be significant handicaps that impede successful operations.

Notes

1. Ozawa, T. *International transfer of technology by Japan's small and medium-sized enterprises in developing countries.* UNCTAD, Geneva. 1985.
    Onida, F. et al. *Technological transfer to developing countries by Italian small and medium-size enterprises.* UNCTAD, Geneva. 1985.
2. Buckley, P. and Casson, M. *The economic theory of the multinational enterprise.* London. 1985.
3. Bertsch, R. *Die industrielle Familienunternehmung.* Winterthur. 1964.
    Steinmann, H., Kumar, B., Wasner, A. *Internationalisierung von*

Mittelbetrieben. Eine empirische Untersuchung in Mittelfranken. Wiesbaden. 1977.

Kumar, B., Steinmann, H. 'Internationalisierung von Mittelbetrieben – Managementprobleme und Förderungsmöglichkeiten.' *Betriebswirtschaftliche Forschung und Praxis.* (1985). pp. 515–30.

Kumar, B. 'Investment strategy of German and small and medium-sized firms in the USA and the theory of direct investment. *International Trade and Finance. A North American Perpsective.* New York. 1988. pp. 175–89.

4.   Pfohl, H.-Chr. and Kellerwessel, P. 'Abgrenzung der Klein- und Mittelbetriebe von Großbetrieben.' *Betriebswirtschaftslehre der Mittel- und Kleinbetriebe. Berlin.* 1982. pp. 9–34.

Van Hoorn, Th. P. 'Strategic planning in small and medium-sized companies.' *Long Range Planning.* Vol. 12. April 1979. pp. 83–91.

5.   Gantzel, K. *Wesen und Begriff der mittelständischen Unternehmung.* Köln. 1962.

6.   Aharoni, Y. *The foreign investment decision process.* Boston. 1969.

Stopford, J. and Wells, L. *Managing the multinational enterprise.* London. 1972.

7.   Newbould, G., Buckley, P. and Thurwell, J. *Going international – The experience of smaller companies overseas.* London. 1978.

8.   There is no space here to go into these relationships e.g. between R & D and direct investments, or between specialisation and direct investments. See Kumar, B. *Deutsche Unternehmen in den USA. Das Management in den Niederlassungen deutscher Mittelbetriebe. Wiesbaden. 1987.*

9.   Johanson, I. and Vahline, I. 'The internationalisation process of the firm – A model of knowledge development and increasing foreign market commitment.' *Journal of International Business Studies.* Spring/Summer 1977. pp. 23–32.

10.   Kumar, B. 'Die multinationale Unternehmung und das Grundbedürfniskonzept.' *Entwicklungsländer als Handlungsfelder internationaler Unternehmungen.* Stuttgart. 1982. pp. 153–78.

Kumar, B. *Führungsprobleme internationaler Gemeinschaftsunternehmen in den Entwicklungsländern.* Meisenheim. 1975.

Kumar, B., Steinmann, H. 'Future and emergence of German multinationals.' *A multinational look at the transnational corporation.* Sydney/New York. 1978. pp. 235–49.

Steinmann, H. and Kumar, B. 'Personalpolitische Aspekte von im Ausland tätigen Unternehmen.' *Exporte als Herausforderung für die deutsche Wirtschaft.* Köln. 1984. pp. 397–428.

Steinmann, H., Kumar, B. and Wasner, A. 'Entwicklungspolitische Aspekte der Direktinvestitionen deutscher Mittelbetriebe in Brasilien.'*Internationale Unternehmensführung.* Berlin. 1981. pp. 415–29.

11.   Fayerweather, J. *International business strategy and administration.* Cambridge, Mass. 1978.

Daniels, J. and Radebaugh, L. *International business: Environments and operations.* 4. ed. Reading, Mass. 1986.

12.   Berger, M. and Uhlmann, L. *Auslandsinvestitionen kleiner und mittlerer Unternehmen.* Berlin. 1985.

5　Japanese international manufacturing and its local supplier problems

MALCOLM TREVOR
NAGOYA CITY UNIVERSITY

With relatively few exceptions, the literature in English on Japanese business has tended to concentrate on large firms. It has also tended to concentrate on such 'soft', though important, issues as employment systems, employee relations and company welfare systems – which small companies cannot in any case afford. Similarly, it has tended to interpret other phenomena that have significantly contributed to the competitiveness of Japanese manufacturers, such as the quality or Quality Circle movement, from a point of view that has been excessively influenced either by the Human Relations school of personnel management in the West or by the 'culturalist' approach.

The latter is not limited to Japan, and sometimes serves as an alibi for Western managers who are opposed to organisational change, but it has been particularly prominent in Japan, because of the oft-repeated ideology of 'uniqueness'. This naturally makes analysis or comparison impossible but there is now in Japan a trend away from the more stereotyped 'cultural' explanations towards a more concrete and analytical approach. It marks, to use the terminology of Talcott Parsons, a shift from a particularistic towards a universalistic view of business. At the same time, a unified method of analysis, without which no valid international comparisons are possible, does not presuppose that every society has the same industrial structure, the same distribution of power between the various economic actors, let alone such obvious differences as what constitutes acceptable behaviour on the part of managers and employees.

The so far excessive attention paid to large firms in Japan, in other words the market leaders, and some of the ways in which their business behaviour has been analysed has led to the major role played by small and medium-sized enterprises (SMEs) in the Japanese economy being neglected. It has obscured the importance of the sub-contractors and suppliers in the integrated production systems conceived and set up by the large Japanese manufacturers with increasing success since the 1960s. These networks did not come into existence by accident. They were the key element of a conscious competitive strategy, clearly seen in the classic cases of two internationally highly competitive industries: motor vehicles and electronics.

In fact the development of these supplier networks and of effective supply systems for parts and materials has been outlined in the English-language literature[1] and one Japanese report referred, for instance, to these supplier relations and procurement practices as 'key factors in the competitiveness of Japanese auto and auto parts industries in the global market'.[2] One of the most authoritative accounts of the Japanese motor industry's development similarly described what it termed 'The Decision against Vertical Integration' in the following way:– 'In-house manufacturing offered no benefits if it was possible to purchase components of equal or better quality from other firms for less money . . . through specialisation and lower wage scales, even small firms would be able to produce high-quality components at comparable or lower costs than (the big companies) themselves . . . If suppliers were unreliable or expensive, it made sense to integrate vertically, whatever the fixed costs. Yet increased levels of outside manufacturing led to lower costs and higher productivity in Japan because Nissan and Toyota made this strategy work. They risked time more than money to help their suppliers, and learned how to control firms, sometimes without investing in them directly, by despatching executives, providing technical assistance and loans of equipment or money, and arranging purchases of all or nearly all a company's output for extended periods of time.'[3]

Importance of SMEs in Japan

The pattern of supplier relations described above can broadly be taken as an ideal type. Its business rationale, or competitive rationality, is clear and hardly requires special appeals to 'culture', particularly since it arose at a specific moment in Japan's post-war industrial progress that is well documented. But such a pattern also depends on the existence of a considerable SME sector, whose size has also frequently been glossed over in the English-language literature.

In this connection, the White Paper on SMEs published by MITI's own SME Agency – whose existence alone says something about the importance attached to SMEs in Japan – is instructive in showing the extent of employment in SMEs in Japan, including in comparison with the UK and USA.[4] The following tables from the official White Paper respectively show three important things. First, that approximately three quarters of all Japanese employees in manufacturing work in SMEs – and that the proportion rose, not decreased, in the nine years up to 1981. Second, that 52 per cent of all manufacturing output comes from SMEs. Third, that just under a third (30.3 per cent) of Japanese manufacturing employment is in firms with no more than 1-19 people only: a vivid contrast with the situation in the USA, and even more in the UK, which has a conspicuous concentration of employment in the large manufacturing firms. These data indicate the contrast between vertical integration in British and American manufacturing, and the large size of many component manufacturers themselves, on the one hand, and the larger pool of competing SMEs, and potential suppliers, in Japan on the other.

Table 1   Employment in small manufacturing firms in Japan 1972-81

	Small and medium companies		Large companies	
	No. of employees	*Per cent*	*No. of employees*	*Per cent*
Year				
1972	9,209,146	69.2	4,088,588	30.8
1975	8,929,979	70.5	3,734,632	29.5
1978	9,194,642	73.5	3,314,464	26.5
1981	9,551,914	74.3	3,311,003	25.7

Table 2   Small firms in Japan: basic statistics

Total secondary and tertiary business establishments = 6.27 million

	Per cent
Small business proportion of above	99.4
Small business proportion of all employment	81.4
Small business proportion of all manufacturing output	52.0
Small business proportion of all wholesale sales (by value)	62.0
Small business proportion of all retail sales (by value)	79.0

Table 3   Employment in small manufacturing firms in UK, USA, Japan 1981-2

	No. of employees in firm					
	1-19	*20-49*	*50-99*	*100-499*	*500-999*	*1000+*
Share of employment (per cent)						
UK	10.0	7.5	7.7	26.4	13.4	34.9
USA	6.7	8.9	10.0	33.1	13.2	28.0
Japan	30.3	16.6	11.5	21.4	7.0	13.2

The share of Japanese SMEs in both manufacturing output and employment shown in the tables clearly demonstrates that they deserve more attention than has often been paid to them, at least outside Japan.

SMEs: the past or the future?

Until recently, there was a tendency to regard the SME sector in Japan as the lower part of the 'dual structure' of the Japanese economy, or as some sort of historical survival that would decline in size and significance as the economy advanced.[5]

It is a truism that in any industrial society the large companies with the famous names and the strong brand images are the best known. People know the names of the leading Japanese motor manufacturers and producers of consumer electronics goods, for instance, but how many know the names of the makers of the hundreds of components that they contain? Even in their home countries, most people do not know the names of the makers of the parts that go into the products that they buy from domestic firms that are household names to them.

In other words, general recognition of the importance of suppliers is low, while in the Japanese case there is the added problem that they have been associated with economic 'backwardness' and a financial weakness that makes it impossible for them to offer the same salaries, fringe benefits and career opportunities that are so frequently alluded to in the case of the big corporations. The lower status associated with SMEs in Japan has led to some apologists skating over them and denigrating their importance; while others would rather study those sectors that they believe represent the future instead of what they see as representative of the past.

But it must be asked whether this deterministic view of the industrial structure of the past and that of the future is the correct one. As Table 1 above showed, employment in SMEs in Japan has been growing, while the economy has been advancing, especially overseas, and it may be that the older view of the 'dual structure' is somewhat simplified and does not allow sufficiently for the rationality of the new division of labour that has been pioneered since the 1960s. As one Japanese commentator observed, 'There is a clear division of labour between the big companies and the speciality suppliers and sub-contractors that they rely on.'[6] This was contrasted with the strategy of many large companies in Europe and the USA to make a high percentage of parts in-house. Meanwhile, as another Japanese observer noted, governments in Britain and elsewhere are endeavouring to reduce unemployment by policies to promote SMEs.[7]

There are also changes in industrial structure and employment to consider. Old industrial areas such as South Wales and the North East of England have had some success in attracting new inward investment; but there has been a decisive shift from the old labour-intensive type of industry towards the new capital-intensive and more high-tech or specialised type. Nissan at Sunderland and Sony at Bridgend, the latter employing approximately 1,200 people, are major undertakings but most new companies in these areas are smaller organisations and do not employ the thousands who formerly worked in such typically early industrial concerns as coal, iron and steel, shipbuilding, railways and docks. New technology and automation have made such large organisations redundant and in Japan too there has been a considerable shakeout in these same industries. 'Small is beautiful' is an oversimplification, if not a piece of romanticism. Large organisations are likely to continue to exist in industries such as automobiles, aerospace and electronics but the future is not likely to be theirs alone. Provided the rational division of labour with the smaller specialist firms is effectively pursued, the role of the latter is likely to be more rather than less important in the future.

Supplier pyramids

The following table shows the scope and importance of the SMEs that major Japanese companies, in this case in the motor industry, have at their disposal in their supplier networks or pyramids:–

Table 4   Ratios of SMEs in the Japanese motor industry (1977)

	SMEs Per cent
Primary sub-contractors	20.5
Secondary sub-contractors	88.5
Tertiary sub-contractors	97.5

Source: Dodwell Marketing Consultants, *The Structure of the Japanese Motor Components Industry*, 1979.

The situation contrasts with that in Europe, where more suppliers of motor components, such as Lucas or GKN in England and Bosch in Germany, are themselves large firms. The next figure shows a similar situation in the Japanese electronics industry, where the extensive network of sub-contractors is conspicuous.[8]

The situation in Japan may be contrasted with that in the UK. From the viewpoint of a Japanese researcher, 'British small businesses are relatively isolated . . . (They) lack a vertical link to a parent company . . . (and) are not part of a well-organised and deliberate social division of labour. As a result, although they can keep their "independence", it is difficult for them to afford crucial new and large investments, and such businesses do not seem secure or to expand their market easily.[9]'

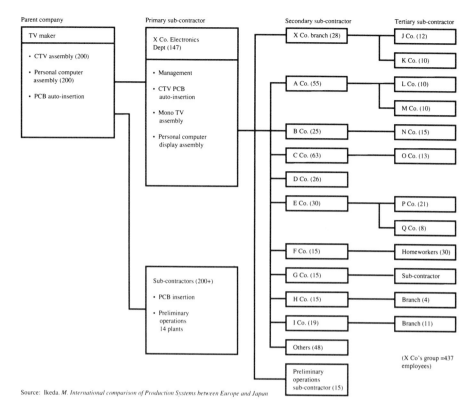

Source: Ikeda. M. *International comparison of Production Systems between Europe and Japan*

Figure 1 A Japanese TV maker and its sub-contractors (numbers in brackets = employees)

The 'deliberate' nature of the division of labour identified by the researcher needs emphasising. What is referred to is of course the manufacturing strategy of large companies, including for example that of Toshiba Consumer Products in Britain. When the business was formerly owned by Rank, there were altogether four factories and a large proportion of components was made in-house. When Toshiba took over the business, such simple processes as coil-winding for transformers were put out to external suppliers and three of the four factories were closed. The strategy was that henceforward 'we are makers of television *sets*, not components'. A new approach to supplier relations was instituted by the company which resembled, allowing for local conditions, that in use in Japan.[10]

Strictly speaking, a supplier is a firm that supplies either finished components or materials to the customer company, while a sub-contractor is one who does work on semi-finished parts, such as PCBs (printed circuit boards), for the customer. There are also differences in shareholding ratios among the different types of suppliers or sub-contractors in Japan;[11] but in practice the two terms are used without distinction and 'supplier relations' is the term in general use.

Business rationales

It is sometimes claimed that supplier relations in Japan are a reflection of 'culture', whatever this nebulous term may mean and in ignorance of the particular time and conditions in which they arose. Fortunately MITI's White Paper provides more precise data on the expectations and gains to both sides involved in a good relationship: data whose rationality is universally recognisable and which has no need of 'culture-bound' explanations.

Table 5   Japanese sub-contractors' reasons for undertaking sub-contract work

		Per cent
1.	Steady amount of orders	59.1
2.	Difficult to design and develop products by oneself	45.8
3.	Difficult to obtain orders by oneself	42.4
4.	Concentrate effort on production activities	38.7
5.	No worries about defaulting on debts	27.7
6.	Enhanced reputation	26.2
7.	Supply of raw materials etc.	21.7
8.	Technical guidance from customer	17.4

Table 6   Japanese customers' reasons for using sub-contractors

		Per cent
1.	Sub-contractor has specialised technical knowledge not held by own company	57.6
2.	Concentrate effort on most appropriate work	48.2
3.	Previous business relations with sub-contractor. Experience of sub-contractor's reliability	46.5
4.	Increased flexibility via size of orders	37.1
5.	Lower personnel costs. Lower unit costs	36.5
6.	Small size of lots. Therefore greater efficiency through production by small firms	30.6
7.	Overly large size of own company would reduce operating rate	9.4
8.	Competition between sub-contractors ensures high quality and lower unit price	8.8

In the best case, this is a relationship in which both sides prosper. SMEs with limited financial and human resources can get technical and managerial assistance from the resource-rich large firms; which feed through into increased productivity and the upgrading of product quality and management. This enhanced competitiveness in turn helps to assure them of the life-blood of regular orders.

It simultaneously provides the customer company with the standard of service and quality that it requires in order to run its own production system without interruption. If the customer company has invested time and effort in the supplier, it naturally wants to recover its investment. Meanwhile, it knows that the SME on its side can only recover its investment in the plant and skills necessary for it to perform to the customer's satisfaction if it has the prospect of repeated orders. Thus the preconditions for a fairly stable relationship are created: an important consideration when the pay back on new products, some of the development work for which can be given to the supplier, cannot be expected in a short period.

The balance of such supplier relations is crucial: too little security for the supplier, and he may have neither the resources nor the incentive to improve; too much security, and the supplier may become complacent and start taking the customer's orders for granted. But in a balanced relationship the customer has a vested interest in the supplier's performance. A maker of VTRs, for instance, does not make one of the most sophisticated parts, the tape head, itself but has farmed the job out to a specialist supplier. It is therefore dependent on the latter; while the latter itself depends on the main maker for its continued orders and prosperity.

In some cases of course, as the Japanese researcher earlier referred to has noted, large firms pressurise suppliers to cut costs and to bear the burden of any downturn in business.[12] But customer companies must also take care not to 'kill the goose that lays the golden eggs'. There is an element of enlightened self-interest.

In an international comparative context, the Far East editor of the *Financial Times* expressed the view that, 'Japan has twice as many small companies as the US – and nearly ten times as many as Britain. For the last 30 years, they have been the critical first stage of the economic rocket that has made Japan a by-word for industrial competition'.[13]

Overseas problems

The nature of the problem of supplier relations for Japanese production operations outside Japan was defined in a report prepared by a Japanese consulting company for the Department of Trade and Industry in the UK. They stressed that:–

The competitiveness of Japanese industries is supported largely by the work provided by the sub-contractors. To be able to maintain their competitiveness, Japanese firms abroad must have the services of local sub-contractors. This is a major concern of Japanese firms seeking advancement in the EC.[14]

The theme has regularly been taken up in the reports now issued in English on the situation of Japanese manufacturing companies in Europe by JETRO. The second report, for instance, stated that, 'The concept of sub-contracting itself, in the Japanese sense, is not well known in Western Europe'.[15]

Although American and European companies may complain about poor supplier performance, most have until recently been reluctant to enter into a closer relationship with them than that described in the traditional British expression 'at arm's length'; based essentially on the well-known procedure of putting orders out to tender, with the signing of the contract as the conclusion of the business and in effect the relationship. An executive of the electronics firm Thorn EMI Ferguson, subsequently taken over by the French company Thomson in 1987, for instance, repeated a widely held type of view when he stated that, 'Having sub-contracting manufacturers would entail possibly having to take responsibility for the operations of these companies. So we do not use them as a policy.' At an international conference in Germany,[16] one representative of a German heavy vehicle manufacturer asserted that it was common practice to discard five per cent of suppliers at regular intervals 'in order to encourage the others'.

Against this is the example of the highly successful, whatever criteria of profitability, market share, growth or return on investment are used, British company Marks and Spencer: a company held up more than once by Peter Drucker as an example of good strategic management, adopted as a case study by the Harvard Business School, and described in a recent study as the country's 'most efficiently managed company'.[17] Frequently characterised as 'a manufacturer without factories', due to its close involvement with its suppliers, the Marks and Spencer chain pioneered its new approach from the 1930s onwards: some thirty years before the Japanese motor industry. Marks' direct approach to its makers was not accomplished without difficulty and had to overcome suspicion and organisational inertia opposed to innovation, not to mention the opposition of the middle-men (comparable to the present well-known situation in the Japanese retail industry). But Marks succeeded in establishing an extremely rational and effective system, in which as in Japan the ability to respond quickly to changes in markets and technology became a key competitive factor: a system described by the company itself in such 'Japanese'-sounding phrases as 'a joint effort for a common purpose' and 'almost like a marriage'. While the approach of a company like Marks and Spencer remains rare, and while British industry has been slow to learn from it, it cannot automatically be assumed that such an approach cannot be introduced because of ill-defined 'cultural' factors.

The future

The JETRO report on manufacturing in Europe referred to above asked Japanese companies to give their main reasons for awarding more contracts

94

to local European suppliers. The largest percentage replied that their main reason was that, 'We found suitable local suppliers.' However, more replied that the trend of Japanese local procurement would remain unchanged than thought it would increase. 57.2 per cent of those who responded replied that they had experience of returning unsatisfactory goods to local suppliers, compared to 26.9 per cent who had not, with 15.9 per cent giving no response. What constitutes 'unsatisfactory' is obviously a problem as far as an objective or mutually acceptable definition is concerned but, for companies that want to get the benefit of Just-in-time production in particular, the usual factors of quality, delivery and price, and what might broadly be termed as 'reliability', have sometimes been contentious issues.

There are therefore unresolved problems but various trends are likely to have an effect on the situation in the future. One is the overseas investments being made by Japanese SMEs, especially in North America and to a lesser extent in Europe, as mentioned for instance in MITI's White Paper on SMEs. In the US there are some 126 wholly-owned or partly-owned Japanese establishments producing motor components, while a report by the US Department of Commerce referred to as many as 300, although this figure also includes materials suppliers. The customers of these Japanese parts makers are not limited to the Japanese motor manufacturers that have set up their own plants in North America but include the Big Three American manufacturers themselves.

Another trend is for more Western firms to adopt the pattern of closer supplier relations. Rover in the UK, influenced by the example of its partner Honda, has introduced the approach of having 'preferred suppliers'. It will 'work with them over the long term in return for sharing both costs and profits': a big change from the traditional 'arm's length' approach. Rover's purchasing managers are attending courses whose aim is 'to broaden their approach from concentration on price to a wider, business awareness': quite a move away from the old almost Pavlovian reaction to accepting the cheapest tender.[18]

General Motors in the US and other major manufacturers have formed suppliers' associations, something previously unheard-of. GM has put new pressure on suppliers to improve performance. One of them, Velcro fasteners, in a case described in the Harvard Business Review, commented that they had had a 90-day deadline within which to improve and that, 'It was no consolation to realise that all three US auto producers were feeling great pressure to upgrade their quality, cut costs, and reduce the number of suppliers.'[19]

Another article in the HBR pointed out what should have been obvious long ago, namely that 'the cheapest component is, in the long run, not necessarily the least expensive'. When all the costs of cheap quality, such as disturbances to the production system, wasted time, legal fees etc are properly calculated 'the cheapest may well be the most costly'. The article began by advising that, 'It is futile for big business to reform their manufacturing operations without the strong support of suppliers . . . Managing suppliers is thus no longer a task for old-style purchasing managers. Strategic manufacturing is becoming a partnership between the big corporations . . . and fewer, smaller, smarter supplilers'.[20]

Changes are taking place and, on the suppliers' side, such firms in the UK as the major motor components producer Lucas and the principal maker of electronic components Mullard have been introducing new quality training systems and new JIT manufacturing systems in order to get closer to their customers.

In official circles too there has been a new interest in what aspects of supplier relations in Japan lead to competitiveness. This includes an EC fact-finding mission on sub-contracting in Japan and courses including factory visits run by the EC-Japan Centre for Industrial Cooperation in Tokyo.[21]

This does not of course mean that a complete convergence between supplier relations in Europe and North America on the one hand and Japan on the other has already taken place: in the highly successful and pioneering case of Marks and Spencer, for example, Marks, as a conscious decision of company policy, does not have any direct financial stake in its suppliers. This is a clear contrast with the situation in Japan, where there are even different terms for different types of suppliers, depending on the degree of the customer company's shareholding in them.[22] But it does mean that new approaches to supplier relations are more acceptable now than they were a few years ago, and this can only make the situation easier for those Japanese companies that want to innovate in this way.

Some, such as Toshiba Consumer Products in Britain, have already been doing this and have found that, as well as concrete benefits to themselves, there has been a favourable reaction on the part of the suppliers. The latter welcome the move away from the old 'arm's length' approach, because they are given more information than before, and more transfer of managerial skills and technology to upgrade their own production systems, and because if they perform well the sounder basis of the relationship enables them to make more definite plans for the future. Unless there is some degree of stability or prospect for the future, suppliers have no incentive or perhaps even ability to invest and to improve; thus trapping them in a vicious circle. On purely rational grounds, strategic manufacturing does now require an approach to supplier relations that is qualitatively different from that of the past, however well the latter may have worked at an earlier stage of industrial development.

Conclusion

Japanese manufacturing first began to exert an influence on industrial management in Europe and America by its widespread introduction of what was originally the American concept of Quality Control[23] and by its further development of this approach to pass responsibility for quality down the line and to

96

involve the whole organisation from top management downwards. It then exerted an impact with its successful introduction of Just-in-time manufacturing; something which Ford had tried without success to introduce into its American operations in the 1920s under the name Short Term Scheduling.

Now the post-1960s approach to supplier relations as part of strategic manufacturing is starting to make itself felt. The hard evidence is the setting up in Europe and North America of either wholly-owned or joint venture operations to supply parts and components to Japanese, and in some cases other, manufacturers. So far, this has predominantly been in the motor and electronics industries, where Japanese manufacturers are most competitive. Further hard evidence is the implementation by companies like Toshiba Consumer Products and its fellow-Japanese competitors in Britain of supplier relations policies similar to those in use in Japan by these same companies; and the moves by major manufacturers like General Motors in the US and Ford and Rover in Britain to switch to a pattern of closer and less short-term relations with their suppliers. This includes the use of such terminology as 'preferred suppliers' and similar, to demonstrate the new strategy of a consciously integrated approach to improving performance. There is a new recognition that strategic manufacturing depends on integrating the efforts of both suppliers and manufacturers and that the total result will be harmed if they both continue to act as if they were not really involved in the same venture.

At the same time there are differences in industrial structure and in patterns of ownership and control between the US and Europe on the one hand and Japan on the other. Some claim that supplier relations in Japan are 'unique' or based on 'unique' Japanese characteristics; in which case, their impact abroad will either be modified or reduced. But if, on the other hand, the essential point of these relations is their rationality and the application of more rational methods than before in order to achieve the aims of strategic manufacturing, then there is the possibility of their spreading.

The results achieved in Japan in terms of competitive edge would seem to indicate their rationality and it is also not at all celar how such highly rational systems as Just-in-Time can be achieved without integrating suppliers, as well of course as functions such as marketing, design and development, information collection and communication, into the process. Some European companies, such as the German manufacturer Stihl, have grasped all that this means, not only for changes in the production system but for changes in their own organisations as well.[24] It will therefore be interesting to watch how companies formulate and implement new strategies in these areas in order to sharpen the competitive edge that they are going to need in the future.

Notes

1. Dodwell Marketing Consultants. *The Structure of the Japanese Motor Components Industry*. Dodwell, Tokyo. 1979. (et seq.)

2. Mitsubishi Research Institute. *The Relationship between Japanese Auto and Auto Parts Makers*. Mitsubishi, Tokyo. 1982.

3. Cusumano, M.A. *The Japanese Automobile Industry. Technology and Management at Nissan and Toyota*. Harvard. 1985. pp. 241–2.

4. MITI (Ministry of International Trade & Industry). *White Paper on Small and Medium Enterprises in Japan*. MITI, Tokyo. 1986.

5. Broadbridge, S. *Industrial Dualism in Japan: a Problem of Economic Growth*. Cass, London. 1966.

6. Kinoshita, H. 'The Role of Small Business.' *Japan*, No. 376. Japanese Embassy, London. 9 October 1986.

7. Mitsui, I. 'First Impressions: a Preliminary Report on a Research into Small Business Policies in Britain.' *Komazawa University Economic Review*, Vol. 20. No. 2. Tokyo. December 1988.

8. Ikeda, M. *International Comparison of Production Systems between Europe and Japan*. Typescript. Chuo University, Tokyo. 1986.

9. Mitsui. op. cit. p. 139.

10. Trevor, M.H. 'The Importance of the Suppliers.' *Toshiba's new British Company*. Policy Studies Institute, London. 1988. Translated into Japanese as *Eikoku Toshiba no Keiei Kakushin*. Toyo Keizai, Tokyo. 1990.

11. Trevor, M.H. and Christie, I.P. *Manufacturers and Suppliers in Britain and Japan*. Policy Studies Institute, London. 1988.

12. Mitsui, I. op. cit. p. 150.

13. Smith, C. 'Why Japan still thinks small.' *Financial Times*, London. 26 April 1982.

14. Technova. *Japanese Direct Investment in the UK: its Possibilities and Problems*. Technova, Tokyo. 1982.

15. JETRO (Japan External Trade Organisation). *Japanese Manufacturing Companies operating in Europe (Second Survey Report)*. JETRO, Tokyo. 1985–6. et. seq.

16. Trevor, M.H. and Holl, U. eds. *Just-in-Time Systems and Euro-Japanese Industrial Collaboration*. Campus, Frankfurt. 1988.

17. Tse, K.K. *Marks and Spencer. Anatomy of Britain's most efficiently managed Company*. Pergamon, Oxford. 1985.

18. Lorenz, A. 'Rover drives towards niche – Honda-style.' *Sunday Times*, London. 8 October 1989.

19. Krantz, K.T. 'How Velcro got hooked on quality.' *Harvard Business Review*, No. 5. September–October 1989.

20. Burt, D.N. 'Managing Suppliers up to Speed.' *Harvard Business Review*, No. 4. July–August 1989.

21. European Community. *EC Fact Finding Mission on Subcontracting in Japan*. EC-Japan Centre for Industrial Cooperation, Tokyo. 1989.

22. Trevor and Christie. op. cit. pp. 35–6.

23. Shewhart, A.L. *The Statistical Control of Manufactured Product*. Bell Laboratories, USA . 1931.

24. Trevor and Holl. eds. op. cit. Stihl, H.P. 'Integrating JIT into a Total Production and Marketing System.' pp. 1–84.

PART 2:

THE MANAGEMENT OF OVERSEAS STAFF

6 The development of Japanese multinationals as European insiders and European managers' job satisfaction

TETSUO AMAKO
YOKOHAMA NATIONAL UNIVERSITY

Introduction

This chapter looks at the following two questions:–

(i)   Is the withdrawal of Japanese expatriates really necessary?
(ii) Is Europeanisation sufficient to increase European managers' job satisfaction?

First it is useful to look at job satisfaction and its various aspects. Satisfaction was measured by considering the following criteria:–

–   salary, fringe benefits
–   relationship with colleagues
–   company (prestige, respect, success etc.)
–   promotion chances
–   availability of information
–   level of worries, stress, pressure
–   motivation to work

It is possible to say that several determinant factors affect job satisfaction; such as personality, salary, colleagues, superiors, promotion, company and work itself, as set out in Figure 1.

Maslow's analysis is useful to look at the human needs levels which contribute to job satisfaction. At the lower end of the scale, it is clear that security, affection and belonging are factors which determine almost all employees' job satisfaction; but it has been suggested that higher in the job

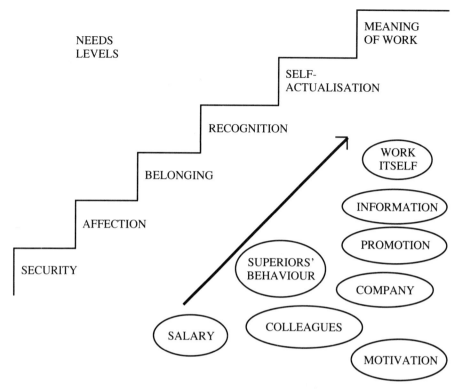

Figure 1   Needs levels and job satisfaction

hierarchy these factors are cumulative and lead to needs beyond these levels, such as recognition (by superiors or by colleagues), self-actualisation (development of one's own capacity) and above all, the meaning of the job one is trying to carry out beyond the needs analysed by Maslow. These things are strongly influenced by the behaviour of one's own superior and this behaviour appears to be the major criterion for measuring managers' job satisfaction. It is clear that to increase the job satisfaction of people at managerial levels, the important elements to concentrate on would appear to be those of promotion, information, work itself, and especially the meaning of work; because they already have a certain success in salary increase and relations with colleagues before reaching this level (see Figure 2).

In Japanese companies in Europe, it is suggested that in companies with a large Japanese presence the level of job satisfaction is low, and conversely, where there is a smaller Japanese presence, the level has a tendency to be much higher. In the intermediate report of this research, this theory was supported, but further results proved that this question was more complex than it had first appeared. The case for supporting the Europeanisation of Japanese companies in Europe is examined in closer detail following these later results, which have

PROMOTION
INFORMATION
WORK ITSELF

V

SALARY
COLLEAGUES

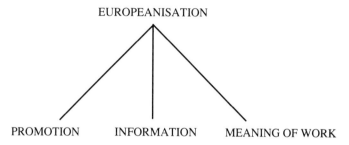

EUROPEANISATION

PROMOTION   INFORMATION   MEANING OF WORK

Figure 2   Ways to increase managers' job satisfaction

brought more interesting conclusions than simply to 'withdraw all Japanese managers'. This Europeanisation is regarded as a means to facilitate the promotion of European managers, the spread of information, and the finding of the meaning of work among company employees.

Discussion

Eighteen companies sent a total of 162 answers to the questionnaire and these answers can be broken up into four categories:–

(i)   those who report to European top managers (9 people)
(ii)   those who report to Japanese top managers (38 people)
(iii)   those who report to European senior or middle managers (37 people)
(iv)   those who report to Japanese senior or middle managers (37 people)

The numbers of completely filled up questionnaires are shown in the brackets above.

The influence of Europeanisation

Here it might be useful to look at this representation of the distribution of job satisfaction according to the company size (see Figure 3). Each company is coded and has a different number on the graph to show its relative position in the responses to the questions relating to job satisfaction. It can be seen that in companies where there are less than 30 people, job satisfaction appears quite high. It drops when the size reaches around 50 people (30–70) and broadens out over a wide spectrum in the larger companies where some results were bad, and some results were very good. From the following table this may look clearer, and it is perhaps surprising to note that where there are fewer Japanese, there are not always good results, as in Figure 4.

It is better to examine only medium-sized and larger companies' answers regarding this aspect, as it is dangerous to represent a smaller company's climate by one or two answers from each company. The following arguments will therefore concern the responses taken from those companies which have over 30 employees.

In plotting the Japanese/European ratio in these companies as far as their answers to the job satisfaction areas are concerned, there is a rough tendency for companies with few Japanese to have a higher rate of job satisfaction, but despite this tendency, one company in this survey falls far outside this assumption, as shown in Figure 5. Company 16 has few Japanese and very low job satisfaction. It is interesting to examine what other criteria might affect the balance.

Language problems fell into a distinct distribution line, as those who found it difficult to communicate with their Japanese superior because of language problems also demonstrated lower job satisfaction, without exception (see Figure 6).

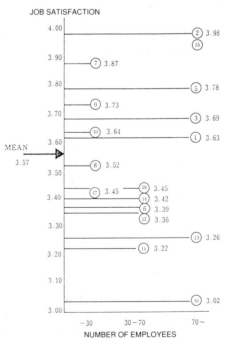

Figure 3 Job satisfaction levels, by company size

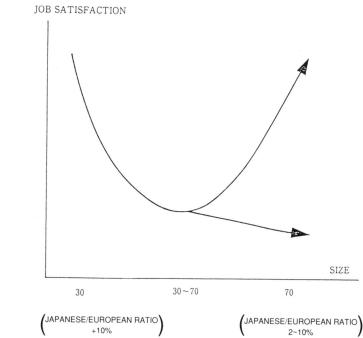

JOB SATISFACTION

SIZE

30   30~70   70

$$\left(\begin{array}{c}\text{JAPANESE/EUROPEAN RATIO}\\ \text{+10\%}\end{array}\right) \qquad \left(\begin{array}{c}\text{JAPANESE/EUROPEAN RATIO}\\ \text{2~10\%}\end{array}\right)$$

Figure 4   Uncertain necessity to withdraw Japanese managers

It was also the case when the questions relating to 'insider efforts' were compared alongside the job satisfaction results (see Figure 7). Those companies which were felt to be making efforts to be a European rather than an entirely Japanese company reflected higher job satisfaction results.

Managerial behaviour was also examined using attitudes evaluation scales developed by Misumi. Significant distribution was also recorded in managerial behaviour and formed a clear pattern where managers who were highly considered reflected a much higher job satisfaction among their subordinates, as in Figure 8.

These results led us to an assumption that a Japanese presence hinders the improvement of job satisfaction of European managers. Japanese managers may not be able to behave as respected managers in a European office situation even if they are highly appreciated as skilful managers in a Japanese office situation.

Differences of European managers' job satisfaction according to their superiors' nationalities are examined separately for top management and middle/senior management in this context. As shown in the graph, European middle/senior managers bring more satisfaction to their subordinates than their Japanese counterparts. As for top management the differences are not so obvious, except for salary and worries items (see Figure 9).

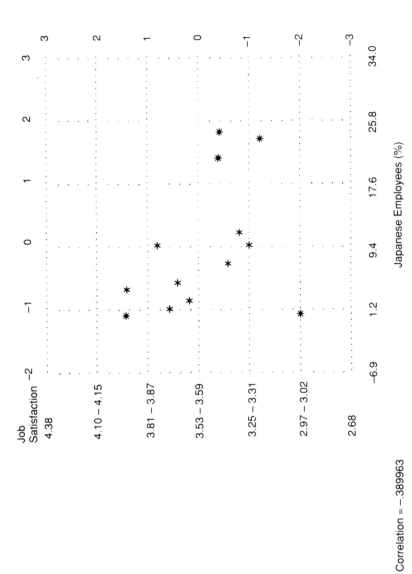

Figure 5 Japanese/European ratio and job satisfaction

Correlation = −.389963

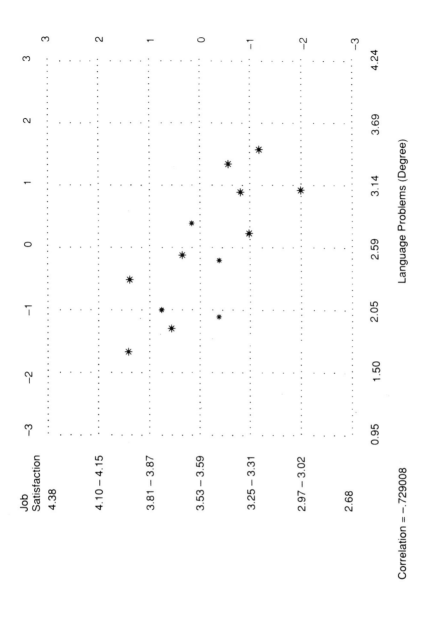

Figure 6   Language problems and job satisfaction

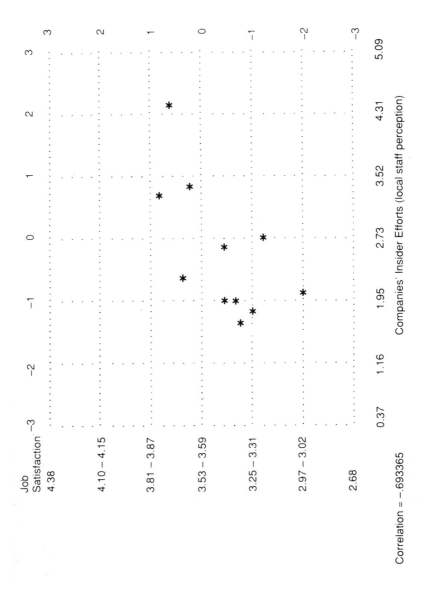

Figure 7 Companies' insider efforts and job satisfaction

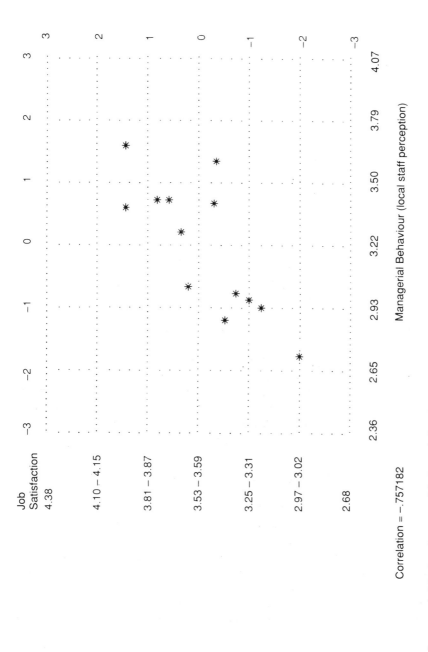

Figure 8 Managerial behaviour and job satisfaction

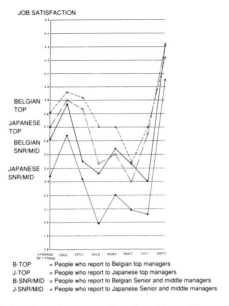

JOB SATISFACTION

B-TOP = People who report to Belgian top managers
J-TOP = People who report to Japanese top managers
B-SNR/MID = People who report to Belgian Senior and middle managers
J-SNR/MID = People who report to Japanese Senior and middle managers

Figure 9 Job satisfaction, by superiors' nationality

All the preceding results would seem to support the case for the efficiency and value of increased Europeanisation, but it is important in this context to look at the distribution of managerial behaviour related to the Japanese/European ratio. It was expected that companies having withdrawn Japanese expatriates would have more skilful managers but, contrary to this assumption, this correlation was not strong (see Figure 10).

Influence of the reliability of the annual plan

The initial theoretical framework was again examined to find the real determinant factors of European managers' job satisfaction. Europeanisation was considered favourable to their job satisfaction because it allows the distribution of higher salaries to European managers, taking into account the high cost of expatriation as well as a bigger chance of promotion. Higher responsibility also gives more of a chance to develop self-actualisation. European superiors may be able to explain the background of the work and its relation to other work which gives more meaning to the jobs done by their subordinates (see Figure 11).

But an important factor has not yet been examined. Despite the skill of superiors, if the initial annual planning and budget is influenced too much by the head office's abstract desk plan without a profound analysis of the European market, it is difficult to give the meaning of work done by their subordinates. The reliability of the annual plan is therefore examined.

110

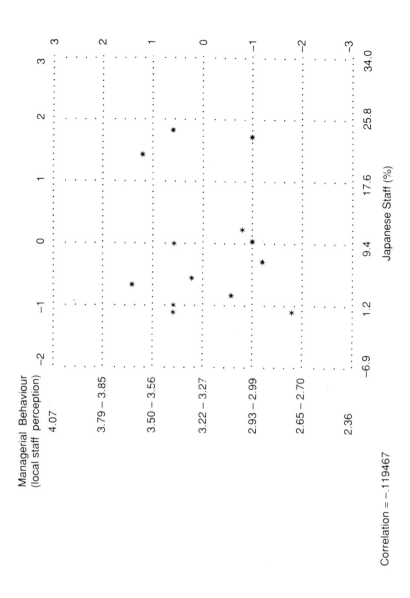

Figure 10 Managerial behaviour and Japanese/European ratio

→ MORE EUROPEAN MANAGERS

$\left(\begin{array}{l}\text{supposed to be more}\\\text{efficient as line managers}\end{array}\right)$

→ PROMOTION

→ INFORMATION

MEANING OF WORK

given by superior's explanation and

by RELIABLE PLANNING

(new hypothesis)

Figure 11 Initial theoretical framework of Europeanisation

There was a marked correlation with increased job satisfaction where planning was regarded as reliable and not changeable by head offices without considering the European situation (see Figure 12). There are no exceptional cases as we found in the relation between the Japanese/European ratio and job satisfaction. Regarding the theoretical framework, the reliability of planning is related to self-actualisation and meaning of work which should influence people in a managerial position. The reliability of planning seems therefore to be a more determinant factor than the Europeanisation factor.

From this point of view, the level of job satisfaction was examined again regarding both factors: the reliability of planning and the Europeanisation level. Each company was plotted on the horizontal axis of the Japanese/ European ratio and on the vertical axis of the reliability level of the planning, as in Figure 13.

It was suggested that in companies where planning was considered reliable, with a low Japanese presence, European managers' job satisfaction would be high; and that, on the other hand, in companies where planning was considered less reliable, with a high Japanese presence, their job satisfaction would be lower. For these cases these assumptions were confirmed.

As for extreme cases, such as company 14 which has a very high presence of Japanese (more than 20 per cent) and company 16 which has the lowest score of reliability of the planning, it was suggested that their job satisfaction was low, which was also confirmed by the data.

For companies 5 and 12 which have a relatively higher reliability of planning but also a higher presence of Japanese expatriates, and for company 3 which has relatively less reliable planning but a low Japanese presence, their job satisfaction was examined relating to managerial behaviour. Company 5 and Company 3 have relatively more skilful managers but

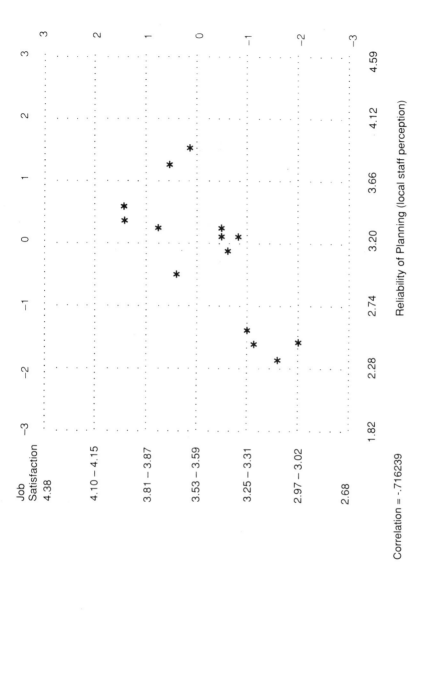

Figure 12 Reliability of planning and job satisfaction

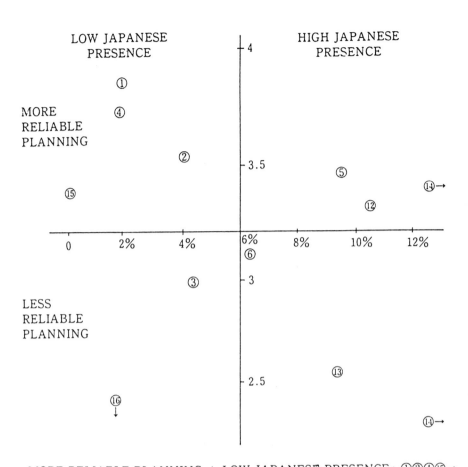

MORE RELIABLE PLANNING + LOW JAPANESE PRESENCE: ①②④⑮→
HIGH JOB SATISFACTION
LESS RELIABLE PLANNING + HIGH JAPANESE PRESENCE: ⑥⑬⑭→
LOW JOB SATISFACTION
EXTREME CASES⑯⑭→ LOW JOB SATISFACTION
IN-BETWEEN CASES
    HIGH MANAGERIAL BEHAVIOUR③⑤→ HIGH JOB SATISFACTION
    LOW MANAGERIAL BEHAVIOUR⑫→ LOW JOB SATISFACTION

Figure 13 Europeanisation + reliability of planning

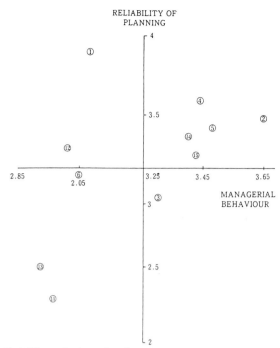

Figure 14 Reliability of planning/managerial behaviour

company 12 has relatively less skilful managers. Companies 5 and 3 enjoy higher job satisfaction but company 12 does not.

These results led to an assumption that three factors i.e. reliability of planning, managerial behaviour, and Japanese presence, are the three determinant factors of European managers' job satisfaction.

To verify the effectiveness of this assumption, each company was again plotted on the horizontal axis of managerial behaviour and on the vertical axis of reliability of planning, as in Figure 14. Companies having more reliable planning and more skilful managers enjoy higher job satisfaction, except for only one case (company 18) which has a very high Japanese/European ratio (more than 20 per cent). On the other hand, those which have less reliable planning and fewer skilful managers do not enjoy high job satisfaction.

Company 3 has more skilful managers than the average but less reliable planning than the average. In this case its low presence of Japanese expatriates favourably influences job satisfaction. For Company 1, as well having reliable planning but fewer skilful managers, its lower Japanese presence favourably influences job satisfaction. As for company 12, it has relatively reliable planning but fewer skilful managers. Its high Japanese presence unfavourably influences its European managers' job satisfaction.

Conclusion

The previous discussion led us to the conclusion that the reliability of the annual plan, the relative number of skilful managers, and the level of Japanese presence are the three determining factors of the different levels of European managers' job satisfaction. The withdrawal of Japanese expatriates by itself cannot have a large influence on European managers' job satisfaction. The reliability of the annual plan and the relative number of skilful managers are the predominant factors. The level of the Japanese presence has only a secondary influence.

As the withdrawal of the Japanese staff does not automatically allow the improvement of reliability of the annual plan and the employment of skilful European managers, this conclusion, obtained from all the eighteen companies, is better suited to our intermediate conclusion obtained from only the first thirteen companies' data.

Europeanisation in fact prepares the environment for employing more skilful European managers and establishing a more reliable annual plan, reflecting more reliable European market information analysed by European managers. However it does not automatically promise to improve them. If communication channels and decision-making processes are improved and/or the behaviour of Japanese expatriates is improved by certain types of training, companies can enjoy improvements in European managers' job satisfaction.

However, job satisfaction itself is not companies' first preoccupation; without good financial results it has no meaning, and many previous studies show its strong correlation with efficiency. The more Japanese business activities in Europe grow, the more European managers' competence becomes necessary for most industries. But for companies or industries which do not need European managers' skill and knowledge the latter's job satisfaction is not the primary concern.

Financial results cannot be sacrificed for the improvement of job satisfaction in our economic environment but as long as financial results are not unfavourably influenced, job satisfaction should be improved even in these industries. Our complementary interview study showed that the recent withdrawal of Japanese expatriates in the banking industry, where the Japanese presence is considered very important, did not unfavourably influence financial results over successive years.

As Europeanisation has a secondary but definite influence on European managers' job satisfaction, the possibility of withdrawing Japanese staff and replacing them with European managers should be seriously examined, keeping, of course, head office control because the combination of the world's global business resources is the most important competitive advantage of multinational companies.

After trade friction has passed its peak, investment friction is becoming a prime concern. Even for companies which have already started manufacturing in Europe, investigations under anti-dumping laws have recently been undertaken. If companies' own managers are not eager to support their employers' position in their own countries, Japanese multinationals will have difficulty in presenting convincing arguments abroad when problems occur.

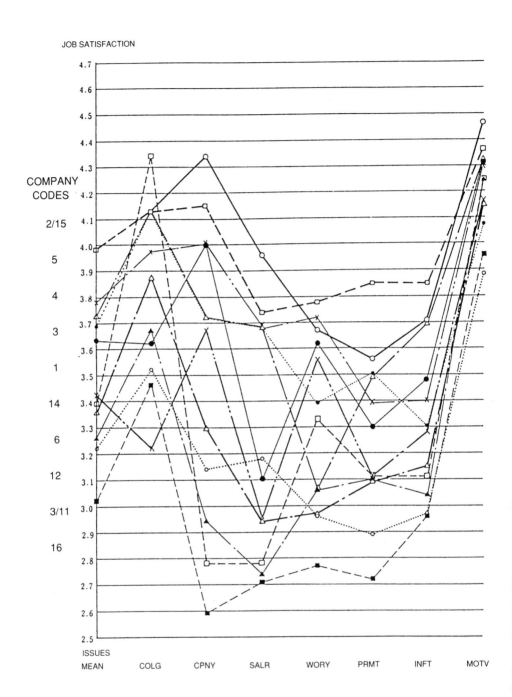

Annexe 1 Job satisfaction in medium and larger companies

118

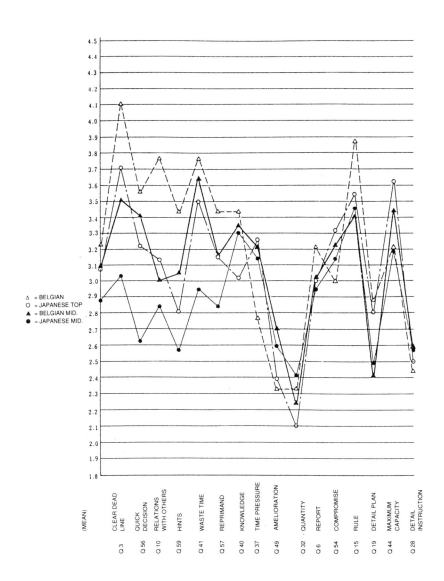

Annexe 2 Performance behaviour differences, by nationality

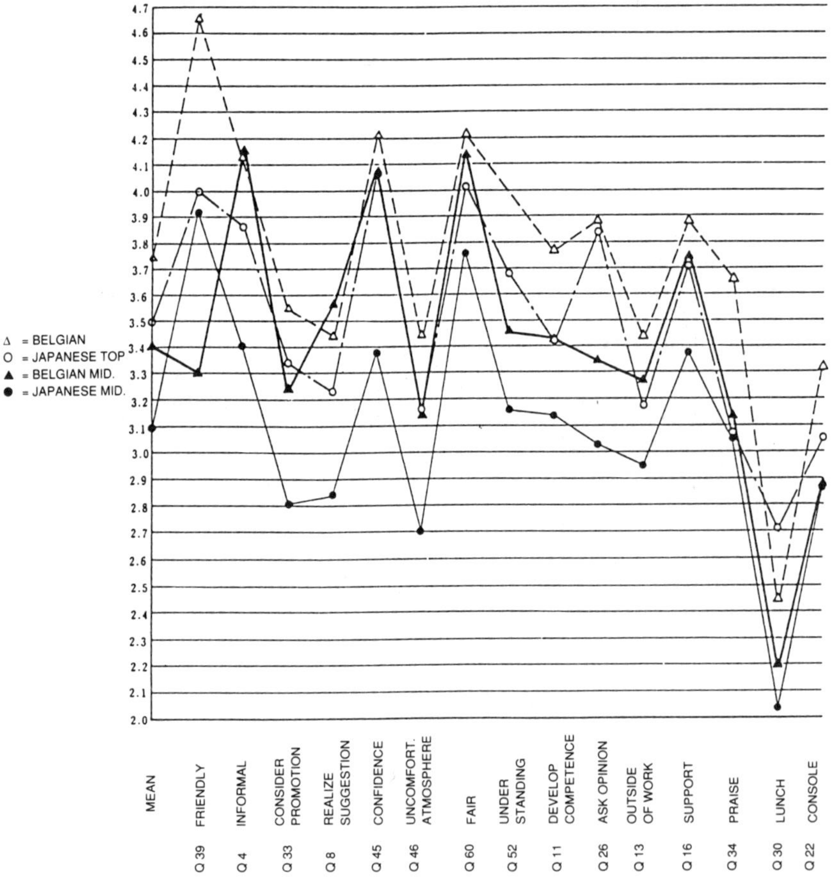

Δ = BELGIAN
O = JAPANESE TOP
▲ = BELGIAN MID.
● = JAPANESE MID.
4.7
4.6
4.5
4.4
4.3
4.2
4.1
4.0
3.9
3.8
3.7
3.6
3.5
3.4
3.3
3.2
3.1
3.0
2.9
2.8
2.7
2.6
2.5
2.4
2.3
2.2
2.1
2.0
MEAN
Q 39 FRIENDLY
Q 4 INFORMAL
Q 33 CONSIDER PROMOTION
Q 8 REALIZE SUGGESTION
Q 45 CONFIDENCE
Q 46 UNCOMFORT. ATMOSPHERE
Q 60 FAIR
Q 52 UNDER STANDING
Q 11 DEVELOP COMPETENCE
Q 26 ASK OPINION
Q 13 OUTSIDE OF WORK
Q 16 SUPPORT
Q 34 PRAISE
Q 30 LUNCH
Q 22 CONSOLE

Annexe 3 Maintenance behaviour differences, by nationality

7 The intra-organisational transferability of Japanese-style management

TERUHIKO TOMITA
SHIGA UNIVERSITY

The most critical international economic issues which Japan currently faces are how to mitigate the increasing criticism of its chronic trade surplus vis-à-vis its trading partners, and how to cope with the emergence of the single EC market in 1992. This implies that the competitive advantage of Japan's exports will be weakened in the long-run, and hence will no longer be as promising a means of adding value for Japanese firms as before. To cope with this situation, Japanese manufacturing firms have increasingly set up production bases outside Japan to supplement or substitute for their exports.

However, these changes alone will not assure successful production overseas. There are at least two other conditions for Japanese firms to expand production activities abroad:–

(i)   The management resources accumulated in Japanese firms must be perceived to have some competitive advantages over indigenous firms in actual or potential host countries.

(ii)   Management resources are abundantly endowed in Japanese firms due to the failure of the international management resources market.[1]

In these conditions, a firm is able to transfer part of its competitive management resources to other countries via non-equity participation, such as licencing and technical service agreements. A firm is also able to transfer a package of its management resources to other countries through equity participation[2] i.e., to internalise management resources in international markets into an intra-firm organisation by setting up subsidiaries outside national boundaries.[3]

In the case of non-equity participation, however, 'The return for a specific proprietary asset, or group of assets, can be fully captured through a market transaction where uncertainty (= uninsurable risk) arises . . . Markets may also fail because they cannot capture the benefits and costs external to a specific transaction . . .'.[4] Therefore, Japanese firms generally prefer equity participation, preferably in the form of wholly-owned subsidiaries, to non-equity participation, so as to optimise, or at least sub-optimise, the use of their management resources, particularly management practices.

However, the relevance of their management practices, when transferred intra-organisationally to other countries, has not yet been well examined as to whether such practices elaborated in a Japanese environment still possess competitive advantages over those developed in the different environment of the host country, with which local employees are familiar.

Mainly from the viewpoint of transaction costs and resource allocation, the aim here is to clarify the relevance of intra-organisational transferability of what is referred to as the Japanese-style management system, defined as an organism of various Japanese management practices, to other countries. The extent to which Japanese management practices are implemented in overseas subsidiaries and are accepted by indigenous local middle managers, and the extent to which they function along with corporate objectives, were the objects of the research.

It is assumed here that the transaction cost[5] of the Japanese-style management system within the intra-firm organisational market is small, when its practices are smoothly implemented in the overseas subsidiaries and are well accepted. Hence smooth implementation and a high degree of acceptability are the necessary conditions for evaluating transferability. But even if the practices are implemented and accepted, the transferability of the system is not necessarily assured, unless the practices function effectively as an organism. Hence it is also assumed that the effective organic functioning of the practices is imperative for the relevance of internal transferability.

The discussion is based on findings from Japanese top managers and local middle managers working for Japanese manufacturing subsidiaries in Britain, with occasional reference to those in East and Southeast Asian countries.[6]

Middle managers were surveyed because their functions are crucial for smooth corporate operations under Japanese management. But there is a prevailing hypothesis among researchers that Japanese-style management overseas is welcomed by rank and file workers, but not by middle and/or senior managers, or that it is more accepted the lower one goes down the company hierarchy.[7] Therefore, it should be investigated whether Japanese-style management is accepted by middle and/or senior local managers and functions effectively. If not, its international intra-firm transferability will not be assured in the long run.

Development of Japanese management

The management system referred to as Japanese-style has not evolved primarily on the basis of socio-cultural values unique to Japan. It has developed through constrained procedural decision-making to respond flexibly to a series of challenges as shown in Figure 1.

From the viewpoint of neo-classical economic theory, the decisions which both management and labour had to make were by no means optimal in terms of resource allocation but were inconsistent and irrational. This was particularly true in the immediate post-war period, when the autonomous stability of labour markets was far-reaching, due to the large surplus of subsistence labour and militant labour movements. Japan was on the verge of social disorder.

In order to avoid this, despite management's position of hiring and firing labour as necessary, patriotic young top managers, not involved in war criminal purges, committed themselves to internalising their employees within the firm, even by sacrificing their managerial goals and sharing employees' poverty (now known as sharing affluence). Thus labour costs became a 'quasi-fixed cost', not variable cost.

The most urgent question for management, therefore, was to develop ways of using labour better so as to lessen its cost. Various practices were therefore introduced for all regular employees, including rank and file workers. They included job security (popularly called 'lifetime employment'), and in-house training and promotion, which have avoided repetitious recruiting and training expenses and accumulated specific skills through the learning effect; also length of service-based company-reward schemes (popularly called the 'seniority reward system'), which has provided living expenses according to age; and job flexibility, which has encouraged employees' commitment to the organisation rather than to particular jobs. By the end of the 1950s, when Japan had recovered its pre-war level of economic activities, these practices had gradually been accepted and conventionalised, and also been found to be effective in pursuing the respective goals of management and labour. This was mainly because employees came to realise that skilful adjustment to an internal labour market was crucial for improving their livelihood. In fact, by then, there were practically no alternative job opportunities in the external market.

In the 1960s, foreign pressure for the liberalisation of trade and direct investment was put on Japan's still fragile industry. In response, such practices as quality circles and suggestion schemes, which expedited the integration of individuals into the group, were introduced and improved to fit into Japanese settings. They greatly strengthened the competitiveness of Japanese industrial products and improved employee welfare.

As a response to the energy crisis and its increasing production costs in the 1970s, the 'just-in-time' system, originally developed by Toyota,

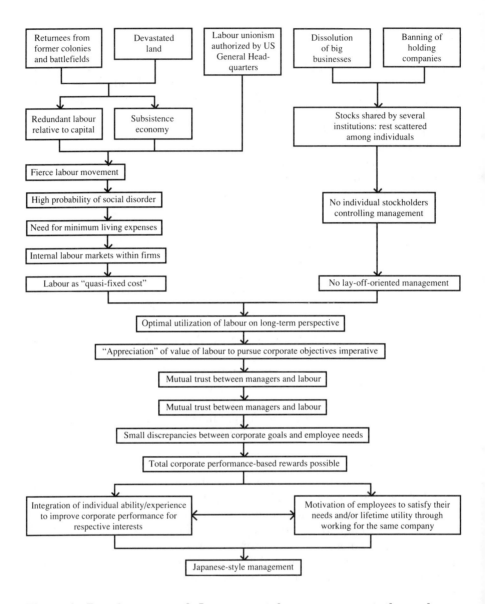

Figure 1 Development of Japanese-style management through responses to environmental changes

was widely adopted to minimise cost and space for carrying inventory. Job reassignments, shifting excess labour into busy sections without reducing salaries, were more actively pursued than before. Initially labour-saving hi-tech equipment, which conventional 'skilled' labour could hardly

124

manage, amplified this process. In the 1980s, length of service-based rewards have been reassessed and have increasingly given way to merit-based rewards, to cope with further change, including the ageing of the work force, slower economic growth and the diversified values of young employees.

These organic components of the Japanese management system were all deliberately created in order to utilise internalised labour to the maximum extent. But they would not have functioned well if there had been no support among workers, or if managers and workers had independently aimed solely at maximising their own respective interests: profit on the part of managers, and satisfying individual needs on the part of workers.

In fact, in the immediate post-war period, management and workers in some companies did try to do this. Some managements were inclined to dismiss redundant labour, while workers insisted on conflicting demands both for no lay-offs and pay rises at the same time. Such actions, however, were fruitless for both parties and worsened their respective situations, leading to the hidden 'Prisoner's Dilemma' solution of mutual distrust.[8] Through this bitter experience, both managers and managed learned that compromise was indispensable for attaining their respective objectives, and realised that mutual trust was the prerequisite for such a compromise. In my view, both 'field'[9] and 'knowledge'[10] played a major role in nurturing this mutual trust.

It is generally believed that individuals' behaviour is constrained by the 'field' of their life space, in other words, by their nature and the environment. This suggests that if individuals' nature is more homogeneous, differences of perception of a particular matter are small; hence differences in behaviour are small. If, therefore, in a given 'field', the behaviour of an individual in a company in accepting a certain management practice produces a desirable result, others are likely to follow; and when the relationship between a certain behaviour and its outcome is increasingly perceived as desirable by many of the members of a company, the cause and effect relationship which the practice carries is likely to be incorporated as 'transmittable knowledge'. Such 'knowledge', even though it may involve some logical inconsistency, develops into 'shared' and/or 'conventional knowledge' implicitly accepted by management and labour for promoting their respective livelihoods. In this way, detailed Japanese management practices have gradually gained the support of workers, as a convention which benefits both managers and managed.

Such practices are deployed on the basis of 'shared knowledge', tacitly supported by mutual trust. Because of this, the practices have been self-enforcing and have functioned effectively. Mutual trust between managers and managed, though sometimes a pretence for their respective benefits, formulates the Japanese management creed, in comparison with the mutual distrust so often observed in Western management.

Functions of Japanese management

Management's basic objective is to pursue profit and Japan is no exception. But management geared too much to profit is generally not socially well received in Japan. Therefore, a certain 'logic' in which profit seeking is skilfully concealed has been needed. What had been formulated by the 1970s can be called a 'logic of human talent' (or a logic of *hito*, literally meaning a logic of man). That is, a 'logic' aimed at long-run optimisation supported by internally developed human resources combined with capital and other resources. This contrasts with the Western 'logic of capital' in which capital is combined with human and other resources.

In order to pursue reasonable profits under the 'logic of human talent', unlike machinery which can be depreciated year after year, the value of each individual's talent must be 'appreciated' over time in line with corporate objectives, or at least its rate 'depreciation' must be minimised. Each individual's ability should be optimally utilised through vertical and across-the-board coordination and the integration of individual activities within the organisational hierarchy. Otherwise, major practices such as 'life-time employment' and length of service-based reward schemes would have no advantages.

Therefore, companies tried to make each individual acquire company-specific skills[11] and wide and compatible views concerning corporate management. They also tried to reduce employees' compatibility with external labour markets.[12] These two strategies enabled firms in the long run to maximise the utilisation of their employees' talents in internal markets. So-called Japanese management can be defined as an organic combination of management practices which together make it possible to maximise such conditions.

Japanese management aims at long-run corporate growth through the 'appreciation' of the value of employees' talents and emphasises high product quality, flexible administrative structure and orderly work discipline. Such a system, in this view, has been supported by two closely interrelated sub-systems, which have worked as a kind of 'quality control' of personnel.

One may be called the system of the 'integration of individuals into the group', in which their achievements are skilfully multiplied. It keeps stimulating the employees' feelings of cooperation through intra-group pressure on the one hand, and friendly but keen competition between colleagues on the other; thus enabling management to 'appreciate' the total value of corporate members.

The other may be called a system of 'the incorporation of individuals into the organisation', in which, while their identification with their own skills is weakened, their identity with the organisation is strengthened. This leads them to expect that their needs and/or long-term utility are best satisfied by the intrinsic and extrinsic rewards they may get through their life-long contribution to a particular company; thus enabling management to skilfully 'manipulate' such expectations for corporate objectives.[13]

These two sub-systems are neither separable nor additive but organic. Their mechanisms are made possible by taking advantage of individual mental processes in accepting management practices. But though inseparable, it is still possible to classify management practices into three rough groups according to their major functions, as is illustrated in Figure 2. The first consists of practices which can provide the basis of support for the two sub-systems. They include annual across-the-board recruitment (or recruitment of all new employees once a year),[14] job security (or 'lifetime employment'), continuous in-house training, in-house promotion, sharing of corporate information, encouraging team spirit, flexibility of job boundaries, and minimisation of status differences between managers and managed. The second group contributes more to 'integrating individuals into a group'. It includes, quality circles, suggestion schemes; *ringi*,[15] consensus decision-making and group meetings. The third group works more toward 'incorporating individuals into the organisation'. It includes length of service-based pay rises and promotion (or seniority reward), job rotation, and job reassignment.

Focus of the research

The generally accepted notion of British management is much concerned with short-run profit maximisation through the optimal allocation of productive resources on the basis of subjective judgement. The major concern in this context is a high return on capital, but not on labour, which would be made possible through 'appreciating' the latter's value in the long run. Hence redundant labour is not as a rule retained.

Employees, on the other hand, aim at satisfying their needs or 'inner preferences' to the maximum extent. Except in instances of high unemployment, long-term discrepancies between employees' inner preferences and actual satisfaction would not usually be acceptable. If the intrinsic and extrinsic rewards do not correspond to their contribution to the company in a subjective sense, they look for other job opportunities in external labour markets, so as to seek higher satisfaction; whereas in Japan, even if employees' inner preferences are not satisfied as they expected at the time of their employment, they still tend to stay in the same company, with the hope that their lifelong utility will thus be maximised.[16]

Such differences in behaviour may be one of the major reasons why Japanese employees tend to complain more about the terms and conditions of the companies they work for than their Western counterparts, as revealed in various surveys.[17] It also implies that the 'field' of the company and the 'knowledge' of its members are quite different between the two countries. British employees are always interacting between internal and external labour markets.

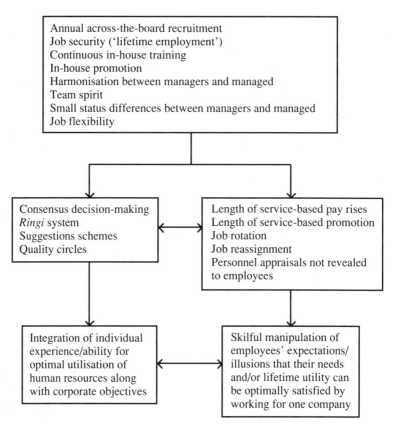

Figure 2 Mechanisms of Japanese management practice

Accordingly, as far as British labour markets remain unchanged, the very mechanisms which the above mentioned Japanese subsidiaries sub-systems carry can hardly be expected to function even in Japanese subsidiaries in Britain; because the prerequisite for Japanese firms to transfer such mechanisms is to impose the nature of the 'Japanese field' on the 'British field'. Hence, the transaction cost of transferring such mechanisms into Britain is not only infinite and Japanese firms will be rejected and bitterly accused if they try to bring such mechanisms straightforwardly into their British subsidiaries. Some cases of US-based multinationals in Western Europe are good examples.[18]

Therefore, the concern should not be to examine whether or not the mechanisms carried in the two sub-systems of Japanese management can be observed in Japanese subsidiaries in Britain, but whether Japanese management practices transferred internationally within intra-firm organisation work efficiently. In this context it is assumed that, if the following three conditions are satisfied, the intra-firm transferability of Japanese-style manage-

128

ment is assured, even though their mechanisms are not identical with those in Japan:–

(i) Management practices are implemented on the basis of the 'logic of human talent' aimed at achieving long-run optimisation through 'appreciating' and 'integrating' the value of human resources within a firm

(ii) The management practices implemented keep satisfying the inner preferences of company members. If they are not continuously satisfied, acceptability of the Japanese management system will not be high; hence the transaction cost is not recouped

(iii) The organic functions of the management practices implemented work to stimulate employees' work motivation. If they do not do so but only make the employees feel comfortable, the efficiency of the Japanese-style management system as an organic entity is not assured, even if the practices are accepted.[19] In this case, allocation of Japanese management resources is not efficient and the transaction cost cannot be recouped

The first two comprise the necessary conditions and the third the sufficient condition for evaluating the relevance of intra-firm transferability of the Japanese-style management system to overseas subsidiaries.

People and companies surveyed

(i) Method and sample

Information was obtained through a questionnaire and interview survey conducted in May and June 1985 in Britain, excluding Northern Ireland. In order to minimise biased evaluation of the Japanese-style management system abroad, opinions of both Japanese and host country nationals must be taken into account. Two questionnaires were therefore prepared; one for top Japanese managers in Britain, and the other for British middle-level managers. In order to avoid biased responses, companies were asked to choose British respondents with neutral attitudes.

Twenty-five Japanese manufacturing firms were asked to fill in the questionnaire, out of the total of thirty firms operating and/or preparing for operation in Britain as of May 1985, and twenty firms responded. Questionnaires were completed by nineteen Japanese top level managers (in effect middle managers in their head offices) plus one locally employed senior level middle manager, and sixty-seven British middle managers, ranging from senior managers to supervisors. Interviews were conducted with a Japanese top level manager and three to five British middle managers working for each of the sixteen firms out of the twenty firms which completed the questionnaires, plus one other firm which terminated its technical service agreement with the British company and took over its whole share by the time of the survey. Thus, the companies surveyed included virtually all Japanese manufacturing companies then operating in Britain with mostly or entirely Japanese equity.

(ii) Profile of Japanese subsidiaries

The companies surveyed were established in Britain between 1966 and 1985, mostly after 1980. Most produced consumer goods, such as TV sets, optical lenses, and fishing tackle; some produced parts and intermediate goods, like batteries and bearings. The major purposes for setting up manufacturing subsidiaries were, (i) to secure the local market, 90 per cent; (ii) to establish a bridgehead for the European market, 80 per cent; and (iii) to make use of local resources, 75 per cent. Their factories were located on industrial estates, where traditional industries such as coal mining had declined, and where the rate of unemployment remained higher than the national average.

The equity of seventeen companies was totally held by the head offices or their affiliates in Japan. Among them, four companies had participated in joint ventures with British capital or technical service agreements to begin with, but later had taken over the whole equity due to bad performance. The majority of the employees of the previous companies were also employed by the new companies. Japanese equity participation in the other three companies was 99.9 per cent, 96 per cent and 75 per cent respectively. The Japanese companies were small to medium size, with less than 599 employees, except one company which had more than 1,000 employees; paid-up capital was £2.8 million on average, ranging from £60,000 to £8.83 million[20], and the number of directors assigned was also limited, as shown in Table 1. On average, 5.4 Japanese staff including directors were assigned to one factory. Companies with shorter experience in Britain had larger numbers of staff sent from Japan, while those with longer experience had reduced their numbers.

Table 1   Distribution of company directors

	Japanese	British	Total
Full-time[1]	1.7	1.2	2.9
Part-time[2]	2.3	0.3	2.6

Notes: 1. Number of Japanese full-time directors ranges from 0 to 6, with 3 companies having none. Number of British full-time directors ranges from 0 to 5, with 12 companies having none.
2. Number of Japanese part-time directors ranges from 0 to 7, with 3 companies having none. Number of British part-time directors ranges from 0 to 2, with 15 companies having none.

130

The average length of service of management level British employees was 4.5 years and of workers 2.6 years. Rates of absenteeism, annual separation and monthly wages are shown in Table 2. Compared with non-Japanese companies in the same area, 47.4 per cent of the Japanese companies set standard wage levels; while 26.3 per cent paid slightly more and 26.3 per cent paid slightly less. A bonus system was in operation in only 37.5 per cent of the Japanese companies, with bonuses averaging the equivalent of 1.24 months' salary per year for managers and 1.12 months for workers. The major reason for introducing bonus systems was to share the fruits of the efforts of both managers and workers.

Eleven companies had trade unions, with nine recognising a 'single union' as the bargaining representative.

Table 2   Work and remuneration

	Managers	Supervisors	Workers
Length of service (years)	4.5	3.3	2.6
Rate of Absenteeism (%)	1.2	2.3	4.2
Annual separation rate (%)	13.1	11.8	11.2
Remuneration (in £ sterling)	13,106	8,406	5,063

(iii)   Profile of British employees

Most employees were recruited from nearby areas; so the nature of company employees was fairly homogeneous. The average age of sixty-seven British respondents was 38.0 years. Those who had graduated from university and/or graduate school were 34.8 per cent; those who had GCSE (General Certificate of Secondary Education) were 31.8 per cent; and the remaining 33.4 per cent were the ones who finished compulsory education, including 9.1 per cent who had some vocational training. Thirty-eight of the respondents were senior middle managers and twenty-eight were junior middle managers, such as assistant managers and supervisors.

Overall, 92.5 per cent of the British respondents had worked elsewhere previously, and had changed their workplaces an average of 3.1 times. Four persons had changed their workplaces as many as seven times, and five persons six times. Both the proportion of middle managers who had changed their workplaces and the average frequency of their changing workplaces were higher than among local middle managers in Japanese subsidiaries in Asia.[21]

Management implemented in Britain

(i) Basic management policies

Seventeen per cent of Japanese corporations in Britain emphasised Japanese management creed and objectives 'strongly' or 'to a considerable extent'; at the same time, 80 per cent of them leaned toward localisation, i.e. adoption of local values and practices. Only 55 per cent emphasised management styles as implemented in Japan, and 15 per cent emphasised a universal management style which could be applied to any Japanese overseas subsidiaries regardless of location. Similar management inclinations were observed in our previous survey of Japanese subsidiaries in Asia.[22] This indicates that Japanese management, as in Japan, adjusts itself flexibly, grafting some Japanese features on to local values and practices.

The precondition that Japanese managers believed most important for the successful grafting of Japanese style is the careful selection of employees. As shown in Table 3, 50 per cent of Japanese companies recruited middle managers and 30 per cent of them hired workers through very careful or more careful selection processes than in Japan. Those which selected middle managers and workers to similar standards as in Japan were 27.8 per cent and 45.5 per cent respectively. In addition to personality and ability, Japanese companies were heavily inclined to recruit persons who, firstly, were considered to be able to conform to Japanese management objectives, namely, persons able to share their 'knowledge' with their Japanese counterparts, and secondly, who seemed to have potential but had so far limited opportunities to demonstrate it due to the fairly low social strata into which they were born.

Table 3   Management attitudes towards selection of local staff compared to in Japan (%)

	Very careful	More careful	About the same	Rather easy	Easy
Managers	16.7	33.3	27.8	22.0	0
Workers	5.0	25.0	45.0	15.0	10.0

Taking the above as the basic management policies of Japanese manufacturing companies in Britain, to what extent have Japanese management practices been implemented, and how far have British middle managers welcomed them? Table 4 shows the answers.[23]

(ii) Practices emphasised and welcomed

Though not directly comparable due to the differences of population, it is noteworthy that most of those defined as the basic practices supporting Japanese-style management were emphasised more heavily in Britain than in Japan. They were job security, continuous in-house training, harmonisation between managers and managed, minimisation of status differences between corporate members, encouragement of team spirit, and the flexibility of job boundaries. These practices are essential in maintaining the long-term stability of management by means of 'appreciating' the value of indi-

Table 4 Degree of implementation/acceptance of Japanese practices (%)

	Japanese responses		British responses	
	Degree of emphasis		Perceived degree of implement-ation	Willingness to accept
	Japanese head office	Subsidiaries in Britain		
	(1)	(2)	(3)	(4)
Japanese management philosophy	67.9	75.0	75.0	72.3
Job security (stable employment)	84.6	94.8	79.3	93.3
Continuous internal training	55.1	84.3	51.6	89.2
In-house promotion	92.3	60.0	61.9	92.4
Harmonisation between managers and managed	63.5	88.9	63.1	95.6
Small status differences	38.5	70.0	70.8	94.0
Encouraging team spirit	51.3	85.0	64.0	90.9
Flexible job demarcation	53.8	63.2	81.6	91.4
Sharing of information	–	55.0	52.4	100.0
Strong emphasis on quality	–	–	96.9	100.0
Consensus decision-making	47.4	33.4	50.9	81.8
ringi	79.5	17.6	50.0	65.7
Quality Circles	67.9	38.9	46.6	79.4
Suggestions schemes	92.3	33.3	34.4	78.8
Length of service-based pay rises	32.1	5.3	24.2	27.2
Length of service-based promotion	44.9	26.3	43.6	53.1
Job rotation	53.8	38.9	31.2	56.1

Notes: Column (1) denotes percentage answering 'emphasised' on 3 point scale.
Columns (2), (3) and (4) denote percentage answering 'strongly' and 'considerably emphasised', 'implemented' and 'welcomed' respectively, on 5 point scale.

vidual abilities, and, since these practices are essential to Japanese-style management but have not been highly emphasised by Western management, Japanese companies in Britain must have emphasised them more strongly than in Japan in the hope that they would assimilate British employees to the Japanese-style approach.

However, in-house promotion and sharing of corporate information were not emphasised relative to other basic practices. Since most of the Japanese companies had a short operating history in Britain, 61 per cent of them were using both in-house promotion and recruitment from the external market to fill vacancies, but none were depending solely on the external market. Those indicating that they would continue to use both internal and external recruitment systems had declined to 39 per cent. They replied that they would gradually shift to internal promotion in accordance with the accumulation of expertise within the firm.

As for information sharing, in addition to the language barrier, Japanese managers were not yet certain what information should be shared with British employees. It may take time for subsidiaries in Britain to reach the degree to which corporate information is shared in Japan.

British respondents did not perceive that some basic management practices, such as continuous internal training and harmonisation between managers and managed, were emphasised to the same extent to which Japanese managers implemented them; but the percentage of British middle managers welcoming these basic practices was quite high. This indicates that basic management practices which support the aims of Japanese-style management – to achieve long-run optimisation through 'appreciation' of the value of human resources – can be implemented in Japanese manufacturing firms in Britain with a limited transaction cost.

(iii) Practices not emphasised

Management practices which mainly work toward the 'integration of individuals into the group' were not emphasised in Britain to the same degree as in Japan. They include consensus decision-making, particularly, *ringi*, suggestion schemes and quality circles. Japanese managers were careful about implementing these group-oriented practices. They were apprehensive that such practices would blur the identity of individuals, and the scope of individual responsibility and individual decision-making; hence would contradict British middle managers' values. They were also afraid that if hasty implementation ends in failure, it would be difficult to gain British support to implement them again and that the consistency of Japanese leadership would be questioned.

A considerable proportion of British respondents showed their willingness to accept these practices but in in-depth interviews, they expressed some ambivalence, as follows:–

(i)   These practices would lessen individual training opportunities for making decisions, and reduce their own confidence in decision-making; hence these practices would work against seeking jobs elsewhere in the future

(ii)   These practices are not compatible with British values, in which individual authority and responsibility attached to the job are respected. If a person asks the opinions of others, including subordinates, about their own job in a meeting, they may be thought incapable. This is quite insulting.

At the same time, British middle managers have gradually come to realise that these practices have advantages in executing their respective jobs and in improving their own performance. They help a middle manager who is responsible for a particular matter to acquire different views from the participants of group discussions. The latter can likewise obtain information on the matter and learn where the company is heading. In this way, participants tend to support ech other, creating a feeling of interdependency within a corporate group.

British middle managers have also come to realise that their satisfaction is greater when a job is done successfully and get praise from a group, instead of only from their respective superior.

Yet, there is still a perception gap or 'knowledge' gap concerning these practices. The ambivalent local 'knowledge' of these practices is formulated on the British 'field'. So their 'knowledge' cannot suddenly be shifted to one where all of them share the feeling that there are more advantages than disadvantages. Therefore, before Japanese managers try to implement these practices, some common 'field' acceptable to both parties must be provided. It should include at least the following:–

–   Clarifying the relationship between the individual and the group so that ultimate authority and responsibility are kept by the person who proposes a course of action

–   Letting middle managers understand what improvements result from 'integrating individual abilities into the group'

–   Establishing rules as to how the fruits resulting from improvements due to these practices are shared between the participants and the company

Time and effort to provide such a 'field' and to get support for it are considered as the transaction cost of implementation.

Relative to the practices for expediting the 'integration of individuals into the group', those which have worked in Japan to stimulate the 'incorporation of individuals into the organisation', were even less emphasised; nor were they welcomed by the majority of the Britons. They included length of service-based pay rises and promotion, and job rotation. In Britain, where differentiation of individual skills is highly evaluated, it is understandable that these practices are not welcomed. Even in Japan, these practices, particularly length of service-based rewards, have been significantly weakened due mainly to the changing values of younger employees and the ageing population.[24] Efforts to make the majority of employees of a uniform nature and to 'incorporate them into the organisation', without much regard for their own identity, are giving way to efforts to 'differentiate' individuals in terms of ability. The system is gradually being modified so that the various attributes of individuals can be harmoniously integrated into the group. In a sense, the Japanese management system implemented in Britain represents a new style which Japanese companies are now trying to explore.

The findings suggest that Japanese manufacturing companies in Britain are trying to implement a mixture of practices, which can expedite 'appreciation' of the value of human resources by preserving individual identity and 'integrate' them for attaining long-term optimisation. This implies that the first condition for evaluating the relevance of the international intra-firm transferability of Japanese management is practically satisfied.

Acceptability of Japanese management

To be clarified next is the degree to which the mixture of Japanese management practices implemented satisfies the inner preferences of British managers. It is assumed that their preferences are shown in their reasons for choosing the company they work for and that they behave in such a way as to satisfy these preferences. Thus, if their preferences are satisfied, the degree of acceptability is high, and vice versa, as shown in Figure 3. According to this Figure, their inner preferences were more satisfied than they had originally expected.

The responses indicate that, with some reservation about promotion, the management practices implemented were fairly well accepted with a fairly low transaction cost. It can therefore be inferred that the second condition for evaluating the relevance of the Japanese-style management system in Britain is satisfied to a significant extent.

This inference is reinforced by responses to the questionnaire item, 'You are glad that you chose this company to work for, over others you were considering.' Twenty-seven per cent answered 'strongly agree', 53 per cent replied 'agree', and only 1.5 per cent responded negatively.

Efficiency of Japanese management

To what extent then does the mix of Japanese management practices implemented at subsidiaries in Britain work efficiently in terms of resource allocation? This is a key issue, because high acceptability with low transaction

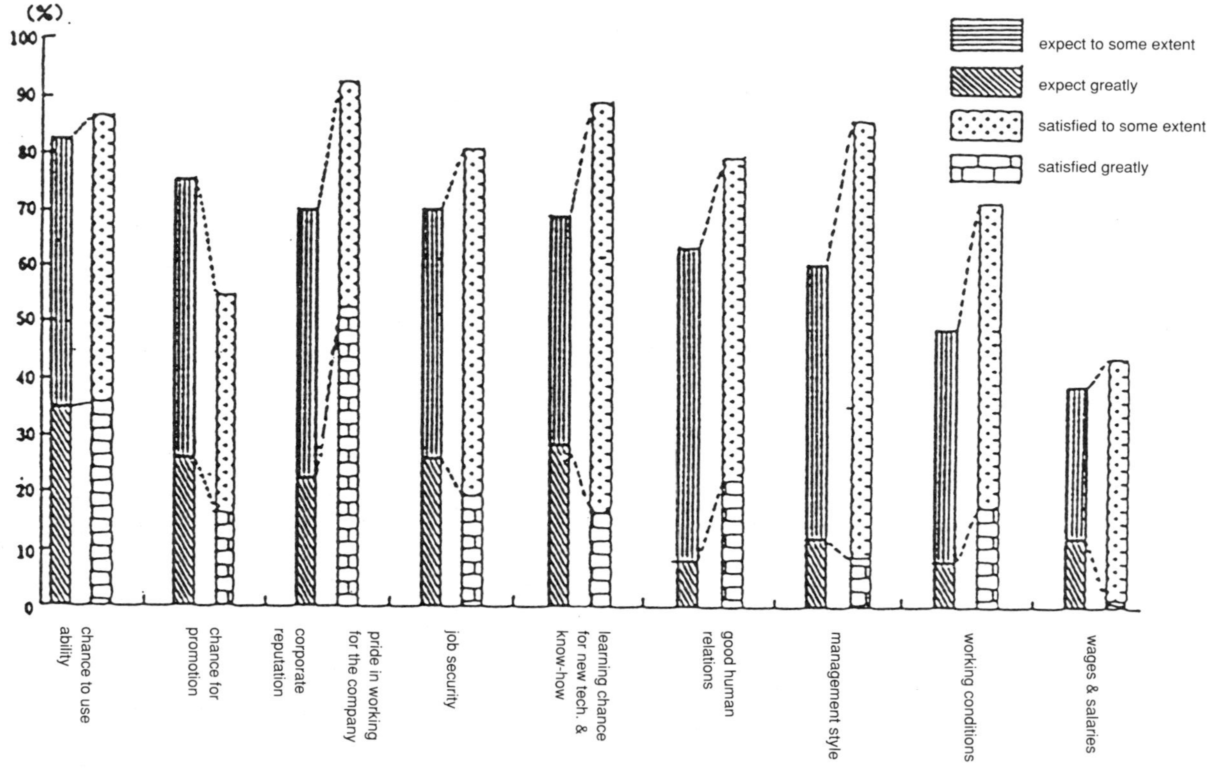
(%)
100
90
80
70
60
50
40
30
20
10
0
expect to some extent
expect greatly
satisfied to some extent
satisfied greatly
chance to use ability
chance for promotion
corporate reputation
pride in working for the company
job security
learning chance for new tech. & know-how
good human relations
management style
working conditions
wages & salaries

Figure 3 British middle managers' preferences: expectations and fulfilment

cost alone does not assure efficient resource allocation, unless the mix works as an incentive to stimulate the motivation of local middle managers.

To the question asking about the incentives for work motivation, the following responses were obtained from British middle managers in the Japanese subsidiaries:–

- Making the job more interesting, 94.0 per cent (The Figure shows the sum of responses marked 'very important' and 'important'. The same applies to the figures below.')
- Good human relations, 84.3 per cent
- Excellent leadership, 81.8 per cent
- Promotion, 79.1 per cent
- Thoroughness of management, 76.1 per cent
- Wages and salaries, 70.1 per cent
- Self-managing work group, 44.8 per cent

If there is a good correlation between the respective incentives and their satisfaction, the mix implemented can be regarded as functioning efficiently in line with corporate objectives. Items 1 to 9 of Table 5 show the satisfaction of the British middle managers with their jobs to be considerable.

However, our survey revealed that many of the British middle managers surveyed were not quite satisfied with the opportunities for promotion and with current salary levels – their other important incentives for work motivation. As many as 79.1 per cent of the British respondents indicated promotion as their incentive for work motivation, but only 54.6 per cent were satisfied with their promotion prospects. Likewise, 70.1 per cent indicated salaries as incentives, but only 44.8 per cent were satisfied. The big discrepancies may imply that the pay and promotion systems were not appropriate motivators. Nevertheless, it is not clear whether the discrepancies really indicate the inappropriateness of Japanese-style pay and promotion systems.

Our previous survey of Japanese subsidiaries in Asian countries showed that the proportion of middle managers in various Asian countries who were satisfied with promotion opportunities and wages corresponded to the levels of economic development. In other words, middle managers in more developed economies tend to grumble over their salary levels and promotion more than those in less developed economies.

The findings may suggest that as the economy matures, the middle class grows and hence opportunities for promotion become fewer, while consumer demand becomes more diversified; hence the potential desire for more income becomes stronger.

Taking this as a general tendency, in Britain, where the stage of economic development is even more matured than in Japan, the British responses in which only 16.7 per cent surveyed were 'very' satisfied with their promotion opportunities and 1.5 per cent with their salaries (see Figure 3) cannot necessarily be attributed to the pay and promotion systems implemented being inappropriate to Britain. This inference is supported by the finding that a small number of British middle managers, relative to those in Japan and Korea, showed dissatisfaction with promotion and wages. It may be said, therefore, that in terms of work motivation the pay and promotion systems in Japanese firms in Britain are not inferior to those implemented in Japan and Korea.

Table 5   British middle managers' preferences and satisfaction (%)

		Strongly agree	Agree	Neutral	Disagree	Strongly disagree
1.	More variety in the job than in previous experience	40.9	34.8	13.6	10.6	0
2.	Job denies any chance to use personal initiative/judgement	1.5	1.5	10.4	50.7	35.8
3.	Satisfied with responsibility given	9.1	63.6	13.6	10.6	3.0
4.	Enough authority to do the job	9.0	61.2	20.9	9.0	0
5.	Feeling of achieving in your job	24.5	59.7	11.9	3.0	0
6.	Ample opportunities to voice opinion at meetings	59.1	27.3	10.6	1.5	1.5
7.	Attention paid to your suggestions	10.4	64.2	20.9	4.5	0
8.	Satisfied with recognition for good work	6.0	49.3	34.3	9.0	1.5
9.	Japanese willing to transfer technology and know-how	16.9	72.3	7.7	0	0
10.	Pride in working for this company	52.2	40.3	7.5	0	0
11.	Work system very humanised	6.2	56.9	33.8	3.1	0
12.	Top managers mix with workers	17.9	64.2	14.9	1.5	1.5
13.	Status differences between management and workers small	10.6	47.0	19.7	19.7	3.0
14.	Japanese staff fair to everyone	19.7	43.9	34.8	1.5	0
15.	Satisfied with your chief	22.4	56.7	17.9	1.5	1.5
16.	Satisfied with peer group	8.1	67.7	19.4	4.8	0
17.	Can make good friends in the company	14.9	62.7	20.9	1.5	0
18.	Lack of Japanese leadership	0	3.1	30.8	49.2	16.9
19.	Management too situation-centred	0	14.8	44.4	38.1	3.2
20.	Good promotion chances	16.7	37.9	33.3	10.6	1.5
21.	Fair promotion system	10.8	52.3	27.7	9.2	0
22.	Pay satisfactory for the job you do	1.5	43.3	28.4	22.4	4.5

This suggests that an organic combination of Japanese-style practices implemented in subsidiaries in Britain can *in toto* stimulate the work motivation of British middle managers. As many as 86.5 per cent of those surveyed had 'a feeling of commitment to the organisation'.

In view of the high proportion of British middle managers who desire more salary increases and promotion compared to Asian middle managers,[25] some improvements are needed to fit the British setting. While 94.6 per cent of Japanese top managers in Britain emphasised 'merit' as a criterion for pay rises and promotion, 83.3 per cent also emphasised 'personality'. This is important when implementing practices such as job flexibility and reassignment but unless objective measures acceptable to local managers are set in evaluating 'personality', there will certainly be friction. Only 54.6 per cent of British middle managers agreed that the 'promotion system is fair'.

28.8 per cent would 'certainly accept', if another organisation offered better pay and position, with 42.2 per cent 'undecided'. Japanese managers must realise the implications. The cost of capable persons changing employers is not small when employees are trained internally through continuous training programmes. Japanese managers should remember the value inherited by the British middle class that 'getting more income through one's own industriousness is a virtue'.[26] They should also think of the well developed British external labour market, contrasted with its immature counterpart in Japan. Otherwise, frustration will remain among capable British employees.

Overall evaluation

(i) British evaluation

According to Table 6, only 3.1 per cent responded negatively to accepting Japanese-style management, with 6.2 per cent hesitating to admit its efficiency. None believed that Japanese-style management was irrational or did not contribute to company performance.

Regarding the weak points, 35.8 per cent mentioned 'slow decisions', and 24.2 per cent 'unclear individual responsibilities'. But when comparing these responses with those of Japanese middle managers in Japan, of whom 36.4 per cent complained about 'slow decisions', and 51.1 per cent 'unclear individual responsibilities', British responses seem quite moderate. However, 24.2 per cent of British respondents were dissatisfied with 'communication based on tacit understandings'. While those not considering 'slow decisions' and 'unclear individual responsibilities' as weak points were 32.9 per cent and 43.9 per cent respectively, only 25.8 per cent considered 'communication based on tacit understandings' was *not* its weak point. This indicates that the 'knowledge' involved in Japanese-style practices is not well shared between British and Japanese staff.

140

Table 6   British middle managers' overall evaluation (%)

	5	4	3	2	1
Generally happy atmosphere in the company	12.1	54.5	28.8	6.1	1.5
Generally satisfied working here	31.8	62.3	3.0	3.0	0
Management style/system generally accepted	9.2	76.9	10.8	3.1	0
Generally efficient work organisation	7.7	73.8	12.3	6.2	0
'Japanese' management standards/practices economically viable and contributing to corporate performance	18.8	64.1	17.2	0	0

Note: 5 = strongly agree, 4 = agree, 3 = neutral, 2 = disagree, 1 = strongly disagree

Thirty-three per cent of Britons answered that there were communication barriers; but this is not surprising in comparison with Asia. Even in Korea and Taiwan, where, relative to Britain, the social and cultural background is more similar to Japan, as many as 60.8 per cent of Korean and 59.9 per cent of Taiwanese middle managers surveyed admitted there were communication barriers between them and Japanese staff. More surprising was the finding that those indicating 'value difference' to be a major factor hindering communication were 30.0 per cent in Korea and 28.9 per cent in Taiwan, but only 20.9 per cent in Britain. The findings imply that the values nurtured in the 'field' of a corporate organisation are not necessarily strongly regulated by cultural factors, or by similar ethnicity. The inference is that the individual sense of economic rationality becomes similar when the level of economic development and the level of maturity of an organisation becomes similar, and hence value differences between different nationals within the same organisation are reduced.

The hypothesis from the above is that, except for highly institutionalised 'knowledge', 'knowledge' related to economic rationality can be shared by nationals at similar stages of economic development if communication is made explicit. The degree of acceptance and efficiency of Japanese-style management systems therefore increases as economic development reaches more mature stages.

Another important finding is that no noticeable differences were observed between senior and junior middle managers. This suggests that the prevailing hypothesis that 'Japanese-style management is more accepted the lower one goes down the company hierarchy' is not applicable to Japanese manufacturing subsidiaries in Britain.

(ii) Japanese evaluation

To the question 'Do you think Japanese-style management is relevant in your British subsidiaries?', 10 per cent of Japanese top managers in Britain replied 'Yes, definitely', 50 per cent answered 'yes', and the remaining 40 per cent 'not decided yet'. No managers responded negatively.

Some of the tangible results attributed to Japanese-style management were as follows:–

– Decrease in defect ratios, 94.3 per cent (The sum of respondents who replied 'improved remarkably' and 'improved considerably'. The same applies to the figures below.)

– Increase in productivity, 88.9 per cent

– Improvement of work process, 83.3 per cent

– Increase of firm's reputation, 82.4 per cent

– Transfer ot technology and know-how, 70.6 per cent

– Increase of employees' commitment to the job, 70.6 per cent

– Increase of employees' commitment to the company, 58.8 per cent

– Decrease of employees' turnover, 55.8 per cent

– Increase of attendance ratios, 50.0 per cent

Major management targets were achieved by the majority of firms, as shown in Table 7.

Table 7   Degree of achievement (%)

	Far beyond target	Beyond target	As planned	Below target	Far below target
Sales	6.2	25.0	50.0	18.8	0
Profits	5.9	17.6	52.9	17.6	5.9
Growth	6.2	12.5	56.2	25.0	0

Taking into account the fairly short experience of Japanese manufacturing subsidiaries in Britain, the findings suggest that Japanese-style management is efficient and that the intra-organisational transferability of Japanese-style management to Britain is relevant.

Concluding remarks

The survey revealed that the intra-firm transferability of the Japanese-style management system to Britain can to a considerable extent be ensured with a limited transaction cost. It is reinforced by careful selection processes and the fairly homogeneous nature of the local staff employed; also by the fairly small size of the subsidiaries, in which there seem to be no noticeable diseconomies of scale in terms of administration.

However, the major reason why Japanese-style management is accepted and functions efficiently is attributable to Japanese management's attitude of not daring to try to transfer practices that would involve 'knowledge' formulated by long-lasting Japanese institutions and hence would not become 'transmittable knowledge' in the British 'field'. Practices which stimulate the 'incorporation of individuals into the organisation' fall into this category.

On the other hand, Japanese staff try to transfer practices that have not existed or have been neglected in Britain but somehow could become 'shared knowledge' even in the British 'field'. Practices which expedite the 'integration of individuals into the group' are in this category.

The Japanese inclination to graft the 'logic of the British field' and the 'logic of the Japanese field in Britain' suggests that British-style management is likely to converge towards Japanese-style with a certain transaction cost. However, there are some necessary conditions for this to take place: Japanese who are well acquainted with the Japanese way must link the 'logic of the British field' and the 'logic of Japanese field in Britain', thus nurturing a 'shared knowledge' between them. Without Japanese staff in Britain, the transaction cost will be enormous.

However, the scenario will be different in all-British companies, where top managers always face a possible take-over. Without nurturing a 'field' in which management has a long-term perspective, it is not easy to get acquainted with Japanese-style management or to share the 'knowledge' which Japanese management practices imply. How to make 'Japanese-style knowledge' transferable to managers in non-Japanese companies while preserving the theory of the 'British field' is the challenge.

Notes

1. Hasegawa, S. 'An Inquiry into a Theory of Multinational Enterprise', Enatsu, K. (ed.)., *Kokusai-keizai Funso to Takokuseki Kigyo (International Economic Conflict and Multinational Enterprise)*, Koyo-shobo. 1987. pp. 321–5.
2. Komiya, R. and Amano, A. *Kokusai Keizai Gaku (International Economics)*. Iwanami Shoten,l Tokyo. 1972. pp. 435–8.
3. Dunning, J.H. 'Trade, Location of Economic Activity and the MNE: A search for an Eclectic Approach', Ohlin, B. et al. (eds.), *The International Allocation of Economic Activity*. Macmillan, London. 1977. ch. 12.
4. Dunning, J.H. *Japanese Participation in British Industry*. Croom Helm, London. 1986. p. 57.
5. Using the concept of transaction cost as a criterion in evaluating the transferability of certain management practices across national boundaries involves many basic questions. See Williamson, O. 'The Economics of Organisation', *A.J.S.* 1981.)
6. Data referred to in this paper were obtained through questionnaire and interview surveys conducted from 1981 to 1985 by researchers organised by Prof.

Shinichi Ichimura, covering Japanese-capital affiliated companies in five ASEAN countries excluding Brunei, three East Asian countries (territories) and their head offices in Japan.

7. See Sasaki, N. *Keiei Kokusai-ka no Riron (Theory of Internationalisation of Management)*. Nihon Keizai Shinbun-sha, Tokyo. 1983. p. 15.

8. Leibenstein, H. *Inside the Firm: The Inefficiencies of Hierarchy*. Harvard University Press, 1987. ch. 5.

9. Lewin, K. *Field Theory in Social Science*. Harper & Brothers, New York. 1951.

10. Polanyi, M. *The Tacit Dimension*. Routledge & Kegan Paul, Boston. 1967.

11. Koike, K. *Nihon no Jukuren (Skill Formation in Japanese Companies)*. Yuhikaku, Tokyo. 1981.

12. Tomita, T. 'Japanese-Style Management in Britain'. Blumenthal, T. (ed.), *Japanese Management at Home and Abroad*. Ben-Gurion University, Beersheva. 1987. p. 176.

13. The organic functions of the *doji issei saiyo seido* (annual across-the-board recruitment system) widely adopted throughout Japan, 'life-time employment', length of service-based reward schemes and Japanese personnel assessments illustrate how effectively their expectations are manipulated and their talents mobilised over the maximum duration. Under the service-based reward schemes, differences of salary and position among employees in the same age group are negligible for a considerable period after hiring; and assessments are not revealed to employees in Japan. This induces younger employees to have expectations, or rather illusions, that there are practically equal opportunities to climb up the promotion ladder. They usually do not therefore complain about their fairly low pecuniary rewards relative to their contribution to the company. Taking advantage of such expectations, management skilfully encourages employees to work harder, so as to enjoy the benefits accruing from the high productivity of younger employees at relatively low cost. Such managerial intentions are camouflaged by an across-the-board recruitment system which hires people with similar abilities once a year. Differentiation of employees' wages and positions by performance is therefore generally considered difficult, and even unfair, for a considerable period. But in reality, performance is strictly evaluated at different management levels immediately after hiring. When managers are convinced, after making appraisals over, say, ten years, that a service-based pay rise for a certain employee is no longer justified by his performance, then the rate amount of his annual pay increase starts to decline relative to his colleagues, and promotion tends to slow down. Such differentiation within the same age bracket is carried out with caution, so as not to lower employee morale at each hierarchical level and not to disturb the 'harmony' among them. Under the 'lifetime' employment system, even though their promotion has stopped, they are, except in extreme cases, given either a title but no real function, or reassigned to a subsidiary. They still receive a salary that they could seldom expect in the external market, so their life long utility will usually be more satisfied by working for the same company throughout their career than otherwise.

14. Every autumn, companies select graduating students. Those selected join the company on 1 April the following year, when the next school year also begins. This system lays the foundations of Japanese management by permit-

ting the companies, firstly, to hire personnel who seem to have traits easily associated with the 'field' of the company; secondly, to train new employees simultaneously, to encourage 'closely knit' group consciousness; thirdly, to stir up feelings of emulation or friendly competition; and fourthly to provide a raison d'être for the implementation of length of service-based pay increase and promotion for a considerable period after hiring.

15. *Ringi* is the system of circulating intra-office memoranda to obtain the approval of all concerned for a proposed course of action, ranging from the purchase of a word processor to a merger. Depending on the type of proposal, it may circulate vertically from the bottom up, or horizontally among managers and directors of related departments before coming up to the president, according to its importance. *Nemawashi* (the groundwork to enlist support or informal consent) is necessary prior to the circulation of the form. Each person approving the proposal puts his seal (*hanko*) on it – the Japanese equivalent of the signature. The advantage of the system is that everyone is involved, so that once a decision is made, company-wide cooperation in its implementation is assured.

16. Regarding extrinsic rewards, employees who work for the same company until retirement age are generally better-off than otherwise. Fringe benefits increase in accordance with length of service and retirement money is much bigger at retirement age than if they quit earlier. In terms of wages and positions, there is an institutionalised framework across industry which makes it disadvantageous to change employers; though this last has gradually been weakened.

17. See *Denki Roren* (Japanese Federation of Electrical Machine Workers' Unions), 'Jukkakoku Denki Rodosha no Ishiki Chosa Chukan Hokoku' (Report on an International Study of Employees in the Electrical and Electronics Industries), *Chosa Jiho*, Vol. 204. December 1985. pp. 168–76.

18. Taira, K., 'The impact on the US of Japanese Management Techniques: With Special Reference to Human Resources and Industrial Relations.' Paper presented at the International Symposium on the *Transferability of the Japanese Management System*, Tokyo, 31 August–2 September 1990. pp. 5, 33–4.

1ᶜ. The survey in Asia revealed that middle managers who thought job security was guaranteed were less committed and more lukewarm towards the company than those who did not.

20. Four companies had a paid-up capital of less than £1 million; six companies between £1 and £1.9 million; four between £2 and £4.9 million; and six had more than £5 million.

21. See *Southeast Asian Studies*, Vol. 22, No. 4. Centre for Southeast Asian Studies, Kyoto University, March 1985. Appendix p. 118.

22. Tomita, T. 'Asia ni Okeru Nihonkigyo no Rommu Keiei' (Labour Management in Japanese Companies in Asia), *Hikone Ronso*. Vol. 245. Shiga University. August 1987. p. 30.

23. Figures shown in Column 1 were obtained from 104 Japanese head offices whose factories in Asia were surveyed.

24. The range of wage differences is small for lower level employees, who are the most numerous. Therefore, as far as the age structure of firms remains a pyramid, firms can take advantage of the higher productivity of younger

employees relative to labour cost, and can even pay off the lower productivity of some older employees relative to their labour cost. But when the population structure becomes a dewdrop shape, the economic rationality of the system can hardly be maintained, since total labour cost may outweigh the sum of labour productivity. Furthermore, when the values of employees become diverse, as currently observed, employees tend to lessen their efforts for material gain and hence 'manipulation' does not work as effectively as before. See also Note 13 above.

25. *Southeast Asian Studies, op. cit.* p. 123.
26. Interview with Mr. Y. Masuoka, President of Beezer Japan Inc.

8 Cross-cultural human resource development: Japanese manufacturing firms in central Japan and central US states

MITSURU WAKABAYASHI AND GEORGE B. GRAEN
NAGOYA UNIVERSITY AND UNIVERSITY OF CINCINNATI

Expansion by Japanese corporations of their manufacturing operations to America is forcing the difficult transfer of core technology from home plants to those in a very different Western culture. Although Japanese manufacturing core technology patterned after the model invented and refined by Toyota was introduced in the US about 1980, it largely remains a mystery to US manufacturing. However, the system has proved a dramatic success at NUMMI in Fremont, California and at other Japanese-owned plants in the US. These successes notwithstanding, little is known about the nature of the transfer process, e.g. what are the major roles in the process, and what are the critical success factors? The purpose here is to explore the answers to these questions based on in-depth interviews with managers of Japanese manufacturing companies both in central Japan and in the central states of the USA.

A key to successful transfers

Recent dramatic increases in Japanese direct investment in the United States has attracted research interests aimed towards understanding how Japanese firms are managing these new businesses.[1] Research attention has also shown renewed interest in the process through which Japanese management practices are made culturally transferable outside Japan.[2] For example, how do Japanese management practices affect attitudes and behaviours of American employees working for the Japanese corporations in the United States[3]?

Kujawa and his associates (1983, 1985) investigated the outcomes of Japanese management practices at ten US plants of Japanese manufacturers.

They argued that Japanese manufacturers have historically improved quality and production efficiency at home by implementing a set of 'unique' management practices. Based on this, their research sought to examine whether the Japanese manufacturing firms in the US were implementing the same management practices employed in Japan or whether different management practices were necessary. If significant variations occurred between the home and US plants, the researchers explored the reasons for these variations.

The major findings of the Kujawa study (1983) indicated that:– firstly, competitive strategy based on production technology was a unique determinant of whether or not Japanese management practices were implemented; secondly, at the larger plants, Japanese management practices were implemented more extensively, e.g. higher job rotation, a lower ratio of minority employees, and a lower rate of employee turnover; thirdly, plant location tended to have a major impact. Compared to plants in California, those in the central states had a significantly lower rate of employee turnover and a lower ratio of minority employees. In addition, the central states' plants tended to be larger, were totally owned by the Japanese parent corporations, were dependent on the US market, and produced goods with significantly more local content; fourthly, the ratio of Japanese nationals to the total workforce was not a relevant factor for the implementation of Japanese-style management; fifthly, the level of small group activities was not significantly affected by any other factor; and, lastly, at plants with fewer job classifications, job rotation was practised more extensively.

Kujawa concluded that implementation decisions will ultimately depend on the judgement and initiative of local management regarding the marketability and usefulness of Japanese-style management practices as a competitive strategy for achieving corporate goals. However, a question remains about what constitutes management judgement in implementing Japanese-style management practices at each US transplant. Ishida (1986) pointed out that strong, entrepreneurial top leadership with a strong drive to succeed in the US market is commonly observed at transplants where Japanese-style management practices are extensively implemented. However, little is known about the actual processes of such transfers, which were the foci of the Nagoya-Cincinnati studies.

Nagoya-Cincinnati studies of manufacturing

The fully integrated production and human resource systems used by leading Japanese manufacturers, patterned after the 'Toyota system', were successfully transferred to the New United Motor Manufacturing, Incorporated (NUMMI) plant in California and other Japanese-owned plants in America. The Toyota system and its adaptations in central US states were the subjects of the Nagoya-Cincinnati Studies of Manufacturing.

The design of these comparative studies employed a two-phase research process. As shown in Table 1, the home plants of ten leading manufacturing firms in central Japan were investigated via 1–3 day visits by both authors to home offices and selected plants. During these visits patterned interviews with operations personnel, and foreign affairs managers were conducted, written documentation and case material were collected, and plant tours were taken. The purpose of this phase was to explore how these firms were doing in globalising their businesses. Specifically, we sought to identify major processes associated with these efforts. In phase two, six US plants of Japanese firms (listed in Table 2) were visited by both authors for at least one day. During this visit, plant management was interviewed, documentation was collected, and plants were toured. Phase three is currently under way.

The present paper deals with results derived from the first and second research phases and involves the cross-cultural transfers of the six manufacturers in the central US states listed in Table 2. All of the transplants were greenfield start-ups and were wholly owned by the parent firms in Japan.

Table 1   Design of comparative study of management practices in home and US plants of leading Japanese manufacturers

Phase One:
1985–1986   In-depth investigations of home plants (N = 10)
- 1-3 days visits to head office and selected plants
- Interviews with operations, personnel, R&D, and Foreign affairs managers
- Collecting documentation
- Plant tours
- Interviews with union officers

Phase Two:
1987–88   In-depth investigations of US plants (N = 6)
- One-day visits to plants
- Interviews with plant managers
- Collection of documentation
- Plant tours

Phase Three:
1989–90   Survey of home plant and US plant practices (N = 200)
- Recruitment and selection
- Job classification and placement
- Training system
- Promotion and wage decisions
- Management development
- Leadership in small groups
- Participation programs
- Equal treatment

Table 2 Profiles of Japanese transplants surveyed

Company	Location	Production Start	Size (employees)	Major Products
A	Battle Creek Michigan	1986	351	Auto Parts
B	Florence Kentucky	1982	560	Machine Tools
C	Seymour Indiana	1986	155	Auto Parts
D	Marysville Ohio	1979 (Motorcycle) 1982 (Auto)	4,530	Auto Assembly
E	Lebanon Ohio	1982	350	Elevator Assembly
F	Walton Kentucky	1983	65	Auto Parts

They all were located in midwestern US states and were engaged in e.g. auto parts production, car assembly, machine tool manufacturing, and elevator assembly operations. The research for this phase required sending a lengthy interview schedule to the participating plants several weeks in advance of the planned visit, so that the participants could gather relevant information. The interview schedule and details of the research procedures are available.[4]

Interview questions concerned:– (i) recruitment procedures and hiring decisions, (ii) job placement and job classification, (iii) training and education programmes, (iv) wage and promotion policies, (v) teamwork and team leaders, (vi) participation and communication, and (vii) egalitarian treatment. The answers are documented elsewhere.[5] Here we focus on the unreported results concerning the processes through which work teams and team leaders were developed:– (a) hiring, (b) training and education, (c) communication, and (d) participation programmes. Specifically, the present study analyses the processes of human resource development of domestic employees for the purpose of facilitating the transfer of core technology and unique work culture practices from Japan to the US.

Hiring, training and organising for team development

In all six plants, an integrated team concept was implemented for hiring, training and organising employees and their jobs. Most importantly, team leaders received special training for their role in socialising and developing their team members. Within the plants, people were specifically hired to be members or leaders of particular work teams. Team leaders, who were mostly skilled and experienced technicians, were carefully selected prior to the recruitment of unskilled, rank-and-file members.

Typically, this skilled group of employees was selected and specifically trained to be future team leaders in the US. The leader was sent to Japanese home plants for more rigorous team leader education and training in Companies A, B, C and D. After returning from Japan, they were appointed team leaders and started building their own teams by training newly recruited team members, who were normally less skilled and had less tenure. Therefore, from the beginning of the greenfield operation, team leaders were developed internally. As the process unfolds and team leaders are promoted, they will be replaced by the internally developed team sub-leaders or experienced senior associates (Companies A, B, D, and E).

Figure 1 displays the framework in which hiring and training practices are designed as integral components of the processes of skill acquisition and team development transferred from Japan to the US plants. Three major roles are played in the transfer processes; those of team leaders, team members, and coaches respectively. At home plants, Japanese coaches help American team leader trainees learn appropriate skills and knowledge. These leaders then work together at the US plants to build effective work teams under the domestic team leaders' direction. The mode of interaction between these actors is carefully designed so that cross-cultural learning of task- and team-relevant skills will be facilitated at each of the four stages of the transfer processes shown in Figure 1.

Preliminary stage

Here skilled and more experienced technicians are hired as vanguards of cross-cultural learning, as well as transfer agents of the target systems from Japan to the US. They also constitute the prime candidates to be future team leaders. In most of the plants we visited (Companies, A, B, and C), these vanguard groups of skilled employees were recruited six to twelve months earlier than the unskilled group, and mostly through local placement service offices. The number of such skilled workers was found to be 30 to 40 in Companies A, B, C and E, and more than 100 in Company D. Most went through the introductory cross-cultural learning about Japanese society and culture, as well as company history and the present situation. They were then sent to the Japanese home plants for on-the-job training in production skills, working side by side with Japanese colleagues. The production lines for on-the-job training at the home plants were those designed for installation at US plants.

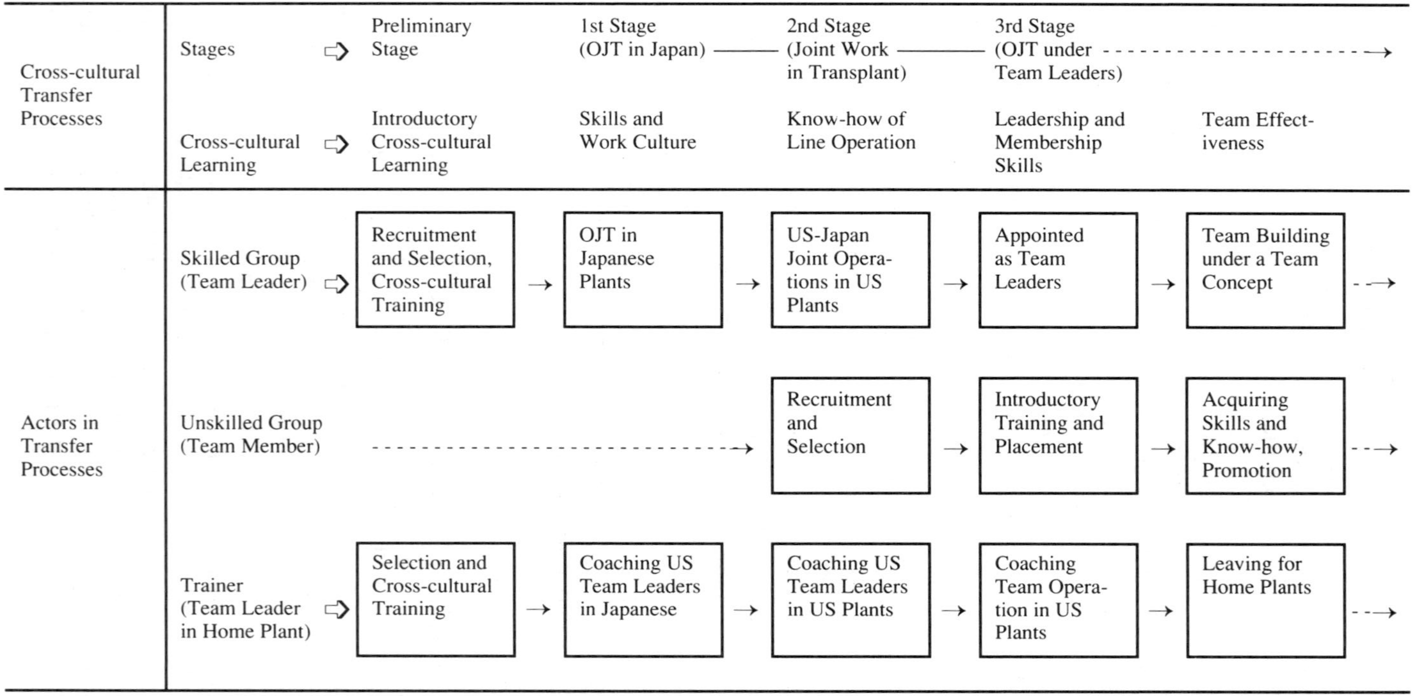

Cross-cultural Transfer Processes

Stages	Preliminary Stage	1st Stage (OJT in Japan)	2nd Stage (Joint Work in Transplant)	3rd Stage (OJT under Team Leaders)	
Cross-cultural Learning	Introductory Cross-cultural Learning	Skills and Work Culture	Know-how of Line Operation	Leadership and Membership Skills	Team Effectiveness

Actors in Transfer Processes

	Preliminary Stage	1st Stage	2nd Stage	3rd Stage	
Skilled Group (Team Leader)	Recruitment and Selection, Cross-cultural Training	OJT in Japanese Plants	US-Japan Joint Operations in US Plants	Appointed as Team Leaders	Team Building under a Team Concept
Unskilled Group (Team Member)			Recruitment and Selection	Introductory Training and Placement	Acquiring Skills and Know-how, Promotion
Trainer (Team Leader in Home Plant)	Selection and Cross-cultural Training	Coaching US Team Leaders in Japanese Plants	Coaching US Team Leaders in US Plants	Coaching Team Operation in US Plants	Leaving for Home Plants

Figure 1 A three-stage model of skill transfer from Japan to transplants in foreign countries

Japanese coaches were carefully selected on the basis of their technical expertise and communication skills. Japanese managers at the home plants emphasised that it is not English proficiency itself that is essential for coaching, but rather an ability to respond to the questions of American co-workers by utilising all means of communication, including non-verbal and paper-and-pencil methods. Sponsor employees selected as coaches for American trainees at home plants also went through a systematic training session to acquire English vocabulary and the idioms necessary for technical communication associated with production and machine operations. Along with language drills, introductory cross-cultural training was provided to these coaches concerning the typical American way of doing business and getting along with Americans.

First stage

At this stage, new groups of selected US trainees were sent to the Japanese home plants for on-the-job training. They worked with Japanese colleagues, who were by now experienced in training Americans on the job and in providing sponsorship on personal issues during their stay of normally two to three months. During this period, trainees usually spent half the day in the classroom, and the other half working on the shop floor. Production lines were the same as or similar to those to be installed in the US plants. It was common that the US plants were to receive slightly modified (to fit Americans) but the most technically advanced production facilities. In addition to technical instruction, American trainees were encouraged to observe and discuss all aspects of the work culture in the Japanese home plant. For example, in Company A, work culture issues involved topics such as working as a team, cooperating with team members, maintaining a clean work environment, working under broader job classification and job rotation systems, customer-oriented services, quality control, corporate philosophies and policies, and so forth.

In addition, American trainees were introduced to such company practices as quality circle activities, suggestion and improvement (*kaizen*) activities, and a *kanban* system (in the home plants of Companies A, B, and C). Specific aspects of work culture were studied using videotapes, written materials, lectures, on-the-job observation and informal discussions with Japanese co-workers. Training officials at one of the home plants in Japan (Company A's) emphasised that the purpose of training Americans about work culture was to provide enhanced understanding of how things were done in the Japanese home plants and why they were done that way.

Second stage

Here production lines were shipped to the US and installed in the plants.

Following the transfer of the hardware, an attempt was made to transplant components of the so-called 'humanware system' by moving a trainee-coach unit from Japanese home plants to the US transplants as the core element of team development. In Companies A and C, in addition to this trainee-coach unit, skilled technicians, engineers and management people were sent to the US plants to help work teams start to operate the new production lines. Frequently the old coach–trainee relationships continued in the US but this time American employees repaid the kindness of their Japanese colleagues who were rather unfamiliar with the US culture. The major goals of the second stage transfer efforts were to establish the basic skills and knowledge needed to operate the new production lines in a different industrial and socio-cultural environment. Also important at this stage was a transfer of team leadership from Japanese to US employees. Trained US employees started to play team leader roles at the transplants, working with coaches, technicians, managers and engineers sent from Japan.

Along with the transfer of men and machaines from Japan, the recruitment process of unskilled team members began at this stage in all six transplants visited. Selection processes for these rank-and-file employees, called 'associates', followed a well-established pattern, involving two or three screening stages with paper-and-pencil tests, interviews, reference checks and physical examinations.[6] It is clear that these procedures were rationalised with a very low selection ratio. All transplants considered this selection stage as the period of initiation of organisational socialisation into their unique corporate society and work culture.[7] This period was also regarded as providing information to modify the unrealistic expectations of over-zealous newcomers desiring to work for a Japanese organisation, some of whom called certain transplant practices 'un-Japanese' after experiencing things that contradicted their initial expectations.

Managers at each plant visited could identify the most desirable types of workers for recruitment; those showing a willingness to develop oneself, to grow with the company, to be a good team player, and to adjust oneself to flexible working conditions.

Third stage

Those who had been trained both in the Japanese home plant and the US plant were formally appointed as team leaders and then began to build their own work teams by organising newly hired team members. Each new team member was assigned to a rather rigorous training programme at a company training centre (Companies A and D) but they were also expected to develop further job mastery while doing their own jobs under a team leader's coaching. In most of the plants visited, one of the important responsibilities of a team leader was to decide what kind of on-the-job training and eventual job assignment each team member should receive. At this stage, Japanese coaches and technicians also helped group members acquire necessary skills and knowledge so that they could grow quickly out of their initially assigned tasks to effective associates who could assume multiple team responsibilities within the group; rapid growth out of initial job limits being a key to the team-building process.

To facilitate smooth on-the-job training and job rotation, all plants had a simplified job classification system. Normally, all hourly workers were grouped into just two broad job categories, e.g. production, and maintenance, and were all called 'associates'. However, jobs were usually structured into a hierarchically ranked system, based on conventional American job titles, for purposes of promotion and wage determination. New group members were expected to start at the bottom level, to acquire skills and knowledge through on-the-job training and job rotation, and to be promoted to higher ranks over time in their work group. Along with this skill development process, group members were exposed to aspects of the 'unique' work culture in the plants concerning corporate philosophies and policies, ideas on quality work, customer orientation, teamwork, and employee relations. In sum, during this stage team leaders were required to function as reliable sponsors for new employees during their socialisation into established team members. Staff from Japan, namely coaches, technicians, engineers and managers, also helped team leaders develop their teams.

Developing team effectiveness: the final stage

By the time people sent from the home plants returned to Japan, work teams in the US plants had grown into self-reliant work groups led by experienced team leaders. It was critical at this stage that management and engineering people provided continuing support to the team concept. They were expected to provide resources for running production systems based on autonomous work groups organised around the team leaders. A team leader, (*hancho*), in the Japanese home plant is commonly provided with broad discretional authority delegated from management in the areas of production, maintenance, and human resource utilisation and development. Thus, team leaders are responsible for producing high quality product on time and on budget and for maintaining a cohesive work team. Therefore, it was critical to establish team control over production processes at the shop floor level under the strong leadership of the group leader at the final stage of team development.

Transfer of technology across vastly different cultures cannot be accomplished without a supportive human organisation. Relevant organisational structures must be developed to support new skills, new patterns of behaviour, a new work culture, and new groups of people. Therefore, organisational development, to provide a supportive environment for practising the team concept in US plants, becomes an important element in facilitating cross-cultural transfers of production systems from Japan to the United States.

Throughout the team-building process, on-the-job training and job rotation were practised in order to develop team leaders. Employees were encouraged to become effective team members, and eventually, to be promoted as team leaders. In fact, it was reported that effective team leaders had been developed internally in Companies A, B and D as a result of implementing an integrated team concept on the shop floor over the past decade.

Developing team organisations in the transplants

Under the Toyota system, the authority hierarchy is shallow and rests on work teams as building blocks. In all the transplants visited, shallow hierarchies were used to facilitate the mobility of the work force and the more flexible utilisation of human resources. Table 3 displays the status hierarchy at Company A, in which there are basically only two status categories: manager and associate. Associates were further differentiated into ranks based on the content of the jobs they held. The key to this system was the different paths through ranks and positions that were used to develop associates within the organisation. For example, in Companies A and D, new technical employees of rank 5, the bottom rank, are expected to move up to hierarchy step-by-step through job rotation and on-the-job training to a team leader position in seven to eight years. Since all jobs were classified into a single associate castegory, no formal barriers existed to prevent associates from moving anywhere in the plant, and this was the case at all plants visited. Promotion decisions and recommendations for job rotation and training were made on the basis of semi-annual evaluations. This made promotions to the team sub-leader and then to the team leader position fairly competitive, based on merit, rather than an automatic progression based on seniority.

Table 3   Status system within the plant

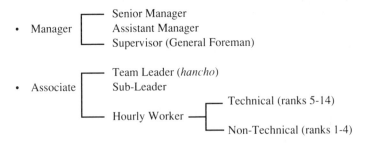

Source: Company A

156

In all plants, in order to attract relatively young, unskilled employees who were eager to develop themselves, the starting wage was set at what they called the 'highest social average'. This was substantially higher than the local average, but slightly lower than the established union wage for manufacturing in the local community. Moreover, the plants provided new employees with an opportunity to surpass the union wage level in a number of years. This could be accomplished through education and training as well as experiences on the job.

Team leader roles

A team leader position belongs to the exempt category, although it is not considered a management position, as Table 3 illustrates. This team leader position is described by the formal job description for the team leader in Company A presented in Table 4. An examination of the content of this job description reveals that a qualified team leader: (i) is expected to have extensive and detailed knowledge of production processes, (ii) can use judgement and problem-solving on interfunctional issues, (iii) is able to implement long-range plans, (iv) can communicate cross-functionally as well as across organisational hierarchies, and (v) is able to direct and train team members. How team leaders keep their teams on time and on budget is discussed elsewhere.[8]

It is clear that the functions of a team leader listed above, although formally not in a management category, overlap with those of manager and engineer. This indicates that a team leader needs to have high qualifications both technically and in team management skills. Table 4 indicates that to reach this high level, potential team leaders must develop first as qualified associates, then acquire the skills needed to be qualified sub-leaders, and finally, make the transformation to team leader.

Moreover, to discharge a team leader's responsibilities successfully, it is critical for a team leader to have authority delegated from managers and engineers. The necessary authority to perform the job successfully includes the authority to write operating rules, to introduce changes in production processes, to handle emergency situations, and to train sub-leaders and associates. These are vital resources for a team leader to function effectively on the shop floor.

In addition to the above formal authority, team leaders in all transplants visited were expected to provide assistance to team members in solving personal problems, including those potentially leading to disciplinary action. In Company A, team leaders were given training to enhance their counselling skills in dealing with these issues, and staff specialists at the personnel department were available to support team leaders' attempts to solve their team members' complicated personal problems. It was emphasised that management and staff made it a rule not to bypass a team leader's authority

Table 4 Job description for associates and team leaders

	QUALIFIED ASSOCIATE	QUALIFIED SUB-LEADER	QUALIFIED TEAM LEADER
KNOWLEDGE	Fundamental technical/industrial knowledge of the job; fundamental SQC knowledge of job standards processes, methods for many processes.	General knowledge of standard work methods/ processes in the area; fundamental knowledge of management methods, consistent with NDUS philosophy.	Detailed knowledge of the product, standards, methods, and processes. General knowledge of the total plant operation. Working knowledge of SQC. Extensive knowledge of management methods consistent with NDUS philosophy. Possible degree/technical degree or equivalent technical experience.
JUDGEMENT	Able to find proper solutions to normal, routine problems, based on past data/experience.	Able to properly analyse and solve routine problems, considering the effect on the area and other departments.	Able to properly analyse and solve routine, and non-routine problems, based on logical thinking and technical expertise, considering the effect on the area, other departments, and the Company.
PLANNING	Makes suggestions to improve production and/or efficiency.	Suggests and implements small improvements/ ideas affecting his/her area.	Suggests and implements long-range plans/ideas based on logic and experience affecting his/her area and other departments.
NEGOTIATION/ INTERPERSONAL RELATIONS	Able to communicate effectively with peers, and supervisors; ask intelligent questions; operate within the parameters of NDUS policies and procedures.	Able to discuss and resolve small problems with associates; communicate effectively with associates and supervisors.	Able to discuss and resolve small and somewhat complicated problems with all others in the organisation. Communicates effectively at all levels.
SKILL	Can perform somewhat complicated varied procedures at standard speeds with reliable quality.	Can perform very complicated, varied procedures with high precision, at standard speeds with reliable quality.	
DIRECTION/TRAINING		Effectively able to train associates, under the direction of the team leader.	Able to train associates and sub-leaders effectively.
EXAMPLE OF WORK	Performs varied procedures; operates complicated or precise machinery; determines simple problems; makes suggestions for improvement.	Handles emergency repair and adjustment of machinery; determines reasons for quality problems and implements simple corrections, directs the activities of associates.	Writes operating manuals, makes improvements in procedures and efficiently handles emergency situations; trains and directs sub-leader and associates.

Source: Company A

on the shop floor. In general, team leaders were given resources (information, decision-making authority, material and budgetary support, etc.), so that they could function as resource persons, rather than as management.

Shop floor control

Figure 2 displays a model of the plant organisation designed to shift managerial resources to the shop floor level where team leaders control day-to-day operations, including production, maintenance, quality control and human relations. As shown, resources are delegated to team leaders so that they can perform the functions specified in Table 2. Using these resources, the following unfolds. First, team leaders provide training opportunities for team members, who learn at different rates to perform the more complex jobs. As a result, hierarchical differences based on skill differences develop among team members. Second, all members gradually learn to solve routine problems by themselves and non-routine ones with the help of team leaders. Also, leaders invite some members of the team to participate in cross-functional problem solving to broaden their perspective. Third, members of the team are trained so that they can make suggestions to continuously improve production processes and productive efficiency. Fourth, team members are encouraged by the team leader to cooperate within their team to discover solutions to problems that confront it. Fifth, team members become members of self-managing teams capable of solving most day-to-day problems, and in emergencies, working together with team leaders to 'trouble shoot' large problems. Finally, managers and engineers realise that helping teams develop themselves so that they can manage routine as well as non-routine problems constitutes a key strategy in achieving corporate goals for product quality, productive efficiency, and flexibility of operation. The team management processes described above are called 'shop floor control' or 'management at the shop floor level' in Japanese home plants.

This team development at the transplants as a process of facilitating skill transfers from Japan to the United States cannot succeed unless control of resources is shifted down to the team leader. To implement shop floor control in the US, plants employ:– (i) a flat hierarchical structure of the production organisation, (ii) A flexible human resource system with supportive job classification, job rotation, on-the-job training, and promotion systems, and (iii) control resources delegated to the shop floor level.

Creating a third culture in US transplants

Successful cross-cultural transfers of complicated technology require rigorous learning and teaching activities by a group of strategically important individuals who can move and communicate effectively across cultural boundaries. Those who can translate their cross-cultural learning into concepts shared by colleagues living in another culture can be vanguards of cross-cultural skill transfers. These people learn two cultures to make a third. If two parties representing two different cultures struggle separately at a transplant trying to overwhelm each other, serious cultural conflict will emerge. On the other hand, if rigorous cross-cultural learning is done by both parties, a third 'hybrid' culture can emerge. Therefore, in the long run, creating the third corporate culture unique to each transplant benefits the organisation by enhancing associates' commitment, promoting associates' participation in corporate issues, and maintaining stable management-employee relations. According to managers working for typical third culture transplants, their associates see themselves neither as Japanese at the home plants nor as other Americans working for the same industry in the United States. Rather, they see themselves as having developed their own unique corporate culture. This finding suggests that cross-cultural human resource development needs to be designed to enhance the continued efforts among employees to learn two different cultures to create a third.

Emerging corporate philosophies

Corporate philosophies serve as criteria to decide what kind of cultural values and practices should be incorporated into the system of a particular corporate culture. Therefore, corporate philosophies constitute core dimensions of the third culture to be created. No sensible Japanese corporation would dare to impose its head office corporate philosophies on a US transplant; nor would the head office let American managers grow whatever philosophies they would prefer within a transplant. These are two extremes. The point is that corporate philosophies must be designed so that they will enable important aspects of Japanese and US cultures and practices to be integrated into a third cultural entity unique to each transplant.

It is often pointed out that strong entrepreneurial top leadership is necessary for the successful implementation of Japanese-style management.[9] According to our observations, powerful moral leadership by top management can help generate core aspects of corporate culture. At Company A, a new value basis for creating corporate philosophy and culture emerged out of the top leader's efforts to integrate Japanese-style management with values held by American employees. Figure 3 illustrates a set of key concepts related to each other according to as coherent value system centred around the issue of employment security.

Figure 3 was drawn based on an interview with Mr. O., a dynamic Japanese vice president who was the key figure in establishing the organisation in the United States. According to him, for the purpose of practising the idea of

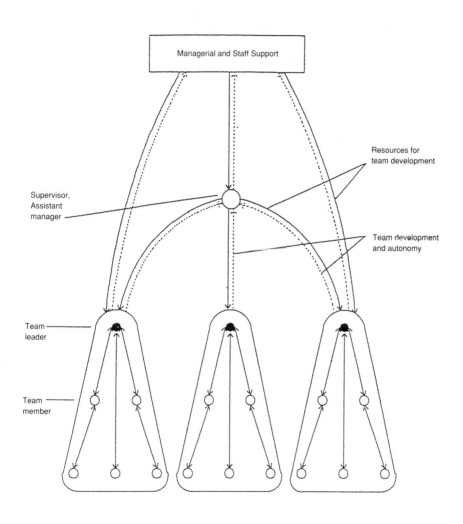

Figure 2 Building up teams under team leaders' initiative

lifetime employment, redefinition or 'translation' of the original Japanese ideas into American terms became necessary to make this basic corporate policy acceptable to American managers and associates. Mr. O. maintained that in his company associates are responsible for their own employment security. Associates' responsibilities start with their efforts to develop themselves, because employee development ensures high job performance and high product quality, customer satisfaction and company reputation in the product market, which leads via company growth to job security and finally to long-term commitment. This means that associates should take a long-range view to develop themselves throughout their careers in Company A. Thus, associates' development stimulates the entire cycle of events toward the higher goals for the company and individual associates, as described in greater detail elsewhere.[10]

Mr. O. preaches his philosophy not only to managers but also to associates at frequent meetings. It represents many of the basic values associated with Japanese-style management, namely lifetime employment, interdependence between company and employees, organisational career development, participation, producing high quality products, commitment to the organisation, self-development, etc. But these ideas are redefined by using the local language, and are reorganised to form a system of values which look unique, but which are acceptable to the associate members of his organisation. In other words, American employees in Company A were told repeatedly, and

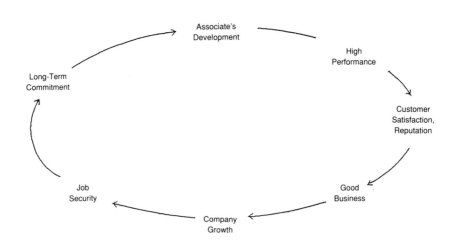

Figure 3 Corporate philosophy on employment security

162

this message was reinforced through their work experience, about the practical values illustrated in Figure 3. As the above example suggests, to create a third corporate culture in a US plant one must:– (i) develop a core value system, (ii) train and socialise employees in it, and (iii) lead both management and associates to work hard to achieve the important payoffs of the value system, namely, employee development, high quality products, company growth, promotion, and job security. Throughout this cyclical process, the cultural values of the corporation become internalised by employees and serve as norms of job behaviour and performance.

It must be emphasised that the third culture can only emerge as a result of joint learning by US and Japanese employees about the respective foreign business culture and through joint efforts to develop a new organisation at the US plant. Moreover, the third corporate culture must be able to provide a set of concrete value concepts, as shown in Figure 3, for guiding the desired behaviour of both associates and managers at the new plant.

Functions of Japanese-style management and its transfer

To study cross-cultural transfers of Japanese-style management, it is important to analyse the various functions that the particular practice generates, rather than to evaluate the nature of the practice itself within a given cultural context.[11] Wakabayashi (1987) identified seven functional areas associated with so-called Japanese-style management and the results of the present study support the finding that all transplants emphasised the importance of achieving these functional goals through a variety of managerial practices. Also, the original practices of the Japanese home plants were modified to a certain extent to meet the American way of doing things:–

(i)   *Training and development functions*
Training and education programmes similar to the Japanese *kenshu* system were implemented in all of the transplants visited, including on-the-job training, job rotation, off-the-job training in the company's *kenshu* house (the employee development centre at Companies A and D), and education through auditing courses and seeking degree programmes at local colleges and universities. Though no systematic comparison is made, the impression is that, in general, average training hours per employee might be greater in the US transplants than in the Japanese home plants, especially for Companies A, C, and D.

(ii) *Welfare programmes*
A list of the Welfare and Benefit Programmes of Company D contained 37 different items including a variety of medical and fringe benefits, a Quality Award Programme, an Associate Service Award, attendance gifts, a family festival, and the like. In other transplants

visited, it was reported that they were recognised by the local community as providing the highest levels of welfare and benefits in the area.

(iii) *Human relations functions*

Activities to support friendly human relations among employees and between the company and employees were undertaken by all transplants. These practices included supporting sports tournaments, club and hobby activities, company picnics, parties and ceremonial meetings, gift giving, birthday cards etc. Activities varied from one transplant to another.

(iv) *Organisational communication*

One of the important missions of Japanese managers at the US plants is to establish an extensive intra-organisational communication network to enhance information sharing among members of the organisation. Thus, as one of the team leaders interviewed pointed out, his people were busy attending various meetings, ranging from a morning team meeting on the shop floor, a weekly team leader meeting, a weekly middle manager's meeting, and a monthly senior manager's meeting. In addition, at all transplants visited, Japanese managers volunteered to wander around the shop to talk to both associates and team leaders. Managers at Company A were asked to spend three days a year working with associate members at the shop floor on the company's plant familiarisation days.

(v) *Equal treatment*

Without exception, equal treatment of employees was practised in the US transplants studied. It involved, first, equality in utilising 'space' such as parking lots, dining halls, rest rooms and spaces in open-plan offices. Second, status symbols tended to be equalised by wearing a common uniform, calling everybody an 'associate', setting the same pay day, and providing equal opportunities to participate in the company's social events. In general, the transplants visited were very reluctant to create any privileged groups of associates in terms of space or symbols.

(vi) *Employee participation*

Quality Circle (QC) activity as one of the typical means of participation was found to be practised only in Companies A and D. Employee suggestions and improvement programmes were reported in all transplants except for Company C. The QC programme in Company A was reported to remain only as a means of morale enhancement at the present stage of development, rather than as an established practice for achieving cost savings and improvements in production processes. On the other hand, in Company D, QC activities were said to be more rigorously practised than at the Japanese home plant.

(vii) *Organisational commitment*

Management practices for organisational commitment are those designed to strengthen long-term employee-organisation linkages.[12] First, all transplants visited had a no lay-off policy. This policy was clearly announced, and only one company shown in Table 2 had ever laid off employees in the past. The 'no lay-off' policy of the US transplants is considered a functional equivalent of the home plant lifetime employment practice. In both cases, lay-offs could happen in exceptionally hard economic circumstances.

Second, the policy of promotion from within was extensively practised among the sample transplants. Especially in Company D, it was reported that those who started their careers at the associate level were now moving into supervisory and management positions; while in Company A, senior team leaders were being promoted to supervisory positions as the company rapidly grew. However, it was reported that years of service had much less weight in making promotion decisions at the US transplant than at the Japanese home plant. In Company B, where technical skills were regarded as counting the most in promotion decisions, technical expertise and task performance constituted the dominant factors in promotion decisions, while tenure was used only as a tie breaker.

Third, financial incentives for long-term organisational commitment were commonly used in all US plants visited. These involved such practices as giving a large year-end bonus, though a much smaller one than given in Japan, to reflect years of service in the company and ownership of company stock (Companies A, B, D, E).

In summary, it must be emphasised that each of the seven functional goals listed above were consciously sought by all transplants visited with varying degrees of success. However, there was no one-to-one relationship between each practice and a particular functional goal. On the contrary, one practice affected several functions, and a particular function was supported by more than one practice. Therefore, a set of managerial practices designed to reinforce each other was expected to produce a system of managerial functions characterised as Japanese-style management. However, it is important to note that acceptable practices can be either Japanese or American in origin, as long as they function to produce the intended effects upon the performance of the plant.

Conclusion

Human Resource Development (HRD) efforts play a catalyst function in the process of producing a third culture in a US transplant. Many studies have pointed out that successful Japanese manufacturers in the United States specify their HRD strategy as a key to adapting and growing in the US.[13] The research also found that Japanese manufacturers were engaging in cross-cultural HRD activities to support the transfer of their managerial and production systems from the Japanese home plants. It was found that active cross-cultural learning among actors in the transfer processes was critically important, since transfers involved not only exporting production facilities but also moving a home plant work culture and team-based work organisation from Japan. Education and training designed to help associate employees become effective members and leaders of work teams constituted major efforts to facilitate the transfer process.

Actors in the process of cross-cultural HRD must acquire key components of two different business cultures to create a third hybrid in the US. Figure 4 illustrates major variables involved in the process of creating a third culture. It indicates that cross-cultural HRD plays the role of catalyst in bringing about a new set of managerial practices, cultural functions, and organisational structures. In other words, knowledge and skill components originally associated with input resources are used by trainees to transform their jobs in the transplants through a process of cross-cultural human resource development. It is people who transform aspects of two different cultures into systems of a third culture through learning and experience. The result of this cross-cultural learning is emerging new practices and cultural functions that characterise the nature of unique corporate culture within the transplant. In addition, a set of new elements of organisational structure must be institutionalised to provide an appropriate work environment for the developing human resources and to accommodate the emerging third culture. The emergent corporate culture and organisational structure may constitute throughput for producing final outcomes for the corporation and employees. In Figure 4, feedback lines are drawn to indicate that outcome information will be brought back to check managerial practices and cultural functions, and to examine the adequacy of the organisational structure at the transplant. Also, information on outcomes as well as on functions and organisational structure is all fed back to the cross-cultural HRD practices to evaluate whether HRD systems were working effectively.

Several limitations of the present study need to be discussed. First, the models developed should be considered appropriate only to manufacturing firms dealing with transfers of large, complex technology from Japan to the United States. Transfers to other host countries, in Europe or Asia for example, may require that additional factors be included in the model. Second, only the positive and socially desirable aspects of transfer operations have been discussed. Some negative and socially undesirable outcomes associated with our transfer model, such as, discrimination in employment, the overpresence of Japanese, labour-management relations, etc.[14] remain to be studied. Third, the results of the interview study identified many problems associated with the human resource development of managers at the US transplants.[15]

The next task is therefore to examine to what extent the present findings derived mainly from the study of technical employees at the shop floor level can be generalised in order to solve problems at the management level.

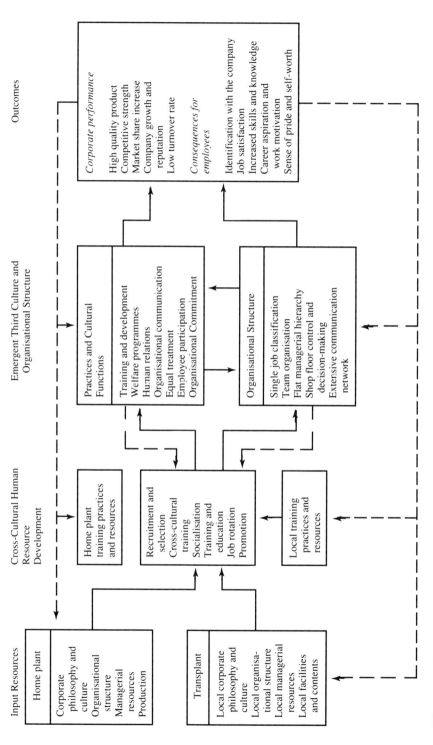

Figure 4 The process of the emerging third culture and its outcomes

Input Resources

Home plant

Corporate philosophy and culture
Organisational structure
Managerial resources
Production

Transplant

Local corporate philosophy and culture
Local organisational structure
Local managerial resources
Local facilities and contents

Cross-Cultural Human Resource Development

Home plant training practices and resources

Recruitment and selection
Cross-cultural training
Socialisation
Training and education
Job rotation
Promotion

Local training practices and resources

Emergent Third Culture and Organisational Structure

Practices and Cultural Functions

Training and development
Welfare programmes
Human relations
Organisational communication
Equal treatment
Employee participation
Organisational Commitment

Organisational Structure

Single job classification
Team organisation
Flat managerial hierarchy
Shop floor control and decision-making
Extensive communication network

Outcomes

Corporate performance

High quality product
Competitive strength
Market share increase
Company growth and reputation
Low turnover rate

Consequences for employees

Identification with the company
Job satisfaction
Increased skills and knowledge
Career aspiration and work motivation
Sense of pride and self-worth

Finally, the present study represents a conceptual generalisation of Japanese-style management at transplants in the central States of the USA based on data derived from interviews, observations, and company documentation. For the next step, empirical examinations of the findings need to be carried out based on quantitative analysis of the survey data to further improve the models of the cross-cultural transfer of production skills and knowledge.[16]

Notes

1. Abo, T. *Local production by Japanese automobile and electric Manufacturers in the United States: Application and adaptability of Japanese-style management practices* (in Japanese). Toyokeizai, Tokyo. 1988.
2. Ishida, H. 'Transferability of Japanese human resource management abroad.' *Human Resource Management*, Vol. 25, Spring 1986. pp. 103–20.
    Itagaki, H. 'Application-adaptation problems in Japanese automobile and electronics plants in the USA.' Shibagaki, K., Trevor, M.H., and Abo, T. (eds.), *Japanese and European Management: Their international adaptability*, University of Tokyo Press. 1989. pp. 118–31.
    Negandi, R. 'The management practices of Japanese subsidiaries overseas.' *California Management Review*, No. 4, Summer. 1985. pp. 125–33.
3. Watanabe, N. 'A pilot study on cross-cultural job training.' *Nanzan Management Studies*, 3. 173–187, (in Japanese). 1988. pp. 173–87.
    Pucik, V. & Hanada, M. *Corporate culture and human resource utilisation of senior managers in Japanese corporations in the United States.* (in Japanese). Egon Zehnder International, Tokyo. 1990.
    Yang, Z. 'Job attitude and human resource policies: A study of employees in Japanese firms operating in America.' *Proceedings for the International Conference on Personnel and Human Resource Management*, Hong Kong. 1989. pp. 511–20.
4. Wakabayashi, M. 'Human resource development strategies of Japanese manufacturing firms in the United States: Focusing upon automobile and machine tool industries in the central states of America.' Nagoya University (Ed.) *Studies on the culture and social structure of the countries surrounding the Pacific Ocean*. Nagoya University Press. 1990.
5. Graen, G.B., & Wakabayashi, M. 'Adapting Japanese management development techniques to their transplants in the United States: Focusing on manufacturing.' Pucik, V. (ed.) *Internationalisation of the Japanese Firm*. In press 1990.
6. *Wall Street Journal*. 24 March 1988.
7. Wanous, J.P. *Organisational entry: Recruitment, selection and socialisation of newcomers*. Addison-Wesley, Reading, Mass. 1980.
8. Graen, G.B. , Wakabayashi, M., and Uhl-Bien, M. 'Making team leaders Toyota Style.' *Harvard Business Review*. In press 1991.
9. Ishida, H. op. cit.
10. Graen, G.B. *Unwritten Rules For Your Career: The 15 Secrets for Fast-Track Success*. Wiley, New York. 1989.

168

11. Marsh, R.W. & Mannari, H. (1977) Organisational commitment and turnover: A prediction study. *Administrative Science Quarterly*, 22, 57–72.
     Rohlen, T.P. (1974) *For harmony and strength*. Berkeley: University of California Press.
12. Mowday, R.T., Porter, L.W., & Steers, W.M. (1981) *Employee-organisation linkages: The psychology of commitment, absenteeism, and turnover*. New York: Academic Press.
13. Abo, T. op. cit.
     Kujawa, D. (1983) Technology strategy and industrial relations: Case study of Japanese multinationals in the United States, *Journal of International Business Studies*, Winter, 92–22.
     Kujawa, D. & Yoshida, M., (1986) Cross-cultural transfer of management practices: Japanese manufacturing plants in the United States. Mimeographed paper.
     Ishida, H. op. cit.
     Watanabe, N. op. cit.
14. *Wall Street Journal*. 10 December 1987.
15. Wakabayashi, M. 'Internationalisation of Japanese corporations: Personnel and human resource management practices of Japanese firms in foreign countries.' *Bulletin of the Faculty of Education*, Nagoya University, *34*. 1987. pp. 173–87.
16. The authors would like to thank Joan Graen, Mike Graen, Marty Graen, and M. Sano, for their research assistance, Mary Uhl-Bien for reading an earlier version of this paper, and the Fulbright Commission, Nagoya University, and the University of Cincinnati for partial support of this project.

PART 3:

THE MANAGEMENT OF CHANGE

9 R & D projects as an information and decision problem: car model design in Japan, Europe and USA

ILARI TYRNI
UNIVERSITY OF TAMPERE

Introduction

R & D projects can be considered as an information and decision problem. A great amount of literature states that an R & D project uses information from the market, from scientific and technical literature, from production and other departments of the firm and creates new knowledge or how to produce a new product. But in order to understand how an R & D project works it is useful to consider it as an information and decision (I & D) problem in the formal sense of decision theory.

A development project using car model development is taken as an example. Since essential (scientific) research is not involved, this choice makes it possible to avoid some difficult problems of uncertainty.[1] Using data from European, Japanese and USA car model designs one can emphasise the importance of the completeness of information and communication; i.e. noise in its different forms. To get as little noise as possible, education in the firm must be appropriate. The same is required for on-the-job training (OJT), rotation etc. Of course participative decision-making is essential in the development of a project team.[2] A successful project organisation is possible only if there exists a base for it in the organisation of the firm; just creating a matrix organisation for the project is not enough.

The idea here came from reading a paper by Clark, Chew and Fujimoto[3] in 1988 while Clark came to give a lecture at Yale University. They had studied 29 car model design projects,[4] of which twelve were Japanese, six American and eleven European. The Japanese used one-third of the engineering hours of the American and European projects but their lead time was two-thirds of the lead time of the Americans and Europeans.

The Japanese cars were smaller but they had more body types per model. The project scope indicators showed that the Japanese had considerably more unique parts in new models, but that they used more sub-suppliers.

Clark and others carefully adjusted the engineering hours and lead times for the above factors but, even after adjustment, the Americans and Europeans used twice the engineering hours of the Japanese. The difference in lead times decreased from 19.9 to 12.5 months mainly due to the sub-supplier factor.

Clark and his colleagues concluded that the remaining differences must be connected to project organisation and technological strategy and they collected data concerning these factors.[5] However, their analysis in this part of paper is not very helpful for understanding the problem and does not give convincing results; therefore another explanation will be put forward here, referring to Clark and others.

Technological strategy and the I & D problem

The goal of R & D projects is to design a product of high quality which can be produced at a reaonable cost. This is dictated by competition in most markets, for example automobiles. Products must also have a wide scope; a car model has different body types, colours, engine types and sizes, extras etc. This means that the production system must be flexible; therefore the requirements of production engineering should also be considered in connection with product design.[6]

However, any firm has constraints on its development projects. There is a limit to the personnel and other resources that can be used on the design project and a time limit within which the new product must come to the market. If the lead time is too long, the product may already be 'old fashioned' when production starts. These limits must be recognised in planning the product design project.

Project planning includes two sides which are tightly connected with each other. The first is technological strategy. There are certain requirements of specialisation and integration in designing products like the models of a car. These requirements determine the extent of parallel design i.e. the overlap which can be used. Much parallel design decreases lead time, but since it might cause many mistakes and a lot of reworking, the number of engineering hours can greatly increase. The conventional wisdom states that there is a tradeoff between these two and consequently some optimal equilibrium. However, Japanese management breaks much conventional wisdom. For example, the Japanese do not accept that there is a tradeoff between product quality and the cost of production. They have devised many methods which at the same time improve quality and decrease production costs; and

174

much the same situation prevails regarding engineering hours and lead times for the same basic reasons.

Technological strategy is connected with the organisation of the project team, but the latter is very much determined by the organisational characteristics of the firm. One cannot expect people suddenly to behave differently in a project team from the way in which they have been accustomed to behave in the firm during many years of service; and that is where the difference between Japanese and Western project teams comes in.

To put it in more detail, technological strategy can be described by PERT analysis, using Figures 1a and 1b. In Figure 1a, on the left side, there is the product concept creation C and, on the right side, production P. Between them there are nine tasks. Task 1 is preliminary design, which can be called the clay model. Then in the first row there is body design, in the second row engine design and in the last row production design. Every task requires a given number of designers and time to be executed. Every task is started when all the necessary information has arrived. For example, task 6 starts when tasks 5 and 8 are ready and the necessary information is given to team members in 6. Task 8 starts when 2, 5 and 7 are completed etc. There is no feedback and therefore tasks must be done in a certain order. By PERT analysis it is possible to calculate the critical path from C to P which gives the lead time. One can also calculate the cost for every task and the change in cost if the task is to be done faster. This makes it possible to compare a shortening of the lead time with a corresponding change in costs.

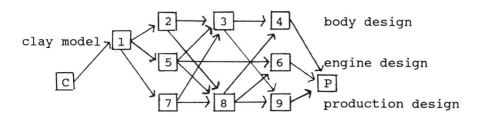

Figure 1a PERT analysis of project technology without feedback

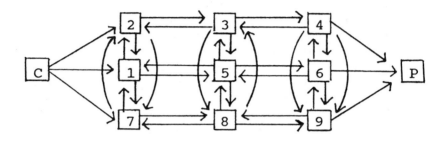

Figure 1b PERT analysis of project technology with feedback

In figure 1b feedback is allowed and therefore tasks can be started when certain advances have been made with other tasks. Tasks are now arranged so that those in the first column can be started at almost the same time and those in the next column can be started well before the tasks in the earlier column are finished. In order not to make the Figure too untidy, not all the possible communication channels have been drawn. Many tasks can be done in parallel, since due to feedback the necessary information comes little by little in small pieces. Therefore lead time is considerably shortened.

Regarding engineering hours, some integration is necessary so that in the worst case the whole job will not be repeated. Up to a certain point, therefore, feedback decreases engineering hours; but how far this happens depends on the project organisation and basically on the organisation of the firm.

The essential point is what happens to the observation and communication of information, and the pattern of decision-making is also connected to this.

The project team needs information from the market about the needs and opinions of customers, and it needs scientific and technological information both about the product and the production system.

The first difficulty comes from incomplete observation. The project team should have experts who understand information from different sources and see what is essential for the project. Thus they would have the possibility of getting almost complete observations $\phi(x) \approx x$, of the relevant state of the world, but at this stage noise $\epsilon^1 = x - \phi(x)$ appears. The difficulties in this respect are similar for Japanese and Western team members in design projects, except that Japanese employees are used to doing more work for observation and gathering of information during their careers in the firm.

Great differences immediately appear when the question is of the communication of observations to the other members of the project team. There are many papers and books with dicussions about special liaison officials, gatekeepers and communication stars needed in Western R & D projects.[7] The need for these people comes from the fact that in Western firms the project members have different backgrounds in departments like marketing, production, engineering and perhaps even finance. In those departments there exist different cultures, with their own terminology etc; so communication specialists are needed to explain information between team members with different backgrounds. Even then, when the contraction, $1 \geq \tau_i^w \geq 0$, of observation, $\tau_i^w \phi(x)$ is sent from team member i, to j a noise ϵ_j^{2w} appears and member j gets $\tau_i^w(x) + \epsilon_i^{2w}$. It is clear that in these circumstances communication takes much time, is troublesome and cannot be done continuously. In our scheme of technological strategy, this is a serious problem for team members engaged in different tasks, especially if the tasks belong to different lines of design like the body, engine and production lines in Figure 1a.

The situation is completely different in regard to Japanese projects. The team members have the same corporate culture regardless of the department in which they last served, and have rotated during their careers from one department to another. They all use the same terms for same concepts, and have experience of work and problem-solving in other departments; so no communication stars or liaison officials etc. are needed. Moreover, in all positions communication and cooperation is an essential part of employees learning, which means that less contracted observations can be sent to the other members of the team than in Western firms, i.e. $\tau_i^J > \tau_i^w$. The noise ϵ_j^{2J} of the receiving member is also much smaller than ϵ_j^{2w}, since there is little if any difficulty in understanding what the received message means.[8] Also the information sent forward does not need as much computation, pooling and other handling as in Western firms; therefore in Japanese (car) design projects, communication can occur very frequently and almost continuously, taking informal verbal forms.

All this means that the Japanese can go much further with parallel design as part of their technological project strategy. Feedback is possible between any pair of tasks and can be very frequent. Therefore any larger unexpected event is likely to increase both engineering hours and lead time. The negative correlation between engineering hours and lead time of the conventional wisdom has turned into a positive one. That is what Clark and others found, although their explanation is not similar to the one above.[9] Meanwhile, in Western systems the negative correlation still prevails for most projects.

Decision-making in R & D projects

Several studies in the Western literature have discussed many points related to organisational structure and decision-making in R & D projects.[10] First, for instance, where in the firm R & D projects should lie.[11] Different locations have been suggested and their (dis)advantages have been discussed; but no definite conclusions have been presented with respect to product development. A more unique opinion is that research should be done in an independent department under the firm's most senior director(s).

Second, the discussion has concerned project management, and whether it should be functional (line) management, pure project organisation or matrix organisation. Again many (dis)advantages have been presented in each case. The matrix form has got most support, although in many applications it has been difficult to separate project and matrix organisation. Some of the points raised in the discussion are central here.

The discussion of all these alternatives, and especially that of the matrix, has more or less implicitly assumed hierarchical top-down decision-making; so the most pressing problem has been how to establish equality between the task forces and between individuals. If that does not succeed some members feel unfairly treated and lose interest in their work.

The most popular solution for this and for some other problems – especially how to prevent conflict between task forces and team members – has been to define clearly the boundaries between task forces and between team members. When everybody knows who can decide what, many difficulties can be avoided.

From the above, it is easy to understand that strong project leaders are usually preferred and that they should be persons who are highly appreciated in the firm in general and in the project team in particular, as Clark and others noted. This kind of project leader can successfully mediate between the project and the firm and can also solve the internal problems between team members with different backgrounds. It is easy to see that this form of organisation and decision-making goes together with information and communication systems in Western projects but it limits communication and cooperation considerably: something that is hardly mentioned in Western writing.

In large Japanese firms, (scientific) research is located as an independent department under the most senior director(s). If the firm is divisionalised (product) development (engineering) departments are in the respective divisions.

In the research department most of the researchers have not rotated outside it but have come straight from college or graduate school. Some have been in research institutes, sometimes abroad, or universities during their career in the firm. It often happens that when a researcher gets a brilliant idea which leads to the development of a new product he follows it to the

178

development department. When the development process is over, he might even follow the designs to the production department; thus he becomes a part of the usual rotation of the firm and is unlikely never to return to the research department.

Development departments consist of people who have very different backgrounds, in e.g. research, production, marketing or other departments, or else straight from university. Most have participated in the usual rotation in the firm and therefore often have experience from two or more departments. Formally, the development department has a similar organisation to other departments and also has the same corporate culture and rotation inside the department. Therefore project teams do not have difficulties in communicating and cooperating with other departments or with each other, and communication is also helped by the presence of ex-development personnel in manufacturing departments.

Decision-making in project teams uses consensus and may be further described as bottom-up: no exact job descriptions and boundaries between the task forces are given. In other words, decision-making is very similar to the other parts of the firm. Strategic decisions – to define and start the project – are top-down and operational decisions – how to run the project – are bottom-up.

This is much more than a matrix organisation; it is a management style in which cooperation and communication of information is central, applied to the organisation of the development project. Many of the decisions evolve during informal communication processes, and this is directly connected to the parallel technological strategy. The Japanese I & D structure described is a prerequisite for really parallel design but is not much needed if parallel design is not used.

Organisational strategy and suppliers in R & D projects

In the study of Clark and others, a great part of the difference in performance between Japanese and American or European projects came from the more extensive use of suppliers by the Japanese. There are reasons why large Japanese firms use more suppliers than Western firms but they are not discussed here.[12] Only factors with a direct bearing on product development are taken up.

Suppliers in Japan produce many of the parts which in USA or Europe are manufactured by original equipment manufacturers (OEM); so it is therefore only natural that a greater portion of parts is also designed by suppliers. There are extremely close contacts between OEMs and suppliers and in cases like Toyota suppliers have formed associations connected to the OEM. What happens during the design process within the supplier and OEM depends on the character of the part and here it is convenient to use

Asunuma's classification of parts in the automobile and electrical industries.[13]

It should be emphasised that the Japanese habit of having close contact with customers is especially true with suppliers, and is of course greatly intensified during the period when the OEM is designing a new product. To explain these contacts, the figure in Appendix 2 below is used, in which the parts are classified according to the degree of the supplier's initiative. The basic division is made in terms of drawings and designs supplied by the OEM (DS) and drawings and designs approved by the OEM (DA). Both DS and DA are divided into three sub-groups in Appendix 2, with practically all the design of parts in sub-group A being done by the OEM. However, in designing the parts the OEM needs detailed knowledge of the production possibilities of the supplier and therefore engineering hours increase as compared to the procurement in the OEM. Communication of information is similar to the case of designing parts for inside procurement only, added by the need for more explanation to people who have no benefit of rotation in the OEM.

Going to sub-groups B and C, part of the design work is done by the supplier (and a large part in C). Contacts with the OEM are extremely frequent, including to a great extent face to face discussions. These close contacts decrease engineering hours indirectly, by preventing rework in the OEM, but increase engineering hours directly. On the other hand, efficient communication makes possible the parallel design of parts with the main product and allows short lead times.

To DA suppliers, the OEM gives the specifications of new parts, using information from their manufacturing processes, and practically all the design work is done by the suppliers. Communication with the designing team of the OEM is quite intense, decreasing from group D to group E, and the intensity of communication varies according to the needs of parallel design. During the 1980s car producers in Japan have practically finished using parts in sub-group G, and nowadays some specifications are given for all parts of new models.

All in all, the relatively high use of sub-suppliers by Japanese car producers does not decrease engineering hours in design as much as Clark and others estimated, due to the time needed for intensive communication. On the other hand, close communication with suppliers might prevent some rework in the design of the OEM and certainly helps to keep lead times short.

180

Appendix 1 Selected data profile, by region

VARIABLES	TOTAL	JAPAN	US	EUROPE
Number of Projects	29	12	6	11
Year of Introduction	1980–87	1981–85	1984–87	1980–87
Engineering Hours (Thousands)				
Average	2577	1155	3478	3636
Minimum	426	426	1041	700
Maximum	7000	2000	7000	6545
Lead Time (Months)				
Average	54.2	42.6	61.9	62.6
Minimum	35.0	35.0	50.2	46.0
Maximum	97.0	51.0	77.0	97.0
Product Complexity Indicators				
Price (Thousand 1987 US dollars. Average)	13591	9238	13193	19720
Body Size (% in number of projects)				
Micro-mini	10%	25%	0%	0%
Small	56%	67%	17%	64%
Medium-Large	34%	8%	83%	36%
Number of Body Types (Average)	2.1	2.3	1.7	2.2
Project Scope Indicators (Average)				
Common Parts Ratio	19%	12%	29%	21%
Carried-over Parts Ratio	10%	7%	9%	14%
Unique Parts Ratio	74%	82%	62%	71%
Share in Parts Procurement Costs by Parts Types				
Supplier Proprietary	7%	8%	3%	7%
Black Box	44%	62%	16%	39%
Detail Controlled	49%	30%	81%	54%

Source: Clark et al. Table 1
Note: for definitions of variables, see Table 1A above.

Appendix 2 Patterns of overlapping and information processing, by region

Table 10

	JAPAN	US	EUROPE*
OVERLAPPING INDICATORS			
Engineering Overlapping Ratio	high (1.63)	middle (1.53)	low (1.37)
Overlapping between Die Design & Prototype	die design starts *before* 1st prototype completes	die design starts *after* 1st prototype completes	die design starts *after* 1st prototype completes
Overlapping between Die Cutting & Prototype	die cutting starts *before* last prototype completes	die cutting starts *after* last prototype completes	die cutting starts *after* last prototype completes
Completeness of Prototypes when Testing starts	prototypes are sufficiently representative but not perfect	prototypes are often *not* representative enough	prototypes are regarded as perfect when tested
	US$300.000/unit	$300.000/unit	$600.000/unit
INFORMATION PROCESSING INDICATOR			
Number of Formal Design Release to Body Engineering	3	2	2–3
Intra-R & D Communication	formal & informal intense through necessity to coordinate	mostly formal through large meetings pretty frequent	mostly informal intense through engineering tradition
Production – R & D Communication	formal & informal intense through necessity to coordinate	mostly formal through large meetings pretty frequent	mostly formal meetings infrequent
INDICATORS ON OVERLAPPING – INFORMATION MISMATCH			
Ratio of Engineering Change Costs in Body Dies	10-20%	30-50%	10-30%
Surprises by Downstream Engineers	moderate	frequent	infrequent
Delay of Introduction Date	1/6 delayed	1/2 delayed	1/3 delayed
Impact of Overlapping on Lead Time	significant (correlation coefficient: –0.64)	not significant (correlation coefficient: 0.12 US and European samples combined)	
SUMMARY			
OVERLAPPING	high	middle	low
INFO INTENSITY	high	low	middle to low

Source: Clark et al. Table 10
Note: *Typically at European companies. Subsidiaries of the US car makers are similar to the parent companies to some extent.

Appendix 3 Classification of parts and suppliers according to the degree of initiative in design of the product and the process

Parts manufactured according to drawings provided by the core firm			Parts manufactured according to drawings provided by the supplier			Parts offered by catalogue ('purchased goods')
A	B	C	D	E	F	G
the core firm provides minute instructions for the manufacturing process	the supplier designs the manufacturing process based on blueprints of products provided by the core firm	the core firm provides only rough drawings and their completion is entrusted to the supplier	the core firm provides specifications and has substantial knowledge of the manufacturing process	intermediate region between D and F	though the core firm issues specifications, it has only limited knowledge concerning the process	the core firm selects from catalogue offered by the supplier
small parts assembled by firms offering assembly service	small outer parts manufactured by firms offering stamping service	small plastic parts used in dashboard	seat	brake, bearing, tyres	radio, electronic fuel injection system, battery	

Source: Asanuma 1986.

Notes

1. Deshmukh, S.D. and Chikte S.D. 'A Unified Approach for Modelling and Analysing New Product R & D Decisions.' *TIMS Studies in the Management Sciences 15*. North-Holland Publishing Company. 1980. pp. 163–82.
2. Klimstra, Paul D. and Potts, Joseph. 'What We've Learned: Managing R & D Projects.' *Research Technology and Management*. Vol. 31. No. 3. May–June 1988. pp. 23–29.
3. Clark, Kim B., Chew, W. Bruce and Fujimoto, Takahiro. *Product Development in the World Auto Industry: Strategy, Organisation and Performance*. November 1987, unpublished.
4. Clark et al. Table 1 in Appendix 1.
5. Clark et al. Table 10 in Appendix 2.
6. There are examples where this was not done e.g. at British Leyland and its predecessor.
7. Tushman, Michael L. and Nadler, David A. 'Communication and Technical Roles in R and D Laboratories: An Information Processing Approach.' *TIMS Studies in the Management Sciences 15*. 1980. pp. 91–112.
8. It is often enough to send a verbal message without any written report or charts. Sometimes even nonverbal communication might be enough.
9. See Clark (1987) figure 4 and its explanation.
10. Klimstra and Potts. op. cit.
11. Vedin, Bengt-Arne. Large Company Organisation and Radical Product Innovation, Institute for Management of Innovation and Technology, Lund 1980. See also Appendix 2.
12. Tyrni, Ilari. 'EX-efficiency in the Short and Long Run: a Consequence of Japanese Human Management.' Blumenthal, T. (ed). *Employer and Employee in Japan and Europe*. Ben-Gurion University, Beersheva. 1989.
13. Asanuma, Banri. 'Transactional Structure of Parts Supply in the Japanese Automobile and Electric Machinery Industries: A Cooperative Analysis.' *Technical Report No. 3*. Socio-Economic Systems Research project. Kyoto University. September 1986. See his Figure 2 in Appendix 3.

10 Micro-electronics in appliances: a part of competitive strategy?

DIETER BESCHORNER
TECHNICAL UNIVERSITY, MUNICH

Introduction

In the last few years many products have become more intelligent as a result of micro-electronic circuits. Besides the substitution of electromechanics, electronisation has led to higher utility for customers e.g. the fully automatic camera or, as a completely new solution of problems, the anti-lock system in motor vehicles. In addition, one can notice a general trend from network intelligent sub-systems to a more intelligent total system.

From the point of view of the European manufacturer, in particular, one must mention household appliances, or White Ware products as they are called. One may ask how a competitive advantage compared with Asian suppliers can be achieved by brand modification. This differentiation is important, because the technical level of appliances is high and for the customer no argument to decide on the product of a particular firm (see Figure 1 below). Even a glance at the market shares do not give a significant element of choice (see Figure 2 a and b), if we compare them with the EDP market for instance, and the beginning process of concentration by merger and acquisition in that market will make the situation worse for the smaller manufacturers.

After the successful penetration of photography, hi-fi equipment and motor vehicles by electronic circuits, the sector of Home Automation, with the sub-systems of Interactive Kitchen Systems (IKS) and Interactive Home Systems (IHS), presents itself as the next strategic unit. Coping with the long development period of electronically equipped appliances on the one hand and the shortening of the product life cycle on the other seems to be problematic. This discrepancy sometimes has a slowdown effect on innovative ideas and it seems imperative to treat the increase of innovative capability in every enterprise as the most important task for management until the turn of the century.

The explanations here seek to show whether the forced use of electronics in the 'White Ware' (WW) market can be regarded as a strategy for attaining competitive advantage. In addition, what kind of additional measures will be necessary for such a technological jump will be discussed.

The argument is based on theoretical studies as well as on discussions with a European manufacturer of WW. A review of technical and costing questions in connection with HA was carried out. In particular, we examined how the calculation of electronic appliances is presented as a function of the number of pieces, in comparison with electro-mechanical appliances. A part of this data has not been released to the public, and therefore this is more an attempt to define the position in this market than a scientific report based on company data.

To analyse the competitive position of a European manufacturer of appliances one can in some respects use Michael Porter's methodology. The competitive climate of any industry is not a matter of accident or luck, but rather it is determined by five fundamental forces:–

- the power of buyers
- the power of suppliers
- the threat of entry
- the threat of substitutes
- the intensity of rivalry of existing competitors

By following a generic strategy of either:–

- differentiation
- overall cost leadership or
- focus

a firm may be able to position itself, in relation to the five fundamental forces, so that it gains competitive advantage.

The study attempted to test theoretically the effects of a highly sophisticated part (intelligent chip) in a WW product as a strategy of differentiation.

Home Automation Systems

The terms 'Integrated Home System' (IHS), and especially 'Domotique' in France and 'Smarthouse' in Britain have also been introduced for HA. A standard definition of these 'intelligent and automatic houses' does not exist, because the houses themselves do not yet exist for the use of the

186

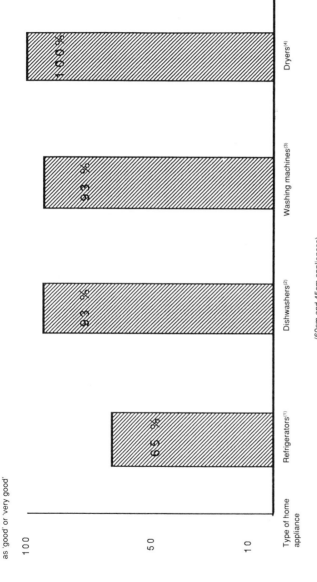

Percentage of appliances evaluated as 'good' or 'very good'

100

50

10

Type of home appliance

Refrigerators[1]   Dishwashers[2]   Washing machines[3]   Dryers[4]

65 %   93 %   93 %   100 %

(60cm and 45cm appliances)

Notes:
Issues of tests of goods of the 'Stiftung Warentest' (goods testing Foundation)

(1) = Issue 6/1989, pp.51–7   (3) = Issue 4/1989, pp.38–44
(2) = Issue 11/1987, pp.26–32   (4) = Issue 1/1988, pp.52–8

Figure 1 Matured technical level of home appliances

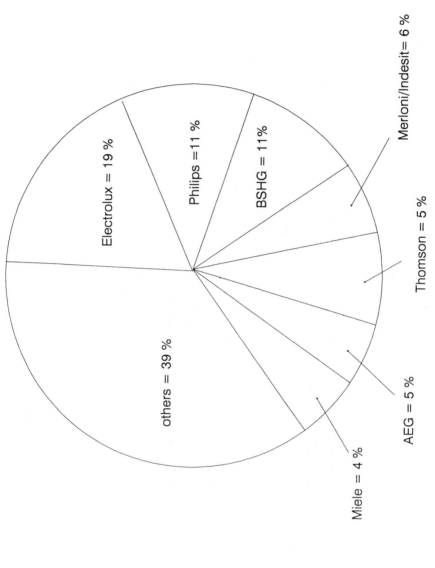

Figure 2a White ware: (Western European) market shares of the seven biggest European manufacturers, 1987

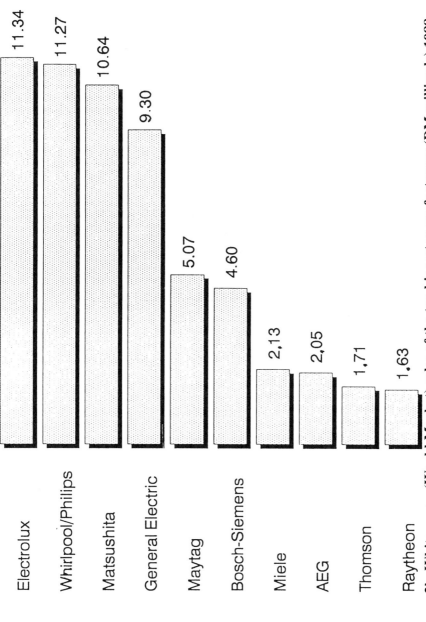

Figure 2b White ware: (World Market) sales of the ten biggest manufacturers (DM milliards) 1988

Source: AEG

future buyers, but only as prototypes. However, in general, one can say that a home computer controls electronic home appliances and home systems which are connected to each other.

The elements of HA concerning their stages of development are:–

– intelligent products
– intelligent sub-systems
– central HA system

Intelligent products and sub-systems can communicate with each other. Here the central HA system is to be regarded as a manager to whom all sub-systems and therefore also products are subordinated (see Figure 3).

For example, such an HA system provides inputs to the following activities when leaving the home:–

(a) Turning on the security systems
(b) Switching over the telephone system
(c) Turning down the heating
(d) Turning off superfluous energy consumers
(e) Turning on the dishwasher at cheap electricity tariff times
(f) Turning on the remote controls to operate appliances by a telephone call from outside the house
(g) etc. etc.

Points (d) and (e) can be united under the generic term 'energy controlling', and this in turn serves housekeeping which is oriented towards the long run for ecological reasons. The customer is here offered a real quantum jump of comfort, security and saving of time, as well as a more environmentally beneficial system. The prerequisites required for introducing HA can be differentiated roughly into technical and market-oriented ones:–

Technical prerequisites:–
The transmission of information for an HA system requires a network which has to perform in the form of a home bus system (HBS) and which has to comply with certain standards. Internationally introduced industry standards are needed to allow the consumer to use products of various manufacturers, which are controlled by microprocessors. That means a standardisation of certain qualities and features:–

– Communication standards for software between sub-systems and home computer
– Physical qualities e.g. medium of transmission, number of outputs, arrangement and outline of plugs, etc.
– Electric characteristics e.g. energy supply, resistance of cables, frequency, etc.
– Priority of signals e.g. emergency signal with priority before other signals
– others

Key sentence: Home appliances are a sub-system of Home Automation

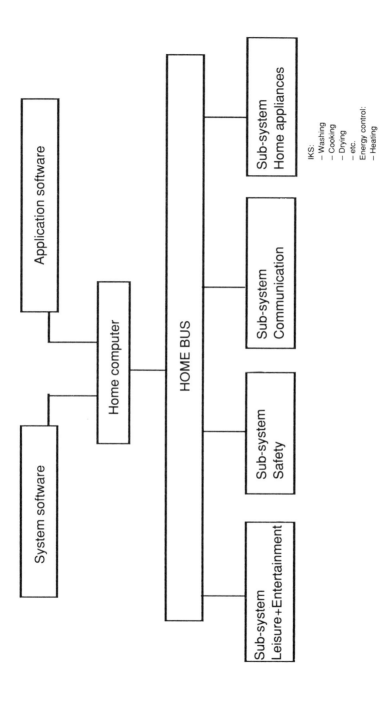

Figure 3 Structure of Home Automation

Japanese efforts for standardisation from the middle of the 1980s resulted at the end of 1988 in an agreement in the Electronic Industries Association/ Consumer Electronics Group (USA), to which belong companies like Panasonic, Sony, Philips, Tandy, Mitsubishi and RCA. The result was the Consumer Electronics Bus (CEBus). Besides the Communication Industries Association of Japan (CIAJ) issued a 'CIAJ Home Bus System Standards Report' in June 1988, which is at present the basis for drawing up final standards.

Market-oriented prerequisites:–
Basically, comprehensive enlightenment and information for the consumer are necessary. This is not only required prior to purchase but also as an accompanying service after purchase and during use. Even very customer-friendly HA systems require a hitherto unknown degree of technical basic know-how.

Insufficient information prevents quick market penetration. This typical mistake was made, for example, in the marketing of PCs by leaving the customer alone with hard and software without clear manuals at the initial phase when these new devices were introduced.

Such factors as market, competition and technology are the driving forces for successful enterprising and are valid too in the area of HA. Looking at these factors intensively creates a list of head-words dealing with the advantages and disadvantages of HA:–

Market:–
In favour of HA:–
(a) Persons with double income in small households
  – not much time for homework
  – safe supply for the children
  – safety of the unoccupied house
  – preparedness to pay more than a proportional price for leisure time
(b) Increasing part-time work among women
  cf. argument regarding persons with double income
(c) Turning of the population pryamid
  – safety in case of illness, accident, fault and wrong operation
  – increasing demands for comfort among healthy and financially strong persons who have taken 'early retirement'
(d) Leisure time society
  – fundamental wish to minimise routine occupations (inconveniences)
  – wish for perfect results
  – more effective after sales service
Against HA:–
There are actually no permanently valid reasons. At most, there are factors conducive to sluggish introduction:–

192

(a)   missing technical standards
(b)   inadequate customer service
(c)   anxiety over uncontrollable intelligence in the house
(d)   too high a price in the introductory phase

Competition:–
Advantages of competition are to be achieved by:–
(a)   new possibilities for differentiation in a more or less saturated market segment
(b)   gain of market share by real innovation e.g. in the sector for sensors; these should facilitate intelligent combinations of the sub-systems
(c)   precaution against increasing environmental regulations, which can be realised only by intelligent electronic circuits e.g. automatic dosage of detergent as a function of the hardness of water

The following disadvantages are to be mentioned:–
(a)   the initially long development time for coping with the technological jump
(b)   the timing of market introduction – the question is not, whether HA is coming but when and how

Technology:–
Prior experience in the electronics sector facilitates offering a high number of pieces at acceptable prices but missing technical standards can slow down the phase of introduction. Therefore, basic feasibility is not questioned but the preparatory work required for it is.

In Japan, prototypes of the intelligent house already exist but the variety of manufacturer standards has hitherto prevented successful distribution.

In the USA, the home observation sub-system is widely available but the lack of compatibility between sub-systems has prevented the distribution of further systems.

In Europe, Zanussi, as a subsidiary of Electrolux, has an exemplary IKS as a sub-system of the IHS but European standards are lacking. However, in the Eureka Programme people are working on them.

Case study (strategy, technology, costs)

The firm looked at for the following statements has aims as follows:–

(i)   Leadership in technology
(ii)   Alignment from exporter to Europe-wide insider
(iii) Verifying of quantum jumps as customer benefits
(iv)   Improvements of the internal performance system (value chain)
(v)   To achieve and protect a second position in the European market

All these sub-aims are dependent on each other and belong to the medium-term time period of planning (up to two years), which has to be seen here as the basis of a long-term strategy, which tries already to realise a part of the technological jump. There is also the question of whether this strategy in the sense of the determinants of potential

- potential for problem solution
- potential for implementation
- potential for diffusion
- potential for differentiation

resulted in a real potential for innovation. Electronic control is an indispensable prerequisite for the use of sensors and the integration of appliances as sub-systems in the intelligent house. Therefore, in the field of washing-up two alternatives must be checked:–

Alternative 1:–
Electronics are put in as an isolated marketing variable in the upper price segment, and are not seen as a strategic argument.

Alternative 2:–
Electronics are used in a large number of pieces in the basic types (altogether over $1/2$ million pieces per year). Even if this alternative is not a direct increase of benefits for the customer in each of the three basic types concerned, this alternative will be examined because of the strategic aspect.

The aim of the second alternative is to make use of the Boston effect for electronic WW, controls and regulations. This effect consists of:–

- learning effects (referring to employees)
- quantity effects (referring to materials)
- forming effects (referring to production processes)

An overview of the most interesting criteria concerning electro-mechanical versus electronic control circuits is shown in Figure 4.

The nature of the firm's calculation is at the moment in a phase of change and of extension to a decision-oriented system of information. The investigations carried out are based on the hitherto used job costing or order costing system. Four different products are examined:–

(i)   60cm dishwasher
(ii) 45cm dishwaster
(iii) Parts for cooling
(iv) Completely knocked down units

To make the calculation, only the example of the 60cm dishwashing machine was considered, as the product bearing all the costs. A more detailed and proven calculation of the two alternatives brought as a result a surplus of costs of approximately DM five million; by this, company costs mount

Key sentence: Increasing advantages of electronic control circuits

	Circuit-speed	Size of elements	Consumption of energy	Sensitivity of temperature	Maintenance	Price	Amplifier required	Consumption	Complex Wiring possible	Control elem. Lifetime
microelectronic control circuit	very small +++	very small +++	very small +++	very sensitive – –	barely neces-sary ++	very cheap +++	yes –	no ++	yes ++	very high ++
electromechanical control circuit	medium +	medium +	medium +	not sensitive +	neces-sary –	– medium +	no ++	medium –	difficult –	low –

Note

+++
++ = advantageous
+

-
-- = disadvantageous

Figure 4 Comparison of electro-mechanical and electronic control systems

on the basis of the quantity calculated of five hundred thousand pieces by about DM 10,– per appliance.

A qualitative judgement of the alternatives shows the following picture:–

Alternative 1:–
Advantages:–
(a)   higher profit in the short run; especially during the time of spare part requirements
(b)   small investment

Disadvantages:–
(a)   low learning effect in the electronics area
(b)   no bulk discount in buying
(c)   a more waiting/remaining than a creative/structuring position concerning new technologies

Alternative 2:–
Advantages:–
(a)   electronics as a basis for the protection of existing and of new markets
(b)   active creation of the technical prerequisites for a higher extra benefit from sensors and for HA
(c)   strong learning effect in the field of electronics
(d)   foundation of know-how of one's own
(e)   company goal of 'leadership in technology' will be fulfilled
(f)   bulk discount in buying

Disadvantages:–
(a)   coping with the difficulties of:–
        –   know-how transfer
        –   organisation
        –   personnel
(b)   technology jump possibly too early

Measures to verify in the strategic area:–

(a)   Pushing existing electronic regulation and control mechanisms
        aim: to create a basis for points B and C below to achieve technological leadership
(b)   Development of sensors
        aim: to make quantum jumps in benefits for the customer
(c)   Developing and fixing technical standards concerning HA together with
        –   important manufacturers of WW
        –   manufacturers of other electronic sub-systems
        –   kitchen manufacturers
        –   others

aim: here too, as above, the achievement of more benefits for the customer
(d) Cooperation in the field of electronics with European partners
aim: reduction of technological dependence on non-European manufacturers

To summarise at this point means identifying the following statements as a trend:–
– the attractiveness of innovation is much higher when using electronics, in comparison with the pure substitution nowadays of electro-mechanical regulation by electronics
– the degree of relative innovation strength will only become sufficient by joining with a powerful partner (see Figure 5).

Technological jump

To translate the above mentioned strategies into action requires the fulfilment of several prerequisites. This can be seen in particular from the model of the value chain of a firm and its integration into a value system (see Figure 6). The change of technology in the product, as discussed in the example, calls for an optimisation of the total system of the firm to realise the competitive advantages striven for. Strategy development and technology planning therefore require a corresponding layout of organisation and personnel planning.

The layout of the organisation has to take into account:

(i) obtaining the know-how for the planned technological jump
(ii) reduction of resistance to innovation

In regard to personnel planning, the aim should be to strive for strictly job- and strategy-oriented training. With this planned innovation, the number of working places should be kept stable (as considered in the calculation done); that means a reduction of personnel costs will be realised in the long run, i.e. that with a constant number of employees, output will be increased.

Conclusion

The problems for European manufacturers at the moment are:

– in the main, markets are saturated as regards e.g. cooling and washing. At the moment there is a spare parts boom, bringing good earning possibilities even to newcomers, but no chance of growth

Key sentence: High innovation potential only by electronics,
sensors and co-operation, intelligence and partnership

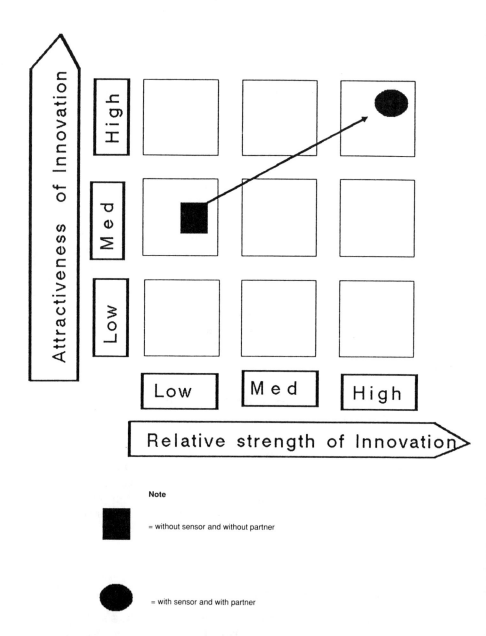

Figure 5 Innovation potential

Key sentence: Changes in technology stipulate new optimisation of all other activities

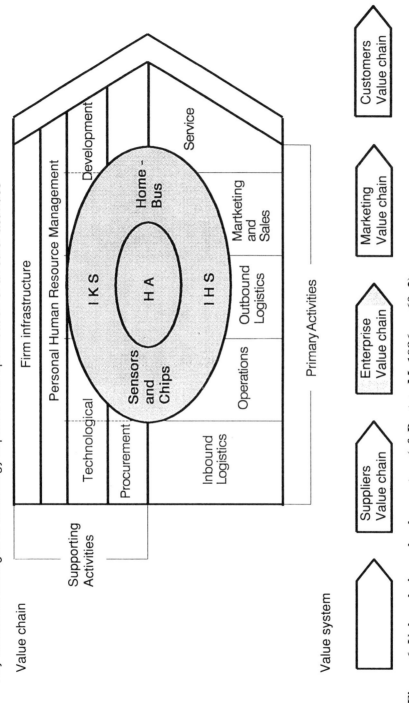

Figure 6 Value chain and value system (cf. Porter, M. 1986 pp.60–2)

- new market shares can only be realised by additional benefits for the customer, if at all. Own brand differentiation in the WW sector is aggravated by increasing globalisation

One possibility for solving the problems discussed under the generic term 'technology as a competitive factor' is the innovation potential of electronic regulation and control. These are prerequisites for the intelligent processing of measurement from sensors and the integration of the IKS sub-system into the IHS.

For the future the following points are important:–

- modern appliances have to be economical and environmentally beneficial
- at the same time, the benefit for the customer has to increase

These requirements can cannot be realised using mechanics or electro-mechanics. As shown, these requirements are to be fulfilled by the installation of micro-electronic circuits (chips). The possibility of networking all these appliances in the HA system is important and in the long term indispensable. The transition from mechanical to electronic/intelligent stand-alone appliances is only an intermediate stage on the way to the network of the intelligent house.

Concerning the question asked at the beginning, whether a strategy to reach advantages in competition can be seen in the forced use of electronics in the WW sector, the following can be noted:–

- 'White Ware', especially washing machines, are already a highly developed and widely diffused product in Europe. Asian suppliers are, at the moment, not competitors in this field. Especially concerning Japan, this technology was taken over from the USA and was pursued further without any ambition – possibly because of the traditional roles of the sexes and because the use of washing-machines was not well established in the public's consciousness
- experience has shown that Japanese companies first serve the home market and then include foreign countries in their strategy. Washing has not so far been an interesting market and washing machines are not an export item with high value added – they have a high weight and no or not much electronics
- the strategy of Asian competitors has often pushed electronics as an export hit to the foreground – and then with extreme power
- as the camera, hi-fi and television equipment sectors have shown, the extensive use of electronics with a correspondingly high value added is favourable to commercialisation when sales over the counter are easily possible; while for the HA sector and the appliances it requires this has hitherto only been possible with microwave ovens
- today's tendency concerning HA becomes apparent on the Asian side in

large scale projects e.g. industrial construction, hotel construction, and could be the first step from the strategic point of view to going in the long run into the wider consumer market too

For European manufacturers therefore, the chance is given by the timely building up of the appropriate electronically equipped appliances in parallel with the pursuit of the network idea to make the threat of entry manifest and to protect their chances in this market.

Notes

Hennig-Cardinal von Widdern, Georg. *Elektronik als Wettbewerbsfaktor in der Weiße-Ware-Industrie: Strategisches Konzept zur Bewältigung eines Technologiesprunges.* Master thesis. Technische Universität, München. 1989.

Kieser, A. 'Die innovative Unternehmung als Voraussetzung der internationalen Wettbewerbsfähigkeit.' *Wirtschaftswissenschaftliches Studium.* 7. 1985. pp. 354–8.

Maréchal, S. 'Le Marché Du Comfort Interactif.' *Micro-Systèmes* 4. 1988. pp. 156–62.

Michel, K. *Technologie im stratequischen Management – Ein Portfolio-Ansatz zur integrierten Technologie- und Marktplanung.* Berlin. 1987.

No author. 'Mörtel für die Akzeptanz.' *High Tech.* 11. 1989. pp. 88–90.

Parks, P. 'Home Automation: A View From A Marketer.' *International Journal of Digital and Analog Cabled System.* 1. 1988. pp. 29–32.

Porter, M.E. *Wettbewerbsvorteile – Spitzenleistungen erreichen und behaupten.* Frankfurt/Main. 1986.

Romer, K.-H. 'Strategische Planung in gesättigten Märkten.' Beschorner, D. und Heinhold, M. (eds.): *Hochschulschriften zur Betriebswirtschaftslehre.* Bd. 49. München. 1987.

Schlauersbach, G. 'A view from Europe.' *Appliance* Part 2. November 1988.

Servatius, H.-G. *New Venture Management – Erfolgrieche Lösung von Innovationsproblemen für Technologie-Unternehmen.* Wiesbaden. 1988.

Viehöver, U. 'Hausgeräte: AEG schwimmt gegen den Strom – Mercedes der Küche.' *Wirtschaftswoche.* Nr. 7. 9 February 1990.

11 Economic effects of robotisation in Japan

TUVIA BLUMENTHAL
BEN-GURION UNIVERSITY

Introduction

Japan has been the leading country in the introduction of industrial robots. At the end of 1986 the number of industrial robots in operation in Japan was larger than that in all other countries combined. This leads to the following questions:–

– What is the economic distinction of robots?
– What are the economic problems which robotisation can solve?
– What is the explanation for the rapid speed of robotisation in Japan?
– What are the future prospects in this field?

Economic aspects of robotisation

The definition of industrial robots is, 'Those devices which provide versatile and flexible moving functions similar to those of human limbs and/or which provide flexible moving functions through their sensing and recognising capabilities'.[1] The robot must be seen as one element in a Flexible Manufacturing System (FMS). A Flexible Manufacturing System consists of a group of processing stations (numerically controlled) connected together by an automated workpart handling system. It operates as an integrated system under computer control.[2] Some of the characteristics of FMS are: production of families of workparts on a series of machines; random launching i.e. no need for downtime setup for handling part families; reduction of non-operation time between work stations; reduction of in-process inventory; and an increase in machine utilisation. FMS reduces the requirement for direct and indirect labour, since labour is only needed for supervision. The system also helps production planners and controllers to achieve better management control.

Robots are divided into the five following categories:–

(i) Operating robots – a robot having controllers and actuators for mobility and/or manipulation, remotely controlled by a human operator

(ii) Sequence controlled robots – a robot that operates sequentially in compliance with present information

(iii) Playback robots – a robot than can repeat an operation on the basis of instructions my moving the robot under operating control

(iv) Numerically controlled (NC) robots – a robot that can execute the commanded operation in compliance with information loaded numerically or by programme without being moved

(v) Intelligent robots – a robot that can determine its own actions through artificial intelligence

Robots have several advantages over human beings in performing a wide range of jobs. These include continuous operation with no need of rest; precision; not being affected by hazardous conditions; and not suffering from boredom or sickness. Robots can replace human beings to do dangerous, repetitive and monotonous tasks.

The main functions performed today by industrial robots are assembly, plastic moulding, welding, machining, pressing, casting and painting.

The introduction of robots may have the following effects on the factory and on its products:– savings of labour; improvement in work content and environment e.g. freedom from dirty, noisy or night work; facilitation of production technology; and rises in production efficiency in the firm's degree of competitiveness.

What is the difference between robots and other machines? The keyword here is flexibility. From the economic point of view, the factor of 'capital' has been described as 'putty-clay'; namely, before a machine is produced all options are open as to which machine should be created with a given amount of expenditure, so it has the quality of 'putty'. Once the machine has been built, it becomes 'clay'; i.e. not amenable to change. Robots introduce the 'putty-putty' concept; that is, a single robot can be used to produce a wide range of products, thus introducing flexibility into the system.

When conventional machines are used, a change in design or model means major changes in the machine or even the need to build a new machine. With robots, a change in the operating programme makes it possible to introduce the desired change in design or model, which enables the firm to adjust production to changing demand conditions. Robots are thus an important element in the introduction of small-batch production; replacing mass production, which has been the essence of cost reduction since the days of Henry Ford.

With the substantial reduction in the cost of robots, they can be introduced in small and medium-sized firms, thus enabling these firms to increase variation in the number of products made by them.

Industrial robots in Japan

The production of industrial robots has increased from 4,400 in 1975 to 45,100 in 1987: in value terms from ¥11.1 billion in 1975 to ¥300.6 billion in 1987. Twenty per cent of these robots were exported. The remainder were absorbed by domestic manufacturers, primarily those of electrical machinery (30 per cent) and automobiles (19 per cent). Other industries, such as metal-working machinery and plastic moulding, each used five per cent or less of the total amount. As mentioned above, the number of industrial robots operating in Japan was by far the largest among all industrial countries: at the end of 1986 there were 116,000 in Japan compared with 25,000 in the US and 12,400 in West Germany. There has also been a change in the composition of robots, thus the percentage of operating and fixed sequence robots went down from 77 per cent in 1980 to 24 per cent in 1987, while the share of NC and intelligent robots went up from 6 per cent in 1960 to 30 per cent in 1987.[3]

How can this rapid propagation of robots in Japan be explained? The following factors seem to shed light on this question:–

(a) Shortage of labour. This has developed in Japan due to an increase in demand for skilled labour on the one hand and a relatively low rate of natural increase in population, of around 1 per cent, together with an increase in the number of students in higher learning institutions on the other hand. Labour shortages have caused an increase in labour costs, which have driven firms to replace workers by robots

(b) Reduction in the price of robots. It has been estimated that the ratio of the average price of a robot to labour cost went down from 4.6 in 1970 to 1.7 in 1978[4]

(c) Social pressure. This has helped reduce industrial accidents and improve working conditions, but it has also caused a reduction in the number of workers willing to do dangerous jobs

(d) Lack of immigrant labour. The Japanese government has adopted a negative attitude toward allowing the immigration of cheap labour into Japan; unlike the policy of some European countries

(e) No effective resistance to robots on the part of Japanese labour unions. The introduction of robots has caused very little negative attitude or resistance by labour because, first, the lifetime employment system in large companies guarantees continuous employment; and, second, the system of company unions ensures that workers have a better understanding of a company's needs

(f)   Government policy. It is the policy of the Japanese government to promote the introduction of robots in small and medium-sized companies

(g)   Land costs. The high price of land in Japan calls for reduction of the land-output ratio. Due to the flexibility of robots, it is possible to adapt a factory to manufacture a different product without building a new one

Effect of robot introduction on employment

Since the Industrial Revolution, when workers demolished machines to protect their jobs, there has been a presumption that technological progress has an adverse effect on employment. Macro data show, that in spite of the much larger number of industrial robots in Japan, overall unemployment figures are smaller. Looked at from theoretical considerations, in a growing economy with a shortage of labour the introduction of robots causes an increase in output and labour productivity, rather than an increase in unemployment. This is because robots are substituting for ageing workers who leave their jobs or workers who move to other functions, such as inspection or maintenance.

According to Moriguchi, robots have not actually replaced workers in large numbers, but have revived small firms who have been suffering from shortages of young workers.[5] Older workers who retire establish the infra-structure needed for the introduction of robots. Robots have also saved some labour-intensive industries that have lost their competitive advantage because of the high increase in labour cost. They regain this advantage by introducing robots: as an example, he cites the cutlery and silverware industry that has been able to compete with its counterparts in Korea and Taiwan by producing low-priced products.

The introduction of robots also serves to create jobs both through the establishment of a robot-producing industry, and by altering working conditions sufficiently so that certain jobs can be offered to handicapped or older workers.

A survey conducted in 1981 by the Japanese National Institute of Employment and Vocational Training on the effects of the introduction of industrial robots in the automobile, electrical machinery and general machinery industries shows that while there was usually a reduction of the workforce at the workplace, this was not often reflected in a reduction of overall employment in the establishment.[6] The reason for this was that there was an increase in total production, causing personnel transfer rather than redundancy.

There was also a change in the nature of work from physical to mental, and special training was given to robot related workers. A limited number of workers were trained by the robot producing company and they were used to give on-the-job training to other workers. The flexibility of the Japanese employment system, based on the lifetime principle and workers' mobility, facilitated the transition.

The three major merits of robot introduction were given as quality improvement, manpower saving and improvement in the working environment in terms of safety and health.

Saito and Nakamura used an econometric model to estimate the effect of robotisation on employment. The total effect of the introduction of robots on employment is the sum of a direct effect, caused by the substitution of robots for labour, and an indirect effect, due to an increase in robot production and investment demand throughout the economy. These two effects partially cancel each other. In their projections, Saito and Nakamura found that the total effect of robot introduction during the period 1985-90 would cause a net reduction of 23,000 workers in manufacturing industries, amounting to less than 0.02 per cent of the total.[7]

Government policy

In 1980, in order to promote the introduction of industrial robots in small and medium-sized companies, the Japanese government established the Japan Robot Leasing Co.; offered financial assistance through the Small Business Finance Corporation and the People's Finance Corporation for the introduction of robots designed to ensure safety; and created a special depreciation system for high performance robots provided with computers. Local government also introduced loans and leasing programs for enterprises to modernise equipment. Since 1984, special interest rates have been provided for loans from the Japan Development Bank to the Japan Robot Leasing Co. for the introduction of Flexible Manufacturing Systems.

Besides receiving loans, small and medium enterprises also get counselling and guidance under the Small Enterprise Guidance Officer System, and these officers also visit business sites and serve as intermediaries between the enterprise and public agencies. The Mechatronics Investment Promotion Tax System enables small enterprises who introduce electronic devices to benefit from special deductions on corporate taxes.

Robots in the automobile industry

Once of the industries in which the introduction of robots has been most successful is the automobile industry. The process of robot introduction into the Nissan factories is vividly recorded by Yamauchi, Nissan's general manager. There were three stages in this process: first, robots were used mainly for spot welding, then they were used in top coat painting, and finally in an automated assembly line. In the beginning, robots were bought from external suppliers but production gradually became indigenous, making it better suited to specific needs.

The advantage of robots is found in four main areas: improvement of quality, improvement of the working environment, cost effectiveness and flexibility. As a result of robot introduction, there has been a substantial decline in accidents, a large reduction in man hours and a rise in cost effectiveness. Over the period there has also been a decrease in the price of robots, whereas wages showed a marked increase. For example, between 1970 and 1987 the price of playback robots went down by 50 per cent while wages went up 500 per cent.[8]

The use of robots makes it possible to develop a Flexible Manufacturing Line (FML) where several models can be produced at the same time, leading to a much shorter period for the introduction of new models.

The advanced robot technology project

This project is now being undertaken by the Agency of Industrial Science and Technology of MITI as a national project. Its aim is to develop robots which can carry out inspection, maintenance and rescue operations in the fields of nuclear power, off-shore oil exploration and disaster fighting.[9] The project was to be carried out within the period 1983-90, with a total expenditure of ¥20 billion. Robots that will function in a nuclear power plant will be designed to perform equipment checks and various tests in a high radiation environment, climb up and down stairs, pass over and under obstacles, turn at right angles, and inspect and repair valves, pumps and other equipment. Robot for underwater operations will have to substitute for human divers in the performance of maintenance and repair work under water, while firefighting robots will extinguish fires in high temperature and heavy smoke environments.

Future developments

Several new directions are being considered in the use of robots:–

(a)   An increase in the degree of automation until a fully automated factory is reached where robots and computer-controlled machines perform with little or no human intervention

(b)   Robots which will perform more complex tasks by having sensors for vision, touch, force and proximity

(c)   Use of robots for non-manufacturing tasks such as helping physically handicapped people, geological surveys under water, fruit harvesting and construction work.

Notes

1.   Yonemoto, Kanji. *Robotization in Japan*. Mimeo. Japan Industrial Robot Association. April 1987.
2.   Boubekri, Nourredin. 'Robots in flexible manufacturing systems.' *Robotics*. 3. 1987. pp. 421–6.
3.   Japan Industrial Robot Association. *General View and Statistics of Industrial Robots*. Mineo. June 1988.
4.   Kuni, Sadamoto. 'Robots in the Japanese economy.' *Survey Japan*. Tokyo. 1981.
5.   Moriguchi, Chikashi. 'Driving forces of economic structural change.' Paper submitted to the IIASA Meeting, November 24–5, 1988.
6.   National Institute of Employment and Vocational Research. *Report of Study Committee Concerning Impacts of Microelectronics on Employment*. Tokyo. March 1984.
7.   Saito, Mitsuo and Nakamura, Shinichiro. *Impact of Robotization on the Japanese Economy*. Mimeo.
8.   Yamauchi, Yasuo. 'Application and Evaluation of Robots at Nissan.' Paper presented at the 19th International Symposium on Industrial Robots. 1988. pp. 189–209.
9.   Okada, Yasushi. 'Major R&D project for advanced robot technology.' Robot. 62. May 1988. pp. 34–43.

12 Strategic information networks for competitive advantage: conversion to network management

YOSHIYA TERAMOTO AND NAOTO IWASAKI
UNIVERSITY OF TSUKUBA AND OBIRIN UNIVERSITY

Introduction

(i) Structural change in maturing societies

Today, in the developed countries, consumers in 'maturing societies' are quantitatively satisfied with fundamental consumption goods and are enjoying a materially rich life. However, with this development consumers are also changing their values and attitudes toward life accordingly. Thus not only quantitative but also qualitative satisfaction is sought in pursuit of the qualitative 'advancement of life'.

Furthermore, in today's information age, consumers have available abundant knowledge of new commodities and life styles through the mass media. Reflecting today's emphasis on individuality, the consumer pattern has changed so that the consumer does not passively accept goods and services offered by the companies but makes an active choice.

To adapt to the market change brought about by the maturity of the market and new consumer patterns, it would be difficult for firms to expand their business through the heretofore existing 'supplier-side logic'. The shift to a 'consumer-side logic' adjusted to changing needs becomes necessary.

One of the most important strategic problems in today's diversified and maturing society is shortening the distance between firms and the market.

(ii) Building up information networks

In order to adapt flexibly to market changes by shortening the distance between the firm and the market, many firms are building up information networks with computers and communication media.

The progress of computer and communication technologies makes it possible, first, to know what commodities are selling best, using POS registers; second, to achieve efficiency in design and development, using CAD/CAM and, third, to rationalise orders, using EOS and so on. Such information networks connecting various business functions, are built up not only within a company, but spread out to other companies, such as subsidiaries or customer companies, making possible a rapid and appropriate response to the market.

Further, information networks can create a new business, which may be called 'network business', by generating variations in the combination of information that produces new meanings and values beyond the original information given. In other words, it is 'information creation'.

For firms to expand in the 21st century, whether strategic management of information networks is possible will be critical. To realise this, a completely new management style that might be termed 'network management' will have to be instituted.

Strategic information networks (SIN) for competitive advantage

(i) Advantage through information networks

Today, as manufacturers expand business activities, the most critical problem is how goods and services needed by customers can be supplied in the required form when necessary. Furthermore, the current consumer market reflects the age of differentiation and customer-consumer needs are diversified, sophisticated and changeable. No longer can customer needs be considered uniformly, as in the past age of mass consumption, nor can firms segment the market unilaterally from the viewpoint of the supply side.

Such changes in the end consumer markets influence the activities of firms that supply the production resources and intermediate products. The suppliers of resources and materials have been forced to adjust their production systems in order to be attuned to the assembly manufacturers' supplied-as-needed or 'Just In Time' (JIT) systems. Assembly manufacturers themselves must in turn form production and distribution systems that are correlated with rapidly changing needs. Similarly, in answer to retailers' demands, food and other consumer product manufacturers are beginning to effect frequent small quantity multi-product deliveries.

For this reason, many companies are faced with the prospect of actualising the increased diversity, or scope, and speed of their business activities so as to meet varied, sophisticated and changeable customer needs. In other words, in addition to economies of scale, as in the past, what might be called economies of scope and economies of speed must be created. In pursuit of these economies, different parts are linked by information networks and in the process new values and meanings are created. They then become the source of a new economy i.e. the 'economy of networks', or economy of linking, and the implementation of the 'network economy' is the basis for gaining competitive advantage.

In fact, in the questionnaire study we carried out, many companies expressed their desire of participating in a business field closer to the customer market than before (see Table 1). Moreover, they wished to build up various types of information networks in cooperation with other companies to cope with market changes; which means that most companies want to accomplish 'adaptation' to varied and rapidly changing markets by building up information networks.

However, if firms persist in merely following market changes, they will be harried by the management of the enormous flow of information and keeping an endless assortment of goods in supply, which in itself imposes enormous expenditure of time and costs. To resolve such an inconsistency, firms should not standardise their market structure one-sidedly, nor consider the firm and the market as being in binary opposition. Rather, a dynamic process of originally fusing firms and markets becomes necessary, signifying the creation of a more flexible and direct information flow between the two.

SIN as a fusion mechanism

To fuse firms and markets by structuring an appropriate SIN, fusion of different functions within firms and across different firms must be realised. In other words, various information networks corresponding to the various levels of business activities should not be considered independently but as interrelated and synchronised in a composite and stratified manner. Fusion between firms and markets is based on networking within the firm and across firms, which are linked and resonant with each other. Fusion between firms and markets builds up 'fusion networks', that originally connect with business resources i.e. personnel, materials, money and information.

Networks for fusion

(i) Fusion within firms

Generally, fusion within the firm is the process of actualising new values and meanings through the fusion of information networks of different business functions, such as purchasing, production, sales, and R & D.

211

Table 1 What business fields are Japanese and American companies planning to move into?

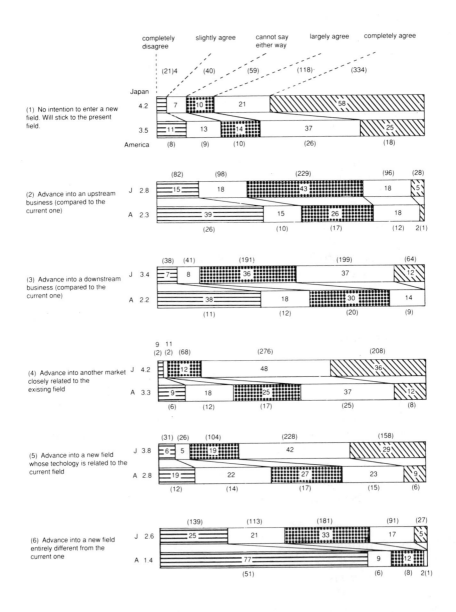

In manufacturing, by synchronising sales, production, purchasing, and R & D information, the fusion of business functions takes place through OA (Office Automation), FA (Factory Automation) and CIM (Computer Integrated Manufacturing) and so on.

Business efficiency, cost- and time-wise, through information networks within the firm is also being promoted in non-manufacturing industries as well. At Nomura Securities, the biggest stock company in Japan, unified management of the information network allows increasing customer orders and business to be dealt with efficiently. Also, the information network sharing within the company as a whole makes it possible to understand the profitability of individual dealings, in spite of the complexity of the investment environment.

In short, the linking of the information within the firm through an intrafirm network destroys the barriers of the sophisticated functional division of labour and leads to the company's rationalisation of business as a whole.

Fusion within the firm not merely promotes business efficiency but also contributes to creating new products and developing new technologies. As can be seen in the automobile industry, for example, information networks can synchronise R & D, design and trial productions (Simultaneous Engineering), shorten the time of R & D and improve the precision of products, by connecting production and design through CAD/CAM.

(ii) Information networks not limited within a single firm

In advanced firms, information networks have grown to encompass related companies and business partners, thus raising the fusion level further. Networks across firms overcome boundaries between firms and sharing the flow of information promotes interaction and speedy and efficient business.

The automobile manufacturing industry is the most typical example. In manufacturing a car, 30,000–40,000 parts are assembled, involving an enormous number of firms. Therefore, unless there is an adequate exchange of information among parts producers and assembly companies, efficient production systems cannot be set up. Information networks across firms are indispensable for JIT systems and efficient production.

Added to the efficiency of production, the efficiency of delivery of the final products and stock commodities is the important factor from the strategic viewpoint. Seven Eleven Japan, the convenience store chain, has about 4,000 shops and each shop stocks many small amounts of commodities (3,000 items per shop). To maintain frequent deliveries, Seven Eleven Japan has constructed a 'joint delivery system', which also builds up information networks across franchised shops and suppliers, so that wholesalers' functions have been rationalised. Seven Eleven Japan manages information flows so as to achieve efficiency in the flow of money and goods.

In other words, information networks across firms have accomplished greater information sharing and unification and faster communication. This in turn has promoted time and cost rationalisation and efficiency in the flow of goods, commerce and money and contributed to the development of new products and technology.

Further, as business activities become more globalised, the importance of networks for fusion increases. In the international division of labour and in international business dealings, distance in time and space acts as a considerable constraint but global information networks play an indispensable role in overcoming such restrictions.

(iii) Fusion of firm and market

Networks within the firm and across firms function more effectively by fusing and linking with other firms and the market. The distance between the market and the firm is considerably shortened by the fusion of intra-inter-firm, market and customer information and in this way a system that swiftly reflects market changes and diversity will be built. Thus, supplying goods and services required by customers when and how they are needed will be possible.

Market and customer information from the market should be transmitted and linked not only to 'front line departments', such as sales and marketing, but also to 'departments at the back', such as production and development, thus making feasible the timely production and development of technology and products to coincide with diverse market needs. For example, at Honda the number of product items increased drastically in response to 'the individualisation of the mass', creating problems with the cost of the necessary inventory to respond to diverse market needs. Therefore, Honda promoted the unification of information within firms and across firms by building up information networks between the market and the production site. Such networks made possible the production of automobiles to order. Similarly, Nissan plans to build an integrated order-production system by gathering customer information on e.g. the attributes and history of purchases, and by constructing an information network.

In this manner, SINs have realised the fusion of market and firms. Information networks have promoted the efficiency of business development by fusing the functions of the 'departments at the back'. Gathering front line department information and swiftly communicating it to the departments 'at the back', the fusion of firms and markets responds quickly to market diversity and change. Fusion of the firm and the market is beginning to change traditional work classification itself; both that of the front line departments, such as sales and services, and that of the departments at the back e.g. production and development. Thus SINs have made business front line, with every facet of business having a direct contact with the market.

Generating new business by network synergy

(i) Network synergy

SINs create bilateral flows of information, while fusing various functions leads to business efficiency and yields new meanings and values. That core process is the 'creation of synergy by networks'.

Synergy has been understood to be the multiplier effect or connective linking effect of resources; but why such an effect is generated is not necessarily clear. SIN has the potential of creating new meanings and values by generating and reforming interaction between heterogeneous departments within and across firms, or between firms and the market. In other words, networks fuse the meanings and values of the heterogeneous information of the constituent members and mutually influence each member, thus creating synergy. For example, NEC's fusing of communication and computer technologies, and its development and expansion of its new 'C & C' business field, is aimed at the creation of synergy.

The valuers and meanings of information are not determined intrinsically in themselves but propagate new ones when they encounter heterogeneous counterparts. The sharing and flow of information between heterogeneous systems fused by a network bring about a 'mutually creative effect' among members, i.e. dynamic synchronisation, or synergy. 'Synergy' is therefore the dynamic fusion process of the constituent members in cooperating in creating new meanings and values.

'Information synergy' and 'learning synergy'

'Network synergy' created in the fusion process can be classified into two types: 'information synergy' and 'learning synergy'. The former is created by the information flow itself and the latter by the accumulation of information and its transfer.

In the former case, by multiple usage of information, information synergy produces different values when fused, rising beyond the individual value of each component factor. This synergy occurs when 'linkage value' is created.

In the latter case, learning synergy is created by utilising the accumulated information. For example, sales information as experience information is utilised for production planning, or for forecasting market changes and customers' purchasing trends. Information does not decrease in quality or quantity by use: the more information is utilised, the more its value and, being used, information itself undergoes change. Accumulated information is shared by others as a database, or transferred to other constituent members as experience information bringing about 'shared learning'.

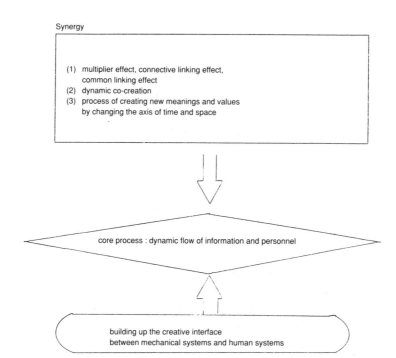

Figure 1 'Network synergy' created by information networks

Moreover, learning synergy is created by information sharing through learning transfer. When Honda builds new plants, it organises a project team which included some persons who have taken part in previous projects. This means that Honda cannot only build a new plant efficiently, but also creates new values by transferring information based on experience over the restrictions of time and space, as well as by rearranging the accumulated information. In other words, this process is designed for creating synergy by learning how to learn: what one might call 'learning by learning'.

Companies using network synergy for new business

(i) Seven Eleven Japan Co. Ltd.

Seven Eleven Japan is a 24 hour convenience store chain that has approximately 4,000 franchised shops all over Japan. It started as a joint venture with the US company but has developed more advanced marketing and sales systems than Seven Eleven US. Seven Eleven Japan has grown on its own: not only that; it has acquired Seven Eleven's US headquarters.

Every Seven Eleven franchised store in Japan orders on the basis of sales data provided by on-line POS registers, and high ordering efficiency is

216

achieved. Such ordering systems using on-line networks complete the joint delivery systems and rationalise the wholesale functions, making it possible to deliver to every shop several times a day; at the same time, the rationalisation of the wholesale functions achieves remarkable reductions in inventory and remarkable increases in profit.

Headquarters processes the data regarding customers and purchasing time, and feeds them back to every store, enabling each store to search for the best selling commodities appropriate to its situation. Thus, Seven Eleven Japan not only integrates information among franchisees and suppliers by POS registers, but also shortens the distance between them. POS data tells every shop what the best selling commodities are.

Moreover, Seven Eleven is developing a new business that utilises multiple networks among different industrires. Payment and collection of bills for public utilities such as TEPCO (Tokyo Electric Power Co.) and Tokyo Gas Company are examples of this; being a multi-use of 24 hour shops. Seven Eleven's ticket reservations for movies and concerts would be in the same vein.

Seven Eleven Japan is creating a new business through placing POS registers in every franchised shop, linking not only information from associated companies but also from other firms in different fields. In short, by changing the combination of factors by means of networks across other industries, it generates business opportunities. Outwards-spreading networks create network synergy and develop new business.

(ii) Yamato Transport Co. Ltd

Yamato is the truck transporation company that started a door-to-door home delivery service, known as 'Takkyubin', for the first time in Japan. Before Yamato began this business, they did not deliver small lots but only large lots for specific customers; for it was thought that a small lot transport system from many consignors to many consignees could not attain economies of scale.

However, Yamato built a previously unthought of efficient small lot truck transport system by using information networks. Such networks allow the flow of transport information on loading, unloading, main line transport and delivery to precede the actual freight flow and, by implementing the new system, Yamato made the transition from being a transport business to being a freight flow information service business.

At the same time, the efficiency of the transport system improved the service for customers by reducing the waiting time for cargo collection and speedily supplying information about individual cargo; which in turn enhanced customer confidence in the company and became a source of competitive advantage.

The integrated management of information completed the just-in-time delivery system, and this created new types of business, such as 'Golf Takkyubin' and 'Ski Takkyubin'.

Yamato's competitive advantage is generated by the multiple use of information networks, that have produced the synergy created by networks, and in turn 'new linking value'.

Moreover, Yamato has developed 'network business', which utilises the transportation and information processing know-how. An example is the 'Collect Service'. This entails the delivery of commodities and collecting payment in place of retailers such as department stores. For consignors, as Yamato settles the payment en bloc, managing individual customer information becomes unnecessary.

Another example is the 'Book Service'; instead of going to a bookstore, and buying books by telephone or fax i.e. a multiple use of the transportation networks. Recently, some regional bookstores have come to place orders with Yamato. By high utilisation of its information networks, Yamato has achieved efficiency in its small lot freight operation and at the same time, in the learning process, recomposition of the meaning of the home delivery business (*Takkyubin*) took place and new business was generated. Yamato's business has been expanded by network synergy.

Creating network management

(i) Heterogeneous and multi-centred structures

The relation between information and network structure is reciprocal. The structure prescribes the flow of information, and the information flow forms the structure.

For example, in a hierarchical structure where relationships among factors are prescribed by strictly vertical authority relations, the information flow becomes vertical. In such cases, the structure inevitably becomes hierarchical. In other words, a rigid hierarchical structure is constructed when there are many recipients to one sender of information, or when the information from many senders is concentrated at one point.

By contrast the network structure is rarely based on strict authority relations, but is laterally based: network structures are constructed when senders and recipients are many and multi-centred. A chain franchise business like Seven Eleven Japan or Pharma is a typical example.

In the case of a chain franchise business, every franchisee is independent and can freely select his stock. The main role of the headquarters is to discover new meanings and values by combining information and to supply management know-how to every franchisee, on the basis of which the latter can undertake individual information creation.

In a network with numerous senders and recipients, where context and meanings are determined by so many, no one member can control information so as to predominate over the others. Therefore, each member of a network coordinates with each other, forming an initiative order by using and sharing information.

Uni-centred hierarchical structures require homogeneity of context and meanings and new values and meanings are not expected. Should a factor introduce different values, or a combination of factors create heterogeneous meanings, such a factor has no choice but to spin out of the system or to be removed from it. By contrast the possibility of creating network synergy is due to structural features that allow networks such heterogeneity.

(ii) Flexible and dynamic relationships

The most important service for customers in the turbulent securities market is to supply timely and accurate trading information. Therefore, securities companies compete by constructing networks for supplying market information and for implementing rapid trading using that information. An example is the 'Fami-Com Trading' system of Nomura Securities Company.

Participating in or leaving such networks is easy because there is hardly any investment and the same phenomenon can be seen among credit card companies. As networks are not restricted by vertical hierarchical relationships, participating or leaving is easy, and flexible and dynamic relationships can be maintained in a pure network structure, avoiding rigid relationships among the factors. The characteristics peculiar to network structures tend to create new relationships, due to the diversity and the flexible recomposition of relationships among the factors.

If the relationships lack flexibility, as in a hierarchical structure, the definition of the structure 'inside' or 'outside' becomes clear. Adaptation to the 'outside' will be in terms of 'structure to structure' or 'one to one' and a recomposition of factors is unlikely to occur.

However, in networks where structural changes are apt to occur because of flexible and dynamic relationships, there is little need to distinguish the borders between 'inside' and 'outside'. Therefore, there is greater variation among the combinations of diverse factors, thus increasing the possibility of creating new knowledge and values. On Seven Eleven Japan's organisational chart, customers are put at the top, with franchisees next, and headquarters at the bottom, reflecting the dynamically changing definition of the networks.

Dynamic processes

(i) Reciprocal interaction

The new value created by networks is the 'linking value' that the interaction of factors creates. It not only generates profit for a specific factor, but may also be shared by all the factors. If firms consider only the benefit to themselves and not the benefit to customers in supplying goods and services, new meanings and 'linking value' will not be created. Similarly, because networks across firms can create linking value by reciprocal interaction, continuous network relationships are built.

For example, the main job of the salesmen of Toyo Sash Co. Ltd. has changed because of networks. Their work is not only to get orders but also to give customers i.e. shop managers, managerial advice, by playing the role of consultants to create reciprocal interaction.

Reciprocal relationships through networks across competitive firms have changed the structure of competition itself. For example, Orion in Shizuoka Prefecture assembled small local wholesalers and started VAN services between wholesalers and retailers; so that new competitive advantages, such as the supply of information for customers and the improvement of trading conditions, have taken the place of traditional competitive advantages. Thus, the process of constructing information networks leads to 'win and win' relationships that change competitive structures and become the driving force for changing the industrial and social structures.

(ii) Learning process of generating synergy

Diverse business activities are significant not only for their results but for the process itself being accumulated as information from experience and it is important for firms to transmit the experience of success or failure through the process of organisational learning. Above all, in the globalisation and diversification of business, the meaning of learning and the transmission of experience continually becomes more important.

Such a learning process can change the context of the learners and recompose the meanings of the learning experience, generating organisational learning synergy. The spread of networks increases not only the variation of experience, but the opportunities of creating new meanings through learning.

For example, Yamato launched a new 'Book Service' and 'Collect Service' by using the transportation and information know-how learnt from the home delivery business. Just as the concept of a delivery system complying with demand created 'Cool Home Delivery', a new type of transportation classified according to temperature, learning experience in other fields has possibilities for creating new value using feedback to the already existing field. The accumulation and transmission of learning through networks gives consistency to the meanings of the relationships among the factors and becomes the process of generating network synergy.

New roles for top management

(i) 'Visions' to create information

In the network society, firms cannot grow if business is run only according to 'supply-side logic' or a firm's own logic. Discarding supply-side logic, business must be run according to a 'society-oriented business vision'; of e.g. what is the firm's role in society? How is the firm to develop while promoting benefits to society?

For example, Nissan changed its vision from 'Technological Nissan' to 'Customer Satisfaction First'. SECOM underwent a transition from 'Guard Security by Men' to 'Safety Industry of Mechanically Controlled Systems' and finally 'Social System Industry using Information Networks'. The above are examples of far-sighted vision by top management.

The business vision, or concept, of top management clarifies the direction that firms should take, and the role of business units and their relationships. Even if networks succeed in producing complex and sophisticated information flows that allow top management all possible information, top managers cannot become involved in every detail. Even if the members of a network share information, not all of them necessarily gain the same meanings and value. Therefore, the new role for top management should be 'leadership by vision (concept) creation', and clarification of the significance of the firm's existence and its role within the network.

Jack Welch, GE's chairman, advocated the 'Three Circle Concept' when GE was restructuring. It meant that GE was concentrating its diversified business fields into core, high-tech and service businesses, and was developing only the top-class business in such fields. To avoid diversifying the business at random, he clarified the direction by 'leadership of vision', promoting the evolution of middle managers and activating the process of organisational information creation.

High-tech companies like IBM and NEC supplying hardware and software advocate the vision of the firm's contribution to society as a whole and disclose technological information that they developed to other companies, including competitors. Their aim is a 'network style of management', where the firm produces goods in cooperation with others and at the same time benefits society.

The visions of top management must consider business not only from the firm-centred point of view (inside out), but also from society-centred viewpoints. Management in a network society should not just meet market needs individually, but meet the needs of social development.

The essence of network management is 'information creation' and this new management process may cause a change not just limited to the firm or the industry but on a large scale in the industrial and social structures. Firms that aspire to network management must lead in promoting information creativity in society as a whole.

(ii) Building top management teams (TOPS)

Top management roles have become complex both within firms and society and it is difficult and sometimes dangerous for one or a few top managers to make all the decisions. Above all, because a large investment is necessary in building them, SIS require complex decisions, as they will strongly influence not only the firm but also associated companies.

It is now impossible for only one CIO (Chief Information Officer) to develop the complicated and large scale SIS within companies constructing integrated global SIS, as for example Nomura Securities. Therefore, all the directors share the responsibility from the strategic viewpoint for decisions on building up SIS.

Information that top management must cope with has become qualitatively complicated and quantitatively enormous in the network society and top management must select high quality information to make appropriate, rapid decisions. In this process, by whom and how the sophisticated information was input and selected becomes important; consequently top management must be concerned with the source of information and its processing. From this standpoint too, it has become inadequate for one top manager to be responsible for SIS construction.

Kao, Marui, and Nomura, the companies that are advanced in utilising SIS, have organised decision-making TOPS, who mutually supplement information that is insufficient, select high quality information and discriminate the process and context of information processing. Free discussion among members with different contexts can produce effective information and decision-making from broader viewpoints.

At a few companies, information networks are beginning to be used for increasing the efficiency of TOPS. In Nihon Seiko, information from CIM is directly linked with the decision-making systems in the directors' room to support precise and rapid decision-making. Kao has set up 'a decision room', where directors can easily get information and freely discuss things. Moreover, in Kao, 24 hour communication among directors is established through information networks.

TOPS which have realised such 'network style decision-making' may be said to be the new style of strategic top management in the information network era.

13 An analysis of mergers among credit co-operatives in Japan

YASUO HOSHINO
NAGOYA CITY UNIVERSITY

(i) Introduction

Credit co-operatives in Japan were established in 1900 based on the Industrial Co-operatives Law. Its objective was mutual financing in co-operative form by small and medium-sized co-operative organisations.

After the Second World War, the majority of the 636 credit co-operatives were converted into credit associations based on the co-operative union law for small and medium-sized firms. The remaining 74 credit co-operatives remain unconverted, mainly under the control of perfectural or metropolitan governments. Later, the number of credit co-operatives increased to 527 by March 1965. Following the reports of the Investigative Committee on Financial Institutions, the so-called 'Two Financial Laws', namely the 'Law on Reforming a Part of the Mutual Loan and Savings Banks and Credit Associations Sectors etc' and the 'Law on Mergers and Conversions among Financial Institutions' were enacted. The former is to cope with internationalisation and improving efficiency. The latter is to promote financial reorganisation in order to raise efficiency not only among the same type, but also among different types of financial institutions, in which mergers had not previously been permitted under any law.

Following the enactment of these laws, the number of mergers and conversions of small and medium-sized financial institution is given in Table 1-1 based on actual execution.

There were 115 mergers among the same type of financial institutions, including 56 mergers for credit co-operatives and 58 for credit associations and only one for mutual loan and savings banks. Among the different types of financial institutions, there were 20 mergers between credit co-operatives and mutual loan and savings banks, 15 between credit co-operatives and credit associations, and only one between credit co-operatives and ordinary banks. The dissolution rate for credit co-operatives is 36/41 = 88 per cent.

Moreover, there were three conversions from credit co-operatives to credit associations, and one to a mutual loan and savings bank. According to Table 1-2, 125 credit co-operatives disappeared, namely, 85 by mergers among the same type of financial institutions, 36 by mergers among different types of institutions, and 4 by conversion.

In 1988 there were nine mergers among 23 credit associations up to April, and three mergers up to the end of the year. It is believed that the local administrative authorities guided and mediated mergers among credit co-operatives to save from bankruptcy credit co-operatives with a rather weak financial basis.

The latest statistics report that as of October 1988 there were 419 credit co-operatives, with 2,914 offices, 45,674 full time staff and employees, and 3,744, 734 members.[1]

Table 1-3 shows the breakdown of the balance of loans for small and medium-sized firms by type of financial institution from March 1983 to March 1988.

The ordinary banks, namely city banks and regional banks, are increasing in number, rising from 48.14 per cent with ¥71,091 billion of loans in 1983, to 59.90 per cent, with ¥145,024 billion of loans in 1988.

While the balance of loans for small and medium-sized financial institutions, mutual loan and savings banks, credit associations, credit co-operatives and governmental financial institutions for small and medium-sized firms is increasing, the percentage of the breakdown is always decreasing. Credit co-operatives especially deceased from 5.50 per cent in 1983 to 4.53 per cent in 1988.

The Report of the Investigative Committee on Financial Institutions, an advisory organ of the Ministry of Finance, stressed the necessity of enlarging co-operative financial institutions through mergers in order to strengthen their financial basis, and to obtain the necessary competitive power to cope with financial liberalisation and internationalisation.[2] However, no empirical research has revealed that temporal enlargement by merger leads to a strengthening of the management base or an increase in competitive power.

The National Central Association of Credit Co-operatives revealed the results of a questionnaire survey about the motives behind their mergers and the financial condition of 35 credit co-operatives which had experienced mergers among the same type of financial institution.

Twenty-one of them improved their situation, to strengthen the management base as the No. 1 reason, and coped with the increasing cost of investment in machines and the increase in the size of loans to local small and medium-sized firms. Over 40 per scent of credit co-operatives acknowledge the positive effects of mergers.

Hoshino[8] showed that the effect of mergers is negative among credit

Table 1-1 Number of mergers among small and medium-sized financial institutions after 1968

Year	1968	1969	1970	1971	1972	1973	1974	1975	1976	1977	1978	1979	1980	1981	1982	1983	1984	1985	1986	1987	Total
Mergers among same type of financial institutions																					
Mutual Loan and Savings Banks				1																	1
Credit Associations	1	10	7	13	2		8	4	1	1	1	3	1	4						2	58
Credit Co-operatives	1	3	1	4	5	5	4	2	1	1	4	2	5	2	4	2	3	2	3	2	56
Subtotal	2	13	8	18	7	5	12	6	2	2	5	5	6	6	4	2	3	2	3	4	115
Mergers among different type institutions																					
Ordinary Banks ● Mutual Loan and Savings Banks									1								1		1		3
Ordinary Bank ● Credit Co-operative							1														1
Mutual Loand and Savings Banks ● Credit Associations		1			1																2
Mutual Loan and Savings Banks ● Credit Co-operatives		1	4	2	5	6	1			1											20
Credit Associations ● Credit Co-operatives	1	5	1		4			1		1	1							1			15
Subtotal	1	7	5	2	10	6	2	1	1	2	1						1	1	1		41
Total of Mergers	3	20	13	20	17	11	14	7	3	4	6	5	6	6	4	2	4	3	4	4	156
Conversions																					
Mutual Loan and Savings Bank › City Bank	1																1				2
Credit Co-operatives › Mutual Banks			1																		1
Credit Co-operatives › Credit Associations		1			2																3
Total of Conversions	1	1	1		2												1				6

Source: Ministry of Finance (1988)

Table 1-2 Number of small and medium-sized financial institutions disappearing after 1968

	Mergers among same type of financial institutions				Mergers among different type of financial institutions						Total
	Mutual Loan and Savings Banks	Credit Associations	Credit Co-operatives	Total	Ordinary Banks ● Mutual Loan and Savings Banks	Ordinary Banks ● Credit Co-operatives	Mutual Loan and Savings Banks ● Credit Associations	Mutual Loan and Savings Banks ● Credit Co-operatives	Credit Associations ● Co-operatives	Total	
Mutual Loan and Savings Banks	1			1	3					3	4
Credit Associations		66		66			2			2	68
Credit Co-operatives			85	85		1		20	15	36	121
Total	1	66	85	152	3	1	2	20	15	41	193

Source: Ministry of Finance (1988)

Table 1-3 Breakdown of the balance of loans for small and medium-sized firms by type of financial institution

(unit: ¥ billion)

Type of Institution / Month / Year	Ordinary Banks	Private Small and Medium Financial Institution				Governmental Small and Medium Financial Institutions	Total
		Mutual Loan and Savings Banks	Credit Associations	Credit Cooperatives	Sub Total		
March 1983	71.091	21,421	30,133	8,120	59,675	16,907	147,674
	(48.14%)	(14.50%)	(20.41%)	(5.50%)	(40.41%)	(11.45%)	(100%)
March 1984	82,294	23,119	32,309	8,710	64,138	17,593	164,016
	(50.17%)	(14.09%)	(19.70%)	(5.31%)	(39.10%)	(10.73%)	(100%)
March 1985	96,180	23,541	34,464	9,158	67,165	18,390	181,736
	(52.92%)	(12.95%)	(18.97%)	(5.04%)	(36.96%)	(10.12%)	(100%)
March 1986	108,439	24,124	35,742	9,655	69,522	18,980	196,942
	(55.06%)	(12.25%)	(18.15%)	(4.90%)	(35.30%)	(9.64%)	(100%)
March 1987	128,430	24,336	37,296	10,055	71,688	19,285	219,404
	(58.54%)	(11.09%)	(17.00%)	(4.58%)	(32.67%)	(8.79%)	(100%)
March 1988	145,024	26,044	40,299	10,959	77,302	19,767	242,094
	(59.90%)	(10.76%)	(16.64%)	(4.53%)	(31.93%)	(8.17%)	(100%)

Source: Bank of Japan (Monetary Economic Statistics)
Department of Investigation of the People's Finance Corporation (Monthly Report of the Department of Investigation)

associations and that the financial characteristics of merging credit associations are inferior to these of non-merging credit associations. The same results among firms listed on the Stock Exchange are exhibited in a series of his study.

In this paper, we analyse whether the performance of mergers is positive or not and whether financial differences between merging credit co-operatives and non-merging credit co-operatives exist or not.

Section ii describes data used for the comparison to measure the performance of mergers among credit co-operatives with five null hypotheses and approach employed.

In Section iii, the comparison between before and after merger among merging credit co-operatives and the comparison between before and after for non-merging credit co-operatives are conducted by univariate analysis with F test and t test, and also by discrimination analysis, relatively.

The same relative comparisons are applied between merging credit co-operatives and non-merging credit co-operatives before merger and between merging credit co-operatives and non-merging credit co-operatives after merger.

In Section iv, an analysis is carried out to examine how the year effect of mergers is changing by a comparison between before and after the year of merger by both univariate and multivariate analysis.

Section v shows the performance of mergers by using the relative financial ratio, namely, the direct differences in the financial variables between merging and paired non-merging credit co-operatives. Additionally, general comparisons of financial characteristics between merging and non-merging credit co-operatives, and general changes in the financial characteristics of credit co-operatives before and after the year of merger are analysed.

(ii) Data, hypotheses and approach

The credit co-operatives analysed are taken only from the mergers of two credit co-operatives which merged between 1974 and 1981, out of a total numbering 18. Corresponding to each merging credit co-operative, a non-merging credit co-operative with the nearest size of deposit in the same prefecture or metropolitan area is chosen in order to make a pair for comparison.[3]

Nineteen financial ratios are compiled for the years between 1969 and 1987 to measure the effects of mergers among credit co-operatives. The added figures of each original financial variable between merging and merged credit co-operatives are used to make the financial ratios of merging credit co-operatives before merger.

A comparative ratio analysis is employed to analyse groups of:–

1. merging credit co-operatives before and after merger
2. non-merging credit co-operatives before and after the year of merger of merging co-operatives
3. merging and non-merging credit co-operatives before merger
4. merging and non-merging credit co-operatives after merger
5. overall merging and non-merging credit co-operatives

Five null hypotheses, that there were no financial differences between them for each pair of groups, are tested using both univariate and multivariate analysis.

Group 1 shows the effects of mergers but may also include changes in financial position due to other factors, such as general economic performance and internal growth.

Group 2 presents changes due to factors other than mergers. The comparison in group 3 indicates whether there are differences in the value of the financial ratios between those co-operatives which subsequently merge and those that do not prior to any effects of mergers. Likewise, group 4 shows the effect of mergers, as well as including the differences in financial ratios between merging and non-merging co-operatives before mergers. Group 5 gives general comparisons of the financial ratios between merging and non-merging co-operatives including the effects of mergers and also describes the original differences between the two groups before merger.

(iii) The performance of mergers

We test the differences of each of the 19 financial ratios of merging credit co-operatives before and after merger, the result of which is given in Table 2-1.[8] There are 10 financial ratios which have statistically significant differences on their means between the two groups.

Those ratios with lower performance after merger than before merger are item (3) yield on loan ($8.67\% \rightarrow 8.28\%$), item (9) gross earnings margin of deposit to loan ($1.58\% \rightarrow 1.04\%$), item (12) gross earnings margin to total assets ($1.02\% \rightarrow 0.60\%$), item (13) net equity ratio ($0.07\% \rightarrow 0.05\%$), item (15) ratio of current expense to current income ($86.08\% \rightarrow 91.67\%$) and item (16) income ratio after tax ($13.40\% \rightarrow 9.30\%$), all of which indicate the negative effects of mergers. While those ratios with higher performance after merger than before merger are item (1) yield of interest received ($4.75\% \rightarrow 5.39\%$), and three ratios of productivity, item (17) deposit per office, item (18) deposit per full-time officer and employee and item (19) deposit per co-operative's member. It is quite natural, however, that three of the productivity ratios increased after merger, reflecting general economic growth and inflation over a long period of years between 1969 and 1988.

The matching 9 non-merging credit co-operatives are compared before and after merger as shown in Table 2-2. By comparing them with the previous table, those ratios, with a statistically significant difference on their means which suffered financial disadvantages after merger are items (3) yield on loan, (9) gross earnings margin of deposit to loan, (12) gross earnings margin to total assets, (15) ratio of current expense to current income, and (16) income ratio after tax, meaning negative effects of mergers. The ratio which gains financial advantage is item (1) yield of interest received. Those ratios with no change in financial advantages are item (13) net equity ratio and three ratios of productivity. Item (6) the non-personnel expenses ratio has a statistically significant difference on its means in the comparison of only non-merging credit co-operatives. Before merger the mean is 0.77 and after merger 0.68, showing the increasing efficiency of cost reduction without merger and no difference between corresponding merging co-operatives, indicating the negative efficiency of mergers.

As far as the standard deviations are concerned, item (2) yield of interest paid has a statistically significant difference at the 5% level with the financial ratios of 0.78% vs. 0.59% for merging credit co-operatives before and after merger, respectively. However, this difference disappears for matching non-merging credit co-operatives, indicating the stabilising effects of mergers on this ratio. Just the opposite trend is observed on item (3) yield on loan.

There are four ratios, items (12) gross earnings margin to total assets, (15) ratio of current expense to current income, (17) deposit per office, and (18) deposit per full-time officer and employee, which have statistically significant differences on their standard deviations for non-merging credit co-operatives, but not for merging credit co-operatives, with a higher value after merger, meaning the stabilising effects of mergers.

Next is the comparative analysis of merging and non-merging credit co-operatives before mergers in Table 2-3, and after mergers in Table 2-4.

The means of items (3) yield on loan and (14) loan-deposit ratio have statistically significant differences between merging and non-merging co-operatives only in Table 2-3 and not in Table 2-4, with higher values for merging co-operatives than for non-merging co-operatives.

This indicates that merging co-operatives lost their superiority in these ratios after mergers, meaning the negative effects of mergers.

On the contrary, there are five ratios which have statistically significant differences only in Table 2-4 and not in Table 2-3, namely, items (1) yield of interest received, (11) total assets cost ratio, (12) gross earnings margin to total assets, (15) ratio of current expense to current income and (16) income ratio after tax. As far as two of these ratios are concerned, such as items (11) total assets cost ratio and (15) ratio of curent expense to current income, their means have become higher statistically for merging credit co-operatives, and as far as two more ratios are concerned, such as (12) gross earnings margin to total assets and (16) income ratio after tax, they became more profitable for non-merging co-operatives; all of which exhibits the negative effects of mergers. Only item (1) yield of interest received from other financial institutions improved for merging co-operatives after merger, showing a positive effect of mergers.

Table 2-5 shows a general comparison between merging and non-merging credit co-operatives ignoring the year of merger. Those ratios with statistically significant differences between means are items (1) yield of interest received, (3) yield on loan, and (14) loan-deposit ratio with positive effect on merging co-operatives, (4) expense ratio, (5) personnel expenses ratios, (8) deposit-cost ratio, (11) total assets cost ratio, (15) ratio of current expense to current income, (16) income ratio after tax, (17) deposit per office, and (18) deposit per full-time officer and employee, all of which have superior values for non-merging co-operatives.

There are eleven financial ratios with statistically significant differences between their standard deviations for merging and non-merging co-operatives, ten of which show higher value for non-merging co-operatives compared with those of merging co-operatives, indicating the higher stability of ratios to merging co-operatives.

Nineteen financial ratios were used to compare the financial characteristics between merging and non-merging credit co-operatives by discriminant analysis.

Table 2-6 shows the classification and accuracy of discriminant analysis. The number of those merging co-operatives with actual data for before merger took place is predicted correctly as before merger in 51 cases, and is predicted incorrectly as after merger in 4 cases, totalling 55 cases.

The sum of diagonal elements, 51 + 43 = 94, represents the total number of correctly discriminated cases which, when divided by the total number of cases 110, yields an accuracy of 85.45%.

The discrimination of non-merging co-operatives before and after the year of merger of merging credit co-operatives, provides an accuracy of 89.91%. The difference between these accuracies indicates the existence of the effects of mergers.

Table 2-7 displays the comparison of merging and non-merging credit co-operatives before and after merger. The accuracies are 77.98% and 85.45% for those cases before merger and after merger, respectively, the difference of which means the existence of the effects of merger, too. These effects lead to the differentiation of the financial characteristics between merging and non-merging co-operatives.

An overall comparison between merging and non-merging credit co-operatives is given in Table 2-8. The discrimination accuracy is 78.54%, which is higher than that of the discrimination between merging and non-merging co-operatives before mergers but lower than that of discrimination after merger. By contrast, the accuracy of the overall comparison of credit co-operatives before and after merger is 84.47%, which is lower than those for merging co-operatives before and after merger (85.45%), and of non-merging co-operatives (89.91%).

(iv) Yearly comparisons of merging credit co-operatives before and after merger

The financial comparison of merging credit co-operatives from one to eleven years before and after merger is examined in Table 3.

For the comparison of merging credit co-operatives one year before and one year after merger, there are no statistically significant differences on their means and standard deviations except for a significant difference in the standard deviations of item (3) yield on loan, which has a higher deviation after merger.

For the two year comparison, seven financial ratios which have statistically significant differences on their means by t test appeared, such as items (1) yield of interest received (4.81% vs. 5.40%), (9) gross earnings margin of deposit to loan (1.43% vs. 0.93%), (11) total assets cost ratio (6.18% vs. 6.68%), (12) gross earnings margin to total assets (0.94% vs. 0.66%), (15) ratio of current expense to current income (86.74% vs. 90.90%), (16) income ratio after tax (13.26% vs. 9.66%) and (18) deposit per full time officer and employee (¥12.56 million vs. ¥16.57 million). Only two ratios, items (1) yield of interest received and (18) deposit full-time officer and employee have superior financial ratios after merger, and the other five ratios show inferiority after merger.

For the three year comparison, new ratios accompanied by statistically significant differences on their means or standard deviations were added, such as, items (2) yield of interest paid with higher burden of interest paid with smaller deviations after merger, (5) personnel expenses ratio with bigger deviation after merger, (7) tax ratio with smaller deviation after merger, and (8) deposit-cost ratio and (13) net equity ratio, both of which show inferiority after merger. For those ratios with significant difference on their means, the level of significance became higher for (1) yield of interest received and (11) total assets cost ratio from 5% to 1%, on (12) gross earnings margin to total assets, (15) ratio of current expense to current income and (16) income ratio after tax from 5% to 0.1%, and (18) deposit per full-time officer and employee from 1% to 0.1%.

For the four year comparison, two more ratios were added which led to a statistically significant difference for their means. They are items (17) deposit per office and (19) deposit per co-operative's member. Three ratios added with significant differences for their standard deviations were items (3) yield on loan, (9) gross earnings margin of deposit to loan and (13) net equity ratio. The expense ratio (4) has a significant difference in its deviations for only this year and the last eleven years' comparison.

Examining the discriminant analysis of the 19 financial ratios for the one to eleven year comparison, the discrimination accuracy is given as follows, 100% for one year, 94.44% for two years, 88.89% for three and four years, 94.44% for five years, 96.26% for six years, 95.83% for seven years, 95.45% for eight years, and 100% for the remaining nine, ten, and eleven years, all of which show high accuracy, and which mean that general economic performance is influencing the measure of performance of merging credit co-operatives to a large extent.

Therefore, there is a strong necessity to eliminate the influence of general economic performance. A comparison of relative financial ratios is used to extract and examine the pure effects of mergers.

(v) Analysis by the relative financial ratios

The relative financial ratios[4] are compiled from the differences in absolute financial ratios between merging and non-merging credit co-operatives as follows:

$$d_{ijk} = M_{ijk} - N_{ijk}$$

d_{ijk} : relative financial ratio k (k = 1, . . ., 19) of (i = 1, . . ., 9) credit co-operative at the jth (j = 1969, . . ., 1987) year.

M_{ijk} : financial ratio k or i merging credit co-operatives at the jth year.

N_{ijk} : corresponding financial ratio k of i non-merging credit co-operatives at the jth year

Table 4 exhibits the comparison of these relative financial ratios before and after merger.

For one year before and one year after merger, there is no significant differences on their means and standard deviations.

For two years before and two years after merger, item (2) yield of interest paid has a significant difference in its standard deviations with the values, 0.79% vs. 0.48% for before and after merger, respectively. This trend does not change even from three years to eleven years before and after merger.

For three years before and three years after mergers, item (7) tax ratio has a significant difference for the three year and eleven year comparison on its standard deviations with higher or equal values before merger compared with after merger for all years.

For the four year comparison, items (4) expense ratio and (9) gross earnings margin of deposit to loan have a statistically significant difference in their standard deviations. However these significant differences are observed only in the ten and eleven year comparison besides this year. Item (12) gross earnings margin to total assets has a statistically significant difference on its means with 0.06% and −0.20% for before and after merger, respectively, indicating the negative effect of mergers. Just the same trend with significance can be observed from six to eleven years before and after merger except for the five year comparison, showing the clearly negative effects of mergers. Item (13) net equity ratio has a statistically significant difference for its standard deviations from four to eleven years before and after merger with higher values for before merger.

For the five year comparison, items (5) personnel expenses ratio, (6) non-personnel expenses ratio, (10) yield on total assets and (11) total assets cost ratio have statistically significant differences on their standard deviations, the latter three ratios of which have statistical differences from five to eleven years before and after merger with higher value for before mergers.

The comparison of six years before and six years after merger has seven ratios added, items (1) yield of interest received, (3) yield on loan, (8) deposit-cost ratio, (15) ratio of current expense to current income, (17) deposit per office, (18) deposit per full-time officer and employee and (19) deposit per co-operative's member, which have significant differences on their standard deviations. The former four ratios have higher values before merger than after merger, indicating the stabilising effects of mergers.

The latter three ratios have higher values after merger, showing the destabilising effects of mergers on productivity-related ratios, except for the nine years before and after mergers of item (18) ratio.

For statistically significant differences on their means from six to eleven years items (12) gross earnings margin to total assets and (16) income ratio after tax are reported to have higher values before merger than after merger, indicating the negative effects of mergers. After seven years before and after mergers, almost the same trend can be observed among the 19 financial ratios.

Therefore, by using relative financial ratios, we could conclude that mergers have negative effects on the profitability of credit co-operatives.

(vi) Conclusion

As the conclusion of this article, we could find the facts that the effect of mergers on the performance of credit co-operatives is negative. However mergers could have the effect of stabilising financial ratios. Secondly, generally speaking, merging credit co-operatives show rather inferior financial characteristics to non-merging co-operatives. These results are consistent with the previous study by Hoshino.[5]

However, the credit co-operatives regard it necessary to achieve tie-up and mergers based upon self judgment in order to pursue the economy of scale, especially when they have enough financial strength in reserve.[6]

Nihon Keizai Shinbun Inc. conducted a questionnaire survey among chairmen of credit associations. Three hundred out of 455 credit associations replied, 47.7% of which mentioned the necessity of mergers among credit associations, and 21.7% of which answered no change in the future.

As to the objectives of firms in Japan, the Ministry of International Trade and Industry (MITI) revealed the result of their investigation, showing that the first is to maximise profit (45.0%), which showed a big difference with the study conducted ten years ago, which said that maximising sales was the most important. Following these objectives are the strengthening of technology, diversification of management, internationalisation of business, maximisation of sales and market share. Among these five objectives of firms, the diversification of management and the internationalisation of business have a close relationship with mergers.

In particular, Japanese corporations are quite willing to buy foreign companies, which is called the 'in–out' type of merger, rather than the 'in–in' type. This is because they would like to, first, save time, second, obtain a group of personnel, third, economise on the amount of investment, and, fourth, gain the benefits of synergy.

Five hundred and ninety-six out of 917 firms that responded to the questionnaire survey conducted by Nippon Keizai Shinbunsha in 1988 have an interest in M&A and 610 firms (65.0%) admit the necessity of mergers for reasons of business diversification (62.1%), the acquisition of new technology (53.1%) and the acquisition of specific assets.

In this article, accounting data are used to measure the performance of mergers, because credit co-operatives are not stock listed corporations. When it comes to analysing listed corporations, to extend our analysis, capital asset pricing theory[7] becomes useful for measuring performance by calculating cumulative average excess return.[8]

Appendix 1 Financial ratios analysed

(1)   Yield of interest received = interest received/deposit × 100
(2)   Yield of interest paid = interest paid/deposit × 100
(3)   Yield on loan = interest on loan/loans × 100
(4)   Expense ratio = (personnel expenses + nonpersonnel expenses + tax)/deposit × 100
(5)   Personnel expenses ratio = personnel expenses/deposit × 100
(6)   Nonpersonnel expenses ratio = nonpersonnel expenses/deposit × 100
(7)   Tax ratio = tax/deposit × 100
(8)   Deposit-cost ratio = interest paid on deposit + expense ratio
(9)   Gross earnings margin of deposit to loan = interest on loan – cost of deposit ratio
(10)   Yield on total assets = recurring profit/total assets × 100
(11)   Total assets cost ratio = ordinary expenditure/total assets × 100
(12)   Gross earnings margin to total assets = yield on total assets – total assets cost ratio
(13)   Net equity ratio = equity/accounts of members × 100
(14)   Loan-deposit ratio = loan/deposit × 100
(15)   Ratio of current expense to current income = current expense/current income
(16)   Income ratio after tax = current income after tax/account of members × 100
(17)   Deposit per office = deposit/number of offices
(18)   Deposit per full-time officer and employee = deposit/number of officers and employees
(19)   Deposit per co-operative's member = deposit/number of members of co-operative

Appendix 2 List of merging and non-merging credit co-operatives

Prefecture	Period of Merger	Merging Credit Co-operatives	Name after Merger	Non-merging Credit Co-operatives
Tokyo	10/1/81	Daiichi Kangyo Hosei	Daiichi Kangyo (Nippon Kangyo till 1970)	Chogin Tokyo (Douwa till 1971)
Tokyo	10/1/78	Keihin Meiwa	Kyoritsu	Nakanogou
Tokyo	4/1/74	Tokyo-Seinan Miyoshi	Seinan*	Katsushika-Shokou
Osaka	4/1/74	Osaka Minami Hirano	Seikyo	Osakafu-Ishi
Hyogo	4/1/82	Seika Kobe Chuo	Minato	Hyogoken Keisatsu (Hyogoken Keisatsu Shokuin till 1973)
Nara	3/1/81	Naraken Naraken Tobacco	Naraken	Nara Chogin
Fukuoka	12/1/79	Minami Fukuoka Futsukaichi	Fukuoka Minami	Fukuokaken-Ishi
Saga	10/1/75	Fujitsu Ariake	Saganishi	Matsuura
Saga	10/1/78	Kanzaki Kojiro	Sagahigashi	Sagaken-Ishi
Nagasaki	8/1/81	Saseho Omura	Nagasaki-Kenmin	Nagasaki-Mitsubishi
Miyazaki	10/1/80	Takachiho Hikage	Miyazakiken-Hokubu	Hyugashi

*Seinan Co-operative merged with Söei Co-operative on 1 February, 1988

Notes

1. See Zenkoku Shinyo Kumiai Chuo Kyokai, Kinyu Zaisei Jijyo Kenkyukai .
2. Kinyuseido Chosakai Kinyuseido Daiichi Iinkai (The First Committee on the Financial System, Investigative Organ of the Financial System) published a report entitled Kyo do Sosiki Kinyukikan no Arikata ni tsuite - - Kinyuseido Daiichi Iinkai Chukan Hokoku (The 'Ought to be' of Co-operative Financial Institutions – An Interim Report of the First Committee on the Financial System).

    Mergers and conversions are included in chapter 5 of this report and in section 1 as follows. It is important for co-operative financial institutions to strengthen their management basis and to obtain the competitive power necessary to cope with the progress of financial liberalisation etc. In this case, the self-helping endeavour of individual co-operative financial institution is important. In addition, it is a useful method of utilising mergers, tie-ups and alliances between organisations. In the case of co-operative financial institutions, considering their increase in size in order to strengthen their management basis because of their previous small size, mergers are expected to be conducted with a forward-looking attitude.

As for the administrative side, it is necessary to pay attention to promoting the appropriate mergers with enough consideration for the self-governing aspect of co-operative financial institutions.

The First Committee points out five important items to be observed.

3. There are several mergers among more than two credit co-operatives at the same time for the period 1975 to 1981 as follows:
   – 1976 Fukuokashi Syoko, Iizuka Syoko, Shimen → Fukuokaken, February
   – 1980 Yoshii (merged by Fuhi and Amaki in 1970) → Ryochiku, April; Higashi, Nashima → Higashi Fukuoka (Consolidation, October)
   – 1981 Nagasaki Sogo, Isahaya, Dai Nagasaki, Tsushima → Nagasaki Daiichi (Consolidation April)

4. The relative financial ratio is defined and compiled to measure the performance of mergers for the first time in English literature in Hoshino.

5. A series of studies is given in Hoshino and the survey of studies of mergers in Japan could also be referred to there. See e.g. 'An Analysis of Mergers among the Credit Associations in Japan'. *Rivista Internazionale di Scienze Economiche e Commerciale*. Vol. 35. No. 2. Bocconi University, Milan. 1988.

   The latest study by Odagiri and Hase reported that they could not find any positive effects of mergers and acquisitions, and could not support the theory that horizontal mergers and acquisitions improve efficiency and increase the wealth of stockholders.

6. Ryutaro Kasahara, the Chairman of Zenkoku Shinyo Kumiai Kyokai (National Association of Credit Co-operatives) expressed his opinion at the Annual Convention of the Association on June 2, 1988. Nippon Kinyu Tsushin sha .

7. There are four studies using Capital Asset Pricing Theory and the stock prices of Japanese corporations to test the performance of mergers. Sudo concluded that mergers have negative effects on a firm's valuation by calculating the monthly cumulative residuals, Sakakibara could not expect synergy's effects on corporate mergers, Pettway and Yamada described the increase in the wealth of stockholders of acquiring firms without statistical significance and the positive effect of the announcement of the increased wealth of the stockholders of acquired firms. Ito mentioned that mergers decrease the valuation of both acquiring and acquired firms.

8. The author would like to thank Ms. Aki Koike, Faculty of Economics, Nagoya City University for help in the initial stages of using the computer. This research was conducted with the assistance of a grant from the Ministry of Education of Japan (Kakenhi general Study C #01530067). For reasons of space, it is not possible to include the complete list of tables and references but this is available on request from the author at: Faculty of Economics, Nagoya City University, Yamanohata, Mizuho-cho, Mizuho-ku, Nagoya 467, Japan.

14 Artificial intelligence: business expert systems in Japan

AKIRA ISHIKAWA
AOYAMA GAKUIN UNIVERSITY

Present situation and prospects

The survey undertaken by the Japanese Information Processing Development Association (JIPDA) in 1988, as partly shown in Figure 1, regarding the present and prospects of artificial intelligence (AI) technology in Japanese firms, produced the following major findings:–

(i)   AI technology is basically applied to seven areas: Expert Systems (ES), Intelligent Robots (IR), Pattern Recognition (PR), Voice Recognition (VR), Natural Language Processing (NLP), and Automatic Programming (AP) Systems

(ii) Concerning the experimental use of these technologies, IR, PR, VR, NLP and APS, but not ES, show approximately the same pattern, in which the peak of experimental use is seen within three years

(iii) On the other hand, the peak of the actual use of these technologies is foreseen within five years, except for IR, which is predicted within ten years

(iv) At present, ten to twenty per cent of the firms surveyed, have advanced to their experimental use, except for ES (> 50%) and NLPS (> 30%)

(v)   On the other hand, the actual use of these technologies is below ten per cent, except for ES, which approaches twenty per cent

In addition, the survey includes the present (1987) and future (1992) prospects of both AI system engineers and knowledge engineers. As to AI system programmers, the present composite is four per cent, whereas the future

238

composite will be seven per cent out of total software specialists. For knowledge engineers, on the other hand, including both single and joint specialists who serve as system engineers as well as knowledge engineers, the number will rise from three per cent to fourteen per cent.

The survey states that while the total number of existing software and AI specialists will increase 1.3 times, the rate of increase of AI specialists will reach four hundred per cent. In regard to knowledge engineers, the number will be six times for joint specialists and 4.2 times for single specialists. Such forecasts indicate that many more knowledge engineers need to be trained.

Present situation and prospects of expert systems

In the above survey, the pattern of ESs is different from that of other AI technologies. Noteworthy is that more than fifty per cent of the companies' surveys have started with the experimental use of ES, while approximately twenty per cent have begun their actual employment.

According to the surveys by Nikkei AI in both 1988 and 1989, 330 companies in 1989 were at the following stages:– prototype (29.8%), field test (26.7%), actual use (38.0%), or commercialisation (4.6%); as compared to:– prototype (43.6%), field test (22.0%) and actual use (34.4%) in 250 companies in 1988.

As far as the developmental hardware is concerned, the ratio of mainframes was reduced from 22.4% to 20% between 1988 and 1989, whereas the use of personal computers increased from 29.6% to 30.7%. The most noticeable transition was that while the percentage of minicomputers decreased (16.0% to 13.6%), that of work stations increased (15.2% to 19.9%). This indicates that ESs have been more easily utilised through personal computers and work stations.

With respect to the change of the type of applications between 1988 and 1989, the findings are as follows:–

(i)   Designing- and planning-type ESs have consistently increased:
      6% (1987) to 12% (1988) to 20% (1989)
(ii) Consolidated ESs have gained popularity.
      Asset Management ES + Customer Services ES = Branch Manager Assisted ES
(iii) ESs which are difficult to classify have appeared.
      Combination of selection-, consultation-, and diagnosis-type

Definition of business expert systems (BES)

A BES is an ES designed to carry out an overall or specific function of business administration as efficiently as possible. Industrial management

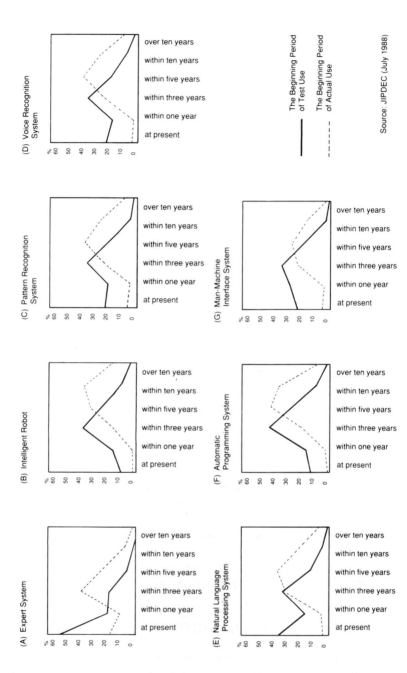

Figure 1.1 Present situation and prospects of AI technology

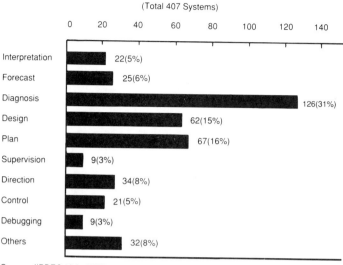

| | 0 | 20 | 40 | 60 | 80 | 100 | 120 | 140 |

Interpretation 22(5%)
Forecast 25(6%)
Diagnosis 126(31%)
Design 62(15%)
Plan 67(16%)
Supervision 9(3%)
Direction 34(8%)
Control 21(5%)
Debugging 9(3%)
Others 32(8%)

Source: JIPDEC (July 1988)

Figure 1.2 Types of ES in all industries (1987)

activities are, in essence, highly intellectual ones. In order to make them successful, pertinent enforcement of responsibility, designation of authority, excellent decision-making, pre-emptive adaptability, keen insight, and endurance are called for. Particularly, as one climbs higher up the organisational tree, more difficult issues need not be resolved. Top management is required to consolidate the capabilities of experts, overcome adverse circumstances, beat the competition, and read contemporary movements on a pre-emptive basis.

If we view such requirements on the basis of the layers of information systems, the lower structure of the information system is transaction-centred and routine information processing has to be performed. In the middle layer, however, DSSs which facilitate specialists are required. This means that middle management needs to deal with information that is non-repetitive and that needs intelligent judgment. As the layering goes higher, the directions to MIS which consolidate personnel, finance, accounting, production, sales, and R & D functions are increased and at the level of the strategic information system, problems are more complicated so that the capabilities of specialists need to be consolidated, part of which can be facilitated by BES. The emergence of BES can be captured on the basis of the development of information systems.[1]

In like manner, ES, the object of which is industrial management or BES, has a prime objective in developing expert systems applicable to management and decision-making. Certainly, developing effective BES is concerned with the survival and development of the organisation. Since corporate strategy is an intelligent activity which strengthens and consolidates personnel, financial, and information resources, while using inexpensive and quality-oriented technology, the design and development of BES are called for.

Next, if we look at BES as a problem-solving resource, it is defined as a practical means of handling management problems which require quality judgment on the basis of knowledge information. For so doing, BES has the capability of exercising the most effective communication within the minimum time through effective dialogues. On the basis of such dialogues, the BES is designed so as to satisfy the needs of users by directing, advising, and justifying the contents which are communicated.

Developing the BES is then an effort to construct the infrastructure of the command, communication and control systems.

Differences between ES and BES

(i) Rule sets and knowledge generation systems

The overall structure of a traditional ES is shown in Figure 2.1. For example, when a user questions the location of malfunctions of an electronic circuit, the ES consisting of inference engine, rule sets (arranged knowledge base), and external knowledge base would ask questions and the user would respond to them.

After all the questions are answered, ES will provide the user with its response and advice, showing the location of malfunctions. Pertinancy, elasticity and inference power between questions and responses in both are depicted as a user interface and indicate the efficiency of interaction.

In this kind of ES, it is conceivable that the more rule sets there are, the more readily available inference will be. However, increases of rule sets alone cannot satisfy all requirements.

Particularly when the object is business administration, problems are diversified and there are problems in many areas where few experts exist. Moreover, responses to the same problem may be subject to experts. Thus, one cannot rely too much upon rule sets only. In order to satisfy such requirements, one has to envisage the BES shown in Figure 2.2.

What is basically different between Figure 2.1 and Figure 2.2 resides in a knowledge generation system and rule set manager. While the former is software that constructs and maintains rule sets, the latter includes spreadsheets which make possible knowledge integration, updating, and processing forms, texts, graphics and use of an external knowledge base.

Inference engine and problem processing systems

When a user raises issues or questions, responses or advice are obtained through inference functions. However, not only in responding to questions but also in letting problem processing systems function, how far the whole system is flexible enough to respond to the processing, interests, and temperaments of users, and how well the security management system is constructed, need to be evaluated.

Problem processing systems should certainly include inference functions. Besides, if inference functions are not used (or in addition to inference functions) database management, spreadsheet analysis, text procesing, computation, quantitative analysis, report generation, communication, form management, graphics and data and knowledge securities need to be functioned, as shown in Figure 2.3.

With respect to data, knowledge and system securities, a password is indispensable for a user to first get access to the system. Next, the user needs to have unique writing and reading codes. While reading codes constrain the domain of the information the user can refer to, writing codes enable the user to record and update the information.

In addition, utility programmes can be arranged along with processing models, and compilation can be performed before execution by the rule set so that the contents of rule sets cannot be referred to by ordinary means.

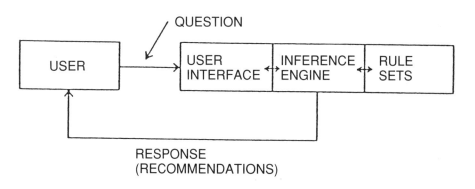

Figure 2.1 Structure of Traditional ES [2]

243

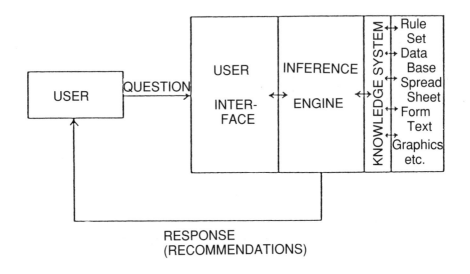

Figure 2.2 Structure of Business ES [2]

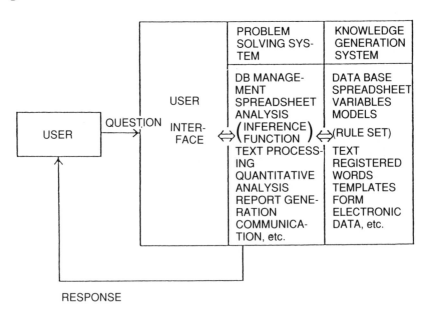

Figure 2.3 BES with DSS [2]

Low level versus high level interface (Command interface vs. natural language interface)

The methods of user interface are varied, including the use of simple diagnostic, direct command, menu guidance, interface through users' definition and natural language. While traditional expert systems have used direct command or menu guidance because of the restraints of technology and simplicity, it is natural that the use of natural languages should be highlighted and expanded.

Moreover, in the case of BES, remote access to an appropriate BES will be increasingly called for and in order to satisfy this requirement, communication networks through VAN and LAN, along with better communication software, are indispensable. Some of the Japanese companies, such as Yahagi Consultants, try to provide access to their BESs in remote areas by means of personal computer networks. By so doing, they use their strategic planning ES from clients' offices or seminar rooms in different cities.

Remarkable cost-performance effects of using BES

The cost-performance effects of BES or ES have been impressive, and may be called 'the principle of ten times effectiveness'. The following are some illustrations in different types of companies:–

Bank: The Daiichi Kangyo Bank has developed a BES for budget assessments. As a result, one day is enough for evaluating budgets, as compared to the ten to twenty required before

Housing: As the result of developing an ES for components deployed in the construction of prefabricated houses, Sekisui Kagaku saved approximately ¥100 million in the six months between the emergence of a new product and its gaining popularity among consumers

Construction: A construction selection ES developed by Kajima Construction Company, attained cost savings of approximately ¥30 million

Insurance: A participant's selection ES for seminars used by the Customer Services Section of Mitsui Life Insurance Company has made the selection process as fast as forty minutes, compared to the two days required before

Chemicals: A production planning ES developed by Sumitomo Chemical Company has been applied to their Ehime factory. As a result, a job previously taking one whole day now only takes ten minutes

Glass: A production planning ES developed by Asahi Glass reduced planning time to as little as three hours, compared to forty hours before

Gas: Tokyo Gas Company has developed a scheduling BES. The result is that scheduling is completed within thirty minutes, compared to the two weeks normally required before

Steel: Tokyo Steel has developed a production planning ES for their steel manufacturing process. While daily production planning normally took one day, monthly planning took more than two days. The institution of the ES has made it possible for both types of planning to be completed within half a day

Aircraft: As a result of introducing their production process design ES, Northrop Aircraft has been successful in shortening the production process design period for parts manufacturing to a few minutes, compared to the one hour they took before

Computers: Savings due to the XCON system developed by DEC (Digital Equipment Corporation) have reached $24 million per year

Food: As a result of developing their list making ES, Myojo Shokuhin have succeeded in making lists for distribution orders in only ten minutes, compared to the more than one hour and a half required before even by experienced workers.

Conclusion – future directions

As partly illustrated in the previous sections, AI in Japan will be continually developed along with each AI technology independently, simultaneously, or combined with other relevant technologies, including neurological, biological, optical, and fuzzy technologies.

Future directions of ES can be summarised as follows:–

(i) in view of the fact that the number of ESs or BESs increased from 100 in 1987 to 250 in 1988, and from 250 in 1988 to 332 in 1989, according to the survey by Nikikei AI, the take-off period of ES seems to have passed and we are now experiencing the period of realisation. If this trend continues, the period of maturity will ensue from the beginning to the middle of the 1990s

(ii) The development of ESs or BESs has commenced with representative, heavy and large scale companies, including steel, electronics and construction. This development trend has gradually shifted to service industries, including banks, securities, and insurance companies. In particular, the development of BES in insurance and securities firms became intensive in 1989. This tendency will be further amplified not only in such service-oriented firms but also knowledge-based ones. By the middle of the 1990s, the development and utilisation of ESs and BESs will be diffused, regardless of the type of industry

(iii) However, as ESs and BESs boom, develop and gain popularity, cost versus performance, cost versus utilities, or cost versus effectiveness will be more strictly sought, completing the era of trial use, whatever the applications may be

(iv)   Not only ES development tools or languages but also application-oriented products will increasingly emerge and be sold to the public as well as the users who will be behind such developments

(v)   Sophisticated planning-type BESs which require profound intelligence and skill will be more intensively sought, while easy-to-use ES development tools and languages will gain more popularity

(vi)   While many small-scale ESs or BESs have been developed and employed, more important and large-scale ones which can really help develop and assess corporate strategy and new product and venture developments have not yet emerged. Developing such highly intelligent ESs and BESs will undoubtedly be one of the future targets in the 1990s

(vii) It is conceivable that the combination and consolidation of new ESs and BESs with the ones developed to date will continually be undertaken so that higher effectiveness or utility may be proven as compared with accumulated costs. Thus, the direction of development will be, on the one hand, to construct unique and advantageous systems and, on the other, to skilfully accumulate added values or incremental effectiveness to existing systems.[3]

Notes

1.   Refer, for example, to future computer and information systems: *The Uses of the Next Generation Computer and Information Systems*. Praeger Publishers, New York. 1986. pp. 4–7, and Ishikawa, Akira. 'Decision Support Systems – Its Role for Efficaciousness of Constructing Strategic Planning.' *Engineers*. No. 378. March 1980. See also Ishikawa, Akira. 'Invitation to the Strategic Information System – I', *Computopia*. December 1987. pp. 115–6.

2.   Adapted from Figures 3.1, 3.2 and Figure 7.1 in C.W. Holsapple and A.B. Winston. *Manager's Guide to Expert Systems Using Guru* (trans.) Diamond, Tokyo. 1986. p. 49 and p. 132.

3.   A complete bibliography is available from the author.

15 Employment problems of the elderly in Japan and their human resource management

TOSHIAKI TACHIBANAKI
KYOTO UNIVERSITY

Introduction

Japan will face a seriously ageing society in the future. Although there are many problems in an ageing society, two issues in particular will be examined here. The first is how to assure employment of the elderly. The second is how to utilise such human resources efficiently within an enterprise.

The first issue is raised by an examination of the employment problems of the elderly. Specifically, several causes of their severe employment problems are discussed and some policy recommendations to overcome such difficulties are suggested. The second issue investigates the human resource management of the elderly, and considers programmes aimed at keeping high levels of productivity even after workers become older. The programmes include various elements, such as training, changes in companies' organisational structures, personnel management, and others.

Employment problems of the elderly

There are many documents and articles on the subject of the ageing trend in Japan and it can be taken for granted that Japan will have a very high proportion of aged people. The study by, for example Okazaki,[1] predicts that the proportion of those whose ages are over 65 will be 23.6 per cent in 2020. Several serious social and economic problems are anticipated and, since the aged currently face a higher degree of difficulty in finding jobs than the young and the middle-aged, some specialists are worried about the ageing trend aggravating the employment problems of the elderly.

Personally, one can be fairly optimistic about the employment problems of the elderly in the future. The reasons for this optimistic view originate from the fact that an ageing society implies a shortage of labour under given conditions. Since an ageing society occurs simply because the proportion of younger generations declines, the number of the working population is diminished; and if the number of working people declined, the growth rate of the Japanese economy would also decline. This is obvious, if we apply the growth-accounting framework. It would therefore be necessary to keep the current level of labour force or employment in order to save the Japanese economy from a declining growth rate. In other words, we have to expect a higher level of labour force or employment of the elderly in the future, if there is a consensus in society that the current level of the growth rate should be maintained.

The author's view is that the Japanese people wish to keep the current level of the growth rate to preserve international competitiveness and living standards, although it is certainly difficult to raise growth beyond the current level. Therefore, the aged are expected to work sufficiently. There are various policies to satisfy this expectation. Postponing the retirement age, extending working hours, and making finding jobs easier for the elderly are examples. To make finding jobs easier for the elderly is the most relevant in view of the current difficulty in finding them. The other policies, such as postponing the retirement age and extending working hours are not appropriate, because they imply further encouragement of the hard-working habits of the Japanese people.

We have to distinguish between postponing the retirement age and providing the elderly with jobs, when we discuss the employment problems of the elderly. On the one hand, there has been a tendency towards early retirement from the labour market for a long time in Japan and the labour force participation rate of the elderly has gradually been declining. On the other hand, older workers currently have great difficulty in finding jobs despite their desire to work, and the great majority of workers in larger firms have to leave their employers at the age of about 60; which is called 'mandatory retirement'. These observations suggest the importance of providing workers aged over 60 with jobs, if they desire to work.

Briefly regarding the labour force participation rate in Japan, and its comparison with other countries, Figure 1 shows the historical changes in the labour force participation rates for older workers. The figure clearly indicates that the male labour force participation rates (ages over 60) have declined constantly, while the female rates have been fairly constant except for the years from 1961 to 1972 in which significant decreases were observed.

Table 1 shows the international comparison of labour force participation rates by sex and age, and suggests that Japan has the highest rate of participation among people over 65. Although this is true for both males and females, the male participation rate is conspicuously higher in Japan than in the other countries.

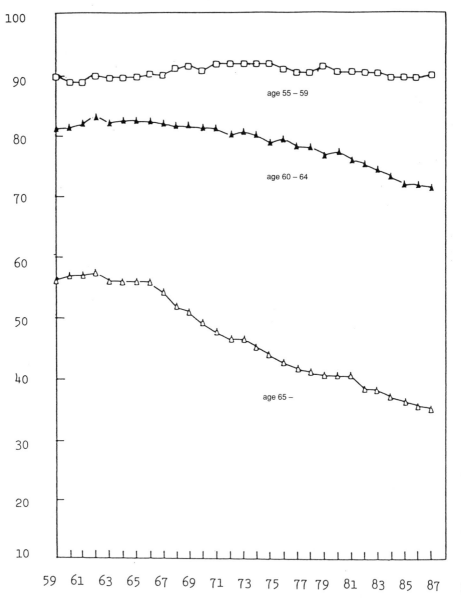

(%)

Source: Management and Cordination Agency, *Labour Force Survey*,
various years

Figure 1 Historical changes in labour force participation rates for older workers

Table 1 International comparison of labour force participation rates, by sex and age (%)

		Canada (1987)	USA (1987)	France (1987)	W. Germany (1986)	Italy (1987)	UK (1986)	Japan (1987)
Male	Rate (all ages)	76.7	73.9	65.4	71.7	65.9	71.9	77.3
	15 - 19	57.6	43.7	15.7	47.0	28.0	58.2	17.4
	20 - 64	88.5	85.8	83.2	86.6	83.6	87.2	91.4
	65 -	11.8	15.7	4.7	5.1	10.1	7.5	35.5
Female	Rate (all ages)	56.2	54.2	45.8	42.0	35.0	48.2	48.6
	15 - 19	54.3	42.8	11.8	40.1	24.9	56.5	16.6
	20 - 64	66.4	66.9	62.2	54.9	45.1	61.0	59.7
	65 -	3.6	6.9	1.9	2.1	3.8	2.7	15.4

Source: ILO. *Year Book of Labour Statistics.* 1988

Two important messages can be formulated on the basis of both Figure 1 and Table 1. They are, first, that while the Japanese labour force participation rate for the elderly has been in a decreasing trend, its level, second, is still much higher than in the other industrialised nations.

Labour supply behaviour of the elderly

The reasons for the two above facts must briefly be examined. There are several factors which have some influence on the supply of labour by the elderly, which are, (i) pensions, (ii) health, (iii) income (or wealth level), (iv) industry, (v) non-economic factors.

(i) Pensions

Two elements affect supply behaviour. First is the amount of public pensions, and second is the pensionable age. Several econometric studies[2] give the estimated labour supply elasticity with respect to public pensions as around −0.2. Although this value is not extraordinarily high, its impact is fairly high. The amount of the old age pension has been significantly increased, and thus it is quite natural that the elderly have lowered their labour supply, as emphasised by Seike. One may, however, be considerably pessimistic about this feature as it concerns the future. It is anticipated that a serious budget deficit in the pension system will occur due to the ageing trend, and that people already recognise a decrease in the amount of payment and a postponement of the starting age. Therefore, the effect of pensions

251

on the labour supply of the elderly will be diminished. It is even possible to predict that this recognition raises the probability of the labour force participation of the elderly some time in the future.

(ii) Health

A large number of studies suggest that the condition of health is crucial in the determination of the retirement age. Table 2 shows it in the simplest way, indicating that 64 per cent of males and 53 per cent of females give their condition of health as a reason for not seeking employment. In particular, illness and injury are much more important than physical hardness among the specific causes. It is quite significant to understand that the condition of health is currently the most important determinant of retirement in Japan, implying that the majority of older Japanese people wish to work semi-permanently so long as their health permits. Why they desire to do so will be discussed later. Finally, it is important to notice that health is a completely personal matter, and that it differs considerably from person to person. In other words, some people face poor health at an earlier age, while others face it later. Therefore, it is largely not controllable, but determined exogenously, and forces people to retire from the labour market in many cases.

(iii) Income and/or wealth

These two variables are important for the determination of the labour supply behaviour of the elderly in any society. If older people had sufficient income, they would desire to retire earlier. Table 3 indicates this clearly, showing that over 80 per cent of Japanese males and about 70 per cent of females who are currently working give 'to get income' as the most important motivation. The ratio declines significantly as people become older.

A somewhat different result appears in Table 3 for older people who are currently seeking jobs. The economic reason, namely 'to get income' is still the highest, but its share is considerably lower for older people who are currently seeking jobs than for older people who are currently working. At the same time, other reasons such as 'for health' and 'to enrich life or participate in society' show significant importance.

It can therefore be concluded that the most crucial motivation for the elderly is the economic reason, namely to earn income by working, although there remains a difference between those currently working and those currently seeking jobs.

One important remark, however, must be added. The economic reason 'to get income' does not necessarily imply that all older people want to earn income for their basic livelihood. Many, but not all, older people in Japan already have sufficient income and wealth, so that their wish to work arises

252

Table 2 Reasons for not seeking employment, by sex and age (%)

	Male				Female			
	55 - 69	55 - 59	60 - 64	65 - 69	55 - 69	55 - 59	60 - 64	65 - 69
Economic Reasons	11.3	5.5	12.8	12.0	9.7	10.2	9.8	9.3
Having pension or retirement allowance	9.3	3.9	11.9	8.9	4.8	3.8	4.9	5.4
Having income from property	0.6	0.4	0.2	1.0	0.9	1.7	0.9	0.5
Children take care	1.2	0.6	0.6	1.9	2.1	1.7	1.9	2.4
Others	0.1	0.6	–	0.1	1.9	3.1	2.0	1.0
Health	64.1	78.1	59.5	63.1	52.7	44.3	52.7	58.9
Illness or injury	48.5	65.6	45.0	45.7	31.3	26.8	32.3	33.7
Physically hard	12.2	10.2	11.4	13.6	16.0	13.6	15.8	18.3
No wish for working	2.2	1.6	1.6	2.9	3.1	2.0	2.5	4.5
Others	1.2	0.9	1.6	0.9	2.1	1.9	2.0	2.4
Skills are obsolete	2.4	2.0	2.9	2.0	0.7	0.9	0.5	0.8
No favourite job	4.2	2.2	5.4	3.9	3.1	3.6	3.2	2.7
Wishing to enjoy hobby or social activity	9.1	3.6	9.1	10.9	10.1	13.1	10.3	7.8
Others	9.0	8.6	10.3	8.0	25.6	27.9	23.5	20.5

Source: Ministry of Labour. *Surveys on Employment of Older Persons.* 1988

Table 3 Reasons for working, and for seeking jobs, by sex and age (%)

	Male					Female			
	55 - 69	55 - 59	60 - 64	65 - 69	55 - 69	55 - 59	60 - 64	65 - 69
Reasons for working	100.0	100.0	100.0	100.0	100.0	100.0	100.0	100.0
To get income	84.5	92.6	77.9	71.6	69.8	76.2	68.3	55.7
To earn a livelihood	77.0	88.9	67.9	57.3	43.9	48.7	42.2	34.4
To supplement a livelihood	6.5	3.0	8.9	12.9	23.8	25.1	24.0	20.1
Others	1.0	0.8	1.2	1.4	2.1	2.4	2.0	1.2
For health	5.3	1.7	8.1	11.6	8.7	5.4	9.7	15.3
To enrich life or participate in society	4.0	2.2	5.6	6.9	6.5	5.6	6.3	9.2
For being asked or having free time	3.1	1.2	4.7	6.0	8.1	6.3	9.2	11.0
Others	3.1	2.4	3.7	4.0	6.9	6.5	6.4	8.8
Reasons for seeking jobs	100.0	100.0	100.0	100.0	100.0	100.0	100.0	100.0
To get income	49.7	68.3	48.1	38.5	43.5	47.5	44.5	35.1
To earn a livelihood	31.7	49.4	29.1	22.5	15.7	16.9	15.6	14.0
To supplement a livelihood	17.6	18.2	18.7	15.6	26.5	29.4	27.4	20.1
Others	0.4	0.7	0.3	0.4	1.2	1.2	1.4	1.0
For health	24.6	15.5	26.7	28.1	21.1	18.6	22.0	23.9
To enrich life or participate in society	18.2	9.1	18.0	25.3	24.2	23.3	23.8	26.2
For being asked or having free time	5.1	3.6	5.3	6.0	6.7	5.5	6.6	9.2
Others	2.4	3.6	1.9	2.1	4.5	5.1	3.1	5.7

Source: Ministry of Labour. *Surveys on Employment of Older Persons*, 1988
Note: Reasons for working are asked to people who are currently working, while reasons for seeking jobs are asked to people who are currently looking for jobs.

from their hope to supplement their living standard, as shown in Table 3, and to increase their savings for the purpose of leaving more as a bequest to their children. The latter purpose is particularly significant and is one of the most important reasons for the higher savings rate in Japan.[3] It is somewhat unfortunate that the elderly in Japan work not for themselves but for their children, and that they do not enjoy their leisure in their sixties or seventies.

(iv) Industry

It is suggested that the self-employed retire fairly late for various reasons. Since Japan's ratio of self-employed to total working population has been high, the average retirement age has obviously been postponed but this is a minor issue here, because the focus is on employees in companies.

(v) Non-economic reasons

There are two views about the elderly in Japan. First, since the Japanese feel satisfasction from working and do not appreciate the value of leisure, the elderly wish to work as long as their health permits. Second, some believe that working is the best way to escape from further sluggishness or ageing. These issues are highly personal and non-economic, and so are not further discussed here but this does not mean that they are unimportant.

Labour demand of firms for the elderly

It is well recognised that older people find great difficulty in finding jobs in comparison with younger and middle-aged people. One simple indicator, which is given by the job openings/active applications ratio, shows that it was 2.77 (ages below 19), 1.23 (ages 20-24), 2.11 (ages 30-34), 1.72 (ages 35-39), 0.78 (ages 50-54), 0.31 (ages 55-59), and 0.16 (ages 60-64) in 1988. These numbers suggest that there is not enough labour demand for the elderly and it is important to consider the reasons for such low demand. Two reasons may be suggested. They are:– (i) lower productivity and (ii) increasing labour cost.

(i) Lower productivity

Briefly, decreasing productivity as one gets older is an unavoidable phenomenon. Not only physical conditions such as quickness, ability of moving, watching and hearing, but also mental conditions such as thinking, memory, and concentration deteriorate, although the degree of deterioration differs greatly among individuals. Firms are not willing to employ older people whose productivity is lower unless they receive some external help or subsidy, so it is inevitable that labour demand for them is lower. The important things are to create or arrange jobs which are suitable even for older people, and to consider the possibility of lowering their labour cost, by providing firms with a subsidy, or by preparing training for the aged.

Koike challenged the view of the lower productivity of the elderly based on extensive field work and proposed in particular that intellectual ability is not so obsolescent as was believed.[4] Thus, it is a good idea to assign supervisory or intellectual jobs to the elderly. This does not necessarily imply, of course, that all of the elderly keep high intellectual abilities forever: obsolescence finally sets in for everybody.

Here one should mention the importance of relatively simply manual work for the elderly, because they are fairly patient, responsible, and accurate compared with younger people. Simple but hard and heavy manual work which requires strong physical ability, however, must be avoided: simple and 'light' manual work fits the elderly relatively well.

(ii) Increasing labour cost

This is the subject with which economists are able to deal, and one of the most crucial factors to determine the employment level of the elderly. Two elements are related to this issue, first, relatively high wage payments to older workers according to the seniority payment system and, second, retirement or severance payment. These issues are fairly peculiar to Japan and thus require careful evaluation.

With respect to the seniority payment system, there is an argument that the steeper wage curve may have to be modified in order to save the labour cost associated with the anticipated ageing trend, because the increase in the amount of wage payments would hurt firms unless modified. In particular, wage curves for workers who are approaching the mandatory retirement age around 60, and wage payments for workers who are rehired on a contract basis after the mandatory retirement are the target of such an argument. Table 4 shows that firms regard a change in the payment system for employees aged over 60 as the most vital subject besides health in the determination of employment for that age class. In fact, 46 per cent of firms mentioned a possible change in the wage system as an effective way of increasing employment opportunities.

This is an opinion expressed by firms and should also be evaluated on the basis of employees' and other viewpoints. To do so, one has to re-evaluate the merits of the seniority payment system. It has been believed that the seniority system, together with the life-time employment "desired" have contributed positively to the workings of industrial relations and the labour market in Japan. Employees did not leave employers, nor shirked work in exchange for higher wage payment or retirement payments at a later stage in their career. Firms provided employees with training without worrying about them quitting, and thus employees' productivity increased consider-ably during their careers. Also, the seniority payment system worked as an egalitarian payment system and contributed to the smooth working of indus-trial relations. The above is a summarised form of the merits of the seniority system.

Table 4 Important determinants of employment for workers aged 60–65 (%)

	All Firms	A	B	C	D	E	F	G
Total	100.0	39.6	17.8	25.1	46.3	37.2	52.4	11.9
5,000 -	100.0	60.4	34.5	69.6	75.0	38.0	49.1	4.7
1,000 - 4,999	100.0	56.2	23.8	51.6	67.6	34.2	53.7	3.1
300 - 999	100.0	47.6	20.2	50.6	62.3	44.5	55.6	3.7
100 - 299	100.0	42.5	17.2	33.7	54.0	41.1	51.1	8.6
30 - 99	100.0	37.5	17.5	19.4	41.9	35.3	52.5	13.9

Source: *Surveys on Employment Management.* 1988

Notes

A: Changes in job assignments and working environment productivity
B: Changes in working hours, and full-time or part-time
C: Available positions and personnel management
D: Changes in wage payment and severance pay

E: Protection of lowering
F: Health
G: No answer

Besides the argument of the seniority system, which is equivalent to a skill hypothesis, there is another school which stresses the importance of a 'liv-ing expenses hypothesis' (*seikatsu-kyu kasetsu*), asserting that higher wage payments for older employees should be explained by their greater need for living expenses such as housing, children, etc.[5]

Both the seniority payment hypothesis and the living expenses hypothesis are prepared to justify that older workers receive higher wage payments; the only difference is in the cause or rationality of such higher wage payments. But as previously stated, employers regard a revision of high wage payments for older employees as vital in order to assure the employment of the elderly at the time of the ageing trend. This requires careful consideration for the following reasons.

First, the current and future older generations received lower wage pay-ments in the past when they were younger, in the hope that they would receive higher wages later. Employers benefited greatly from lower wage payments for younger employees because in the past the majority of employees were younger. Drastic cuts in wages for older employees would therefore violate 'equity' because the particular generations concerned would have to sacrifice themselves twice; namely at both younger and older ages.

Second, since the seniority system has been one of the most important elements which has enabled the Japanese industrial relations system to work rather well, a change in wage payments for older employees might alter the whole course of this industrial relations system. In other words, it is possible that the cost of losing the overall benefit of the seniority system would be larger than the benefit of increasing employment for the elderly; although this requires quantitative assessment of the cost and benefit.

A personal guess is that it would be harmful to implement drastic changes in wage payments for older employees. It is very likely that such drastic changes would not only be unfair on the particular generations concerned, but also detrimental to the workings of the industrial relations system from the long-term point of view. Only a very gradual change would be a justified method, if strong labour demand for the elderly were expected socially.

Employers recognise the detrimental effect of a drastic change and Figure 2 shows that firms hope for only a minor change in the wage rate for older employees. The Figure shows various wage payment courses after a certain age by size of firm and also calculates the proportions of firms, indicating that the most popular course is A (52.4 per cent), and the next most popular B (23.0 per cent). These courses suggest only minor deviations from the normal wage growth path, and that drastic changes such as D and E are adopted only by a small proportion of firms. Therefore, it is concluded that firms also do not intend to alter or lower the wage growth of older employees drastically. However, it is interesting to note that large firms have a stronger wish to lower the wage growth path than smaller firms, when one compares the intention by size of firm.

Next, it is necessary to examine the issue of retirement, or severance, payment. As Table 4 indicates, a change in retirement payments as well as in wages is proposed by enterprises as a useful policy to ensure the employment of the elderly. The effect and justification of a change in retirement payments may be evaluated almost analogously to the arguments given in the case of a change in the wage growth path for older workers. They are not therefore described in detail, but it may be useful to repeat that a drastic decrease in retirement payments is not strongly recommended. In addition to the reasons already referred to, a decrease in the retirement payment implies a transfer of funds from the employee to the employer, because the retirement payment has the property of being a deferred payment of wages. It is not therefore justifiable to cut the wage payment which employees are entitled to.

There is, however, one rational alternative for overcoming this problem: a change in the payment procedure from a one time lump sum payment to an annuity-based payment. A large number of retirees currently prefer one

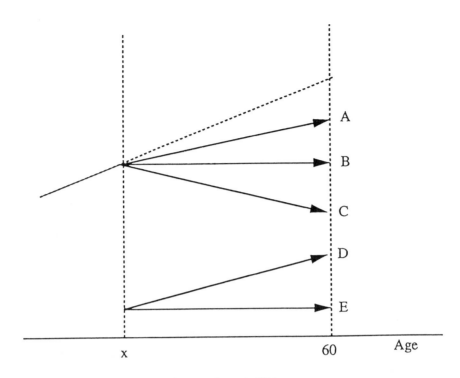

Proportions of firms for each growth path (%)

	Large firms	Medium firms	Small firms	Age x (average)
A	33.1	45.8	57.9	49.3
B	17.3	23.4	23.3	52.1
C	8.5	12.3	6.9	53.0
D	18.2	7.0	4.6	54.7
E	8.0	5.2	4.2	54.1

Source: Ministry of Labour. *Surveys on Wages and Working Hours.* 1987

Note
Age x means that a wage growth path is modified at the age of x.

Figure 2 Changes in wage growth after a certain age

time lump sum payments to annuity payments for the following reasons. First, workers who are 55-60 years old at the mandatory retirement age have higher expenditure on items such as housing, children's education and others. Second, they recognise that the rate of return on annuity income is lower than that on a one time lump sum payment, supposing that they are able to manage their funds efficiently. Third, the effective tax rate on one time lump sum retirement income is lower than that on annuity income because there is a significant allowance for retirement income.

It would be necessary to persuade employees to accept a gradual switch from the one time lump sum payment of retirement money to the annuity form, in order to save the cost to employers, by offering several policy reforms, and one of the most effective ways would be to levy a heavier burden of taxation on lump sum retirement income than on annuity income.

Human resource management (HRM)

(i) Postponement of mandatory retirement

As is well-known, a large number of enterprises in Japan, in particular larger enterprises, have a mandatory retirement age. This used in the past to be 55 but postponing it to 60 has been a national trend and thus the average is approaching 60, which is a favourable trend. Two recent and foreseeable phenomena, first, longer life expectancy i.e. that the current elderly will survive until 80 and, second, the possible postponement of the pensionable age for public pensions, may require the postponement of the mandatory retirement age even further.

Regarding the historical change in the mandatory retirement age and its dispersion by firm size, Table 5 leads to the two following observations:– First, firms whose mandatory retirement age is 55 have shown a decreasing trend; nowadays, more than 50 per cent of firms have a mandatory retirement age of over 60. Second, the share of firms whose retirement age is over 60 is higher in larger firms than in smaller firms; larger firms are more anxious to postpone the mandatory retirement age than smaller firms.

It would be difficult to postpone the mandatory retirement age from age 60 to age 65 in the short run because postponement to age 60 is only a recent event; as a transitional process it would be preferable to prepare a system of rehiring after the mandatory retirement age. Both employers and employees would commit themselves to new contracts, which should be fairly flexible in the determination of not only duration of employment but also of working hours a week or a day, and this contract-based rehiring would probably be the most effective policy for encouraging the employment of the elderly at this stage for various reasons.

First, a new contract after the mandatory retirement age would provide a firm with the introduction of a flexible wage payment and with a cut in the past wage growth path. Second, a new contract would make layoff or discharge of the elderly easier, when business conditions are difficult, in com-

Table 5 **Shares of firms having mandatory retirement ages, by age, class and firm size (%)**

Year	total	Age 54	55	56 - 59	60	61 -	60 -
1967	100.0	0.3	63.2	14.2	20.6	1.5	22.1
1970	100.0	0.7	57.9	18.3	21.7	1.4	23.1
1974	100.0	0.3	52.0	12.3	32.4	3.0	35.4
1976	100.0	0.3	47.3	15.9	32.3	3.6	35.9
1978	100.0	0.1	41.3	19.4	33.7	4.8	38.5
1980	100.0	0.2	39.5	20.1	36.5	3.2	39.7
1981	100.0	0.4	38.0	18.0	39.5	3.1	42.6
1982	100.0	0.5	35.5	18.2	43.0	2.8	45.8
1983	100.0	0.3	31.3	19.0	45.8	3.6	49.4
1984	100.0	0.1	29.6	18.3	48.3	3.8	52.1
1985	100.0	0.1	27.0	17.4	51.0	3.9	55.4
1986	100.0	0.1	26.7	16.6	52.5	4.1	56.6
1987	100.0	0.3	23.0	18.0	53.9	4.8	58.7

Year	Firm Size	Total	Age 54	55	56 - 69	60	61 -	60 -
1987	5,000 -	100.0	–	23.1	11.9	84.3	0.6	84.9
	1,000 - 4,999	100.0	–	10.5	18.2	69.8	1.4	71.2
	300 - 999	100.0	–	23.7	21.4	53.2	1.8	55.0
	100 - 299	100.0	0.6	25.0	19.6	51.9	2.9	54.8
	30 - 99	100.0	0.3	22.8	17.1	54.0	5.6	59.6

Source: Ministry of Labour. *Surveys on Employment Management.* 1988

parison with regular workers. Third, flexible working days or hours would enable employees to prepare their entire retirement smoothly, or encourage them to enjoy lesure more, or relieve the severe health condition of the elderly. A majority of the elderly prefer part-time employment or self-employment;[6] thus, flexible working hours or days would meet their hopes. Fourth, a new contract also enables employees to retire entirely from the labour market without much trouble with employers, in comparison with regular workers. Fifth, it is good to discourage the hard-working Japanese, who are often criticised at home and internationally.

Finally, it is noted that larger firms are more reluctant to prepare for the introduction of rehiring after the mandatory retirement age than smaller firms; in contrast with larger firms being willing to extend the mandatory retirement age to 60. Table 6 shows the proportion of firms which have introduced rehiring after the retirement age of 60 and it should be emphasised that all the firms in the Table have postponed the mandatory retirement age. The Table also clearly indicates that the proportion of smaller firms which had introduced a system of rehiring after the mandatory retirement age of 60 is considerably higher than that of larger firms. In sum, there is a great contrast between smaller firms and larger firms with respect to policies towards employment of the elderly; while smaller firms try to introduce employment on a contract basis, larger firms try to postpone the mandatory retirement age. This is an interesting contrast which characterises industrial relations in Japan, and deserves further consideration.

(ii) Personnel management of the middle-aged and elderly

Since the ageing trend implies that the proportion of the middle-aged (say 40 years old and older) increases within firms, it affects various aspects of management. For example, the lack of superior or supervisory positions on the hierarchical ladder is a serious problem under the prevailing seniority-based promotion system; or the middle-aged are less reluctant to cope with new technology or a new management style. What kind of policies should be considered in facing the above problems?

The lack of superior positions is particularly serious because the previous seniority-based promotion system guaranteed the promotion of educated white-collar workers to at least *kacho* (section head) level and to *bucho* (department manager) level to a lesser extent.[7] As the share of middle-aged or older employees, like the baby boom generation after World War II, in companies increases, it is difficult for firms to promote all their white-collar staff. If the growth of a firm had previously been higher, the number of superior positions would have been increased, but the Japanese economy has ended its period of rapid growth, and thus it would be impossible to anticipate the rapid growth of a firm.

Before arguing the policy issue involved, it is first useful to understand

Table 6 Ratio of enterprises with retirement age of 60 or over according to employment extension system and future plans, by size of industry

Industry size	Enterprises with uniform age limit system over		With system				Without system					
			Total	Employment extended system only	Re-employment system only	Re-employment and employment extended system	Total	Planned to apply system				Not planned to apply system
								Total	Employment extended system only	Re-employment system only	Re-employment and employment extended system	
Total	**(61.9)**	**100.0**	**66.3**	**21.2**	**33.0**	**12.1**	**33.7**	**5.3**	**0.5**	**1.7**	**3.1**	**28.4**
5,000-	(86.4)	100.0	32.3	5.3	24.8	2.3	67.7	2.6	–	2.6	–	65.0
1,000-4,999	(75.1)	100.0	44.1	5.9	32.5	5.6	55.9	3.5	0.2	1.6	1.7	52.4
300 - 999	(65.4)	100.0	56.3	8.7	39.7	7.9	43.7	3.9	0.1	0.9	2.8	39.8
100 - 299	(61.3)	100.0	68.0	17.8	35.5	14.7	32.0	4.2	0.2	1.6	2.4	27.8
30 - 99	(61.2)	100.0	67.8	24.3	31.5	12.0	32.2	5.9	0.6	1.9	3.4	26.3

Source: Ministry of Labour. *Surveys on Employment Management.* 1989

the problem statistically and the 1989 report of the Ministry of Labour gives an interesting figure which indicates its seriousness. When two years, namely 1981 and 1986, are examined with respect to the positions occupied by university graduates, it can be seen that employees aged between 45 and 49 had increased by 42 per cent; but the number of *bucho* (department managers) had increased by only 5 per cent, and the number of *kacho* (section heads) had increased by 56 per cent, while the number of *kakaricho* (heads of the smallest segment) by 114 per cent, and of non-supervisory positions by 59 per cent. The corresponding figures with respect to employees aged between 50 and 54 are 88 per cent for all employees, 85 per cent for *bucho*, 134 per cent for *kacho*, 57 per cent for *kakaricho*, 115 per cent for other supervisory positions and 34 per cent for non-supervisory positions. Similar figures with respect to employees aged between 55 and 59 are 94 per cent for all employees, 65 per cent for *bucho*, 235 per cent for *kacho*, 82 per cent for other supervisory positions, and 96 per cent for non-supervisory positions.

In sum, the above numbers suggest that *bucho* have increased by 39 per cent, and *kacho* by 76 per cent, *kakaricho* by 96 per cent, other supervisory positions by 66 per cent, and non-supervisory positions by 56 per cent. They imply that the majority of the increases are filled by *kacho* and positions lower than *kacho*. In other words, a large number of employees aged around 40 to 50 are not expected to be promoted, and the lack of higher positions, in particular *bucho* and *kacho*, will be a serious problem. Are such employees frustrated and losing incentives? They have to accept such a situation to a certain extent because it is fate but a remedy must also be discussed.

The 1989 Ministry of Labour report and the Hitotsubashi[8] group suggest the following policies:– First, not only seniority-based promotion but also ability- and performance-based promotion must be introduced. Also, equity-oriented promotion may have to be abandoned, and thus selection for promotion may have to be intensified. Second, since promotion is no longer guaranteed, the system of specialists or other methods of qualification should be introduced in exchange for fewer promotions. Third, temporary transfers or permanent transfers to subsidiary firms, or even voluntary retirement and working at other firms may be encouraged.

The present author, unfortunately, considers that the first policy would lower the average productivity of employees, because the majority of them might lose the incentive to work hard and to make a contribution to the firm. Previously, employees were treated nearly equally at least until around age 30 or 35; they had a hope of further promotion after this age and thus worked hard and accepted severe competition. If selection for promotion were made at a relatively younger age, or were intensified, some of the employees who would be condemned to be outside the mainstream of the hierarchy might lose their incentive, and thus the average productivity of all employees might decrease. This would not be good for the firms. Of course, the productivity of employees who are successful at an earlier and intensified selection period would be increased but in my view the gain due to the latter would not cancel out the loss due to the former.

Then, what kind of policies are recommended? The specialist system may be a hopeful candidate but to discuss it would require considerable space, which is not available here. However, at least, the importance of training must be emphasised. Another possibility is to encourage temporary transfers from larger firms, which lack the necessary number of superior positions, to subsidiary i.e. smaller firms, which need skilful managers and heads. Human resources can be used more efficiently at these smaller firms than at larger firms, because such staff are likely to feel a stronger incentive as managers and heads, even if the numbers of their subordinates at smaller firms are also smaller.

Concluding remarks

Having examined the employment problems of the elderly in Japan, where an ageing trend is under way, and human resource management at enterprise level, it can be concluded, first, that the future employment problem is not so serious, on the basis of the examination of the labour supply and demand for the elderly. However, several policy issues such as the postponement of the mandatory retirement age, a very gradual change in the wage growth path for the elderly, flexible rehiring systems after mandatory retirement, a reform of the lump sum retirement, or severance, payment towards annuity income, and others have been discussed in order to cope with the ageing society. Finally,there are the problems of the lack of sufficient superior or supervisory positions at firms to cater for all those who would normally expect to be promoted to be solved.[9]

Notes

1. Okazaki, Y. 'Ageing Society and Population.' Kanamori, H. and Ibe, H. eds. *Economics of Ageing Society*. University of Tokyo Press. 1990. pp. 11–32 (in Japanese).
2. Seike, A. 'Labour Supply Behaviour of the Elderly.' Ministry of Labour ed., *Forecasting of Labour Supply and Demand* (in Japanese). 1987.
   Shimono, K. and Tachibanaki, T. 'An Analysis of the Working Behaviour of the Elderly.' *Kikan shakaihosho Kenkyu*. Vol. 19. No. 4. 1984. pp. 398–413 (in Japanese).
3. Hayashi, F. 'Why is Japan's Saving Rate apparently so High?' Fischer, S. ed., *NBER Macroeconomics Annual*. MIT Press. 1986.
   Ishikawa, T. 'Saving and Labour Supply Behaviour of Aged Households in Japan.' *Journal of Japanese and International Economies*. Vol. 2. 1988. pp. 417–49.
   Shimono, K. and Tachinabaki, T. op. cit. (Note 2 above)

4. Koike, K. (1990), 'Working Ability of the Elderly'. Kanamori, H. and Ibe, H. eds. *Economics of Ageing Society*. University of Tokyo Press. 1990. pp. 107–37 (in Japanese).

5. Ono, A. *Japanese Style Employment Practices and Labour Market*. Toyo Keizai Shinposha, (in Japanese). 1989.

6. Tachibanaki, T. and Shimono, K. 'Labour Supply of the Elderly: Their Desires and Realities about Full-time Jobs, Part-time Jobs, Self-employed Jobs or Retirement.' *Keizai Kenkyu*. Vol. 36, No. 3. 1985. pp. 239–50.

7. Ministry of Labour. *Industry and Labour Report*. (in Japanese). 1989.

    Tachibanaki, T. 'The Determination of the Promotion Process in Organisations and the Earnings Differentials.' *Journal of Economic Behaviour and Organisation*. Vol. 8. 1987. pp. 603–6.

    Tachibanaki, T. 'Education, Occupation, Hierarchy and Earnings.' *Economics of Education Review*. Vol. 9. No. 2. 1988. pp. 221–30.

8. Hitotsubashi Group. *Survey on Personnel Management under the Ageing Trend of Employees*. (in Japanese). 1987.

9. Tachibanaki, T. 'Employment Problems of the Elderly.' Kanamori, H. and Ibe, H. eds. *Economics of Ageing Society*. University of Tokyo Press. 1990. pp. 85–106 (in Japanese).

    Tachibanaki, T. and Shimono, K. 'Wealth Accumulation Process by Income Class.' *Journal of Japanese and International Economies*. 1990.

PART 4:

THE INTERNATIONAL COMPARISON

16 Industrial democracy in Japan and the West: will it survive?

SOLOMON B. LEVINE
NANZAN UNIVERSITY

The 20th century will certainly be remembered for the spread of industrial democracy in the advanced market-oriented economies. In most of these countries there has evolved a wide variety of institutions for workers to participate in and even control directly, or through their own autonomous unions, managerial decisions regarding important aspects of their lives at work. Leading conceptualisations and theories of industrial relations indeed assign workers and their own independent organisations a major role, alongside employers and government, in the making of the rules that guide or control both the substance of wages, hours, and other working conditions, including training and promotion, and the procedures for reaching such decisions. Within advanced market-oriented economies, it is expected that democratic tripartite arrangements will emerge in some form.[1]

Recently, considerable discussion has centred on the need for revising industrial relations theory because of rapid changes in national and international economic structures, technologies, labour market behaviour, and manager and worker attitudes. It is believed that, as a result of this dynamism, the roles of the actors also have been changing and will continue to change. In essence, new paradigms for understanding industrial relations see much of the direction and control of the substance and procedure passing to professional managers, who are expert in human resource administration and socio-technical analysis. While the new managerial approaches and techniques seem to provide for increased individual or small group employee involvement, workers' autonomous union organisations appear to be on the verge of fading out as outdated institutions for strategic decision-making in the world of work – at least in some of the most economically important societies. The new concepts claim to place far more emphasis on informality and variety in the role of employees as individuals or of small groups in influencing or participating in management decision-making at work. At stake, however, may be the continuing viability of democratic tripartitism.[2]

Definition of 'industrial democracy'

This discussion does not plunge directly into the current controversy over the appropriateness of existing theories of industrial relations. Rather, it looks at the institutions which have been built to provide 'industrial democracy', defined broadly as the right of workers to influence important decisions regarding their work, not only in the enterprise and workshops in which they are employed but also in relevant industrial, national, and other super-enterprise bodies. However, the term, industrial democracy, is far from precise, and has had both narrow and broad definitions.[3] A very broad one is taken here. The question is whether, in the transformation that has been going on, industrial democracy is also undergoing substantial changes. Is it declining or about to decline? In certain advanced market economies industrial democracy is still alive and well but limited in extent. While its further growth is in doubt, where industrial democracy is already well institutionalised, any setbacks are likely to be temporary.

Varieties of industrial democracy

Here, for reasons of space, observations are confined to only a few countries, especially the US and Japan, which the author happens to know best, with passing references to the UK, the former West Germany, Scandinavia, Canada and Australasia. All these countries are among the leaders of the democratic industrialised world and, specially since the end of World War II, each has been dedicated to promoting democracy as a national goal, even if in some instances economic growth and development have to be sacrificed (although some contend that growth of both goes together). Within this context, but without completely destroying management 'prerogatives', most have consciously and officially supported the spread of industrial democracy.

The numerous forms of industrial democracy range from direct worker or union control over decisions to allowing employees only a minor 'voice' in deliberations. Autonomous work groups alone deciding on production methods in a shop are an example of the former; while advisory joint employer-employee consultation represents the latter. In between, there are various arrangements for the parties to reach agreement (or disagreement) on decisions. These, of course, would include collective bargaining, co-determination, grievance processing, contract administration, and the like – usually within the establishment or enterprise. Of course, too, there are often institutions outside the firm which provide democratic participation – at the various branches and levels of government and in bipartite or tripartite (and occasionally unilateral) machinery at national, regional, and industrial levels. A full-fledged industrial democracy would include most of these possibilities.

The evolution of industrial democracy

The forms of industrial democracy now well established, and usually sanctioned in law, have evolved over many years and are the product of long-standing campaigns led by worker organisations. Even in the case of Japan and the former West Germany, which underwent drastic labour reforms after World War II, present-day forms of industrial democracy did not suddenly spring up. Usually, when first broached, governments and employers resisted their establishment. Even today, after fifty to a hundred years of experience with worker or union participation, many managements still prefer to avoid such involvements if they can. One suspects that the recent employer enthusiasm in many cases for employee involvement in management decision-making is motivated in part by the desire to weaken, get rid of, or avoid other strong types of industrial democracy, such as union-management collective bargaining. On the other hand, some managements, still small in number, seem to welcome many forms of industrial democracy in the belief that labour's 'voice' is needed to assure vital communication and consensus building within organisations for the purpose of achieving production efficiency and employee satisfaction. But employer-contrived worker participation schemes are seldom democratic in themselves. Usually it takes the initiative of workers and unions to achieve lasting industrial democracy, whatever the form.

Each country covered here has generated a somewhat different set of institutions for industrial democracy.[4] In general, the trend among them has been convergent; in particular detail, however, they diverge. The differences reflect variations in historical origins and timing and in on-going economic, technological, political, and social forces. Indeed, it is somewhat surprising how much similarity there is. Almost universally, for example, union-management collective bargaining is a central or near central activity. While the countries differ in particulars about the levels, scope, and areas of collective bargaining, the distinctions among them lie mainly in still other means for achieving industrial democracy which each country has chosen to emphasise.

For example, West Germany, Sweden, and Norway have legislated variations of co-determination at the enterprise level. This form is almost anathema in the US and Canada from the point of view of all the major industrial relations actors. It has yet to be accepted in the UK, having come close but finally been rejected by the unions themselves. With its conciliation and arbitration tribunals, co-determination is also almost unthinkable in Australia and New Zealand. Such differences, too, can be seen in the use of works councils in their various guises. West Germany and other Western European nations have by law legislated them. Japan, on the other hand, has witnessed their widespread informal development especially within firms without any direct legal underpinning. The US would not accept such non-union worker participation in collective bargaining under its system of 'exclusive' union representation.

The combination of industrial democratic forms found in each country often represents differing strategies and ideologies for the exercise of worker or union influence. As the late Adolf Sturmthal frequently pointed out, the combination which evolved in a country has to be understood along with the more general struggle to achieve political democracy throughout that nation.[5] German co-determination, for example, was an integral part of the effort to establish a comprehensive political democracy in face of a history of rigid class divisions and conflict, industrial elite collaboration with the Nazi leadership, and a labour movement sharply divided along ideological lines. In contrast, in the US, the almost sole emphasis on collective bargaining, and the scant interest in gaining representation on company boards of directors, arose in part because of the acceptance of the existing political system in which workers had already obtained democratic rights even before industrialisation began to develop on a major scale (although it took a civil war to spread the rights to others, notably blacks and women). The American experience, emphasising 'exclusive' collective bargaining representation and 'appropriate' collective bargaining 'units', written into law, occurred within the context of a broad pluralistic two-party system in which unions are only one small influence among many. Highly detailed, decentralised collective bargaining agreements were hammered out within the provinces where 'business' unionism reigned.

Until recently also, legislative enactment of rules for workers and work were fairly meagre in the US, in contrast for example with the UK, where the unions successfully developed their own ruling political party to achieve common rules through legislation. Given these contexts, in neither country is co-determination or works councils, on the German model, apt to be very relevant.

The Japanese case affords still another contrast. Certainly after 1945 a wide set of democratic rights was established as the result of massive reforms initiated by the Allied Occupation. However, except for a short-lived movement by some of the newly formed unions to achieve 'production control', there has never been a serious attempt since to install co-determination and works councils by legislation. These proved unnecessary with the new guarantees of labour rights to organise and engage in collective bargaining and in view of the emergence of 'key' employees in the process of rapid economic growth. Thus, many major industrial enterprises through their 'internal' labour markets in effect became employee-managed; with only secondary consideration for shareholders. In this evolution, especially as union-management collective bargaining solidified, the distinctions and differentials among different categories of permanent employees e.g. white collar, blue collar, gradually diminished to produce a high degree of egalitarianism within many companies. Indeed, Koike calls this process the 'white-collarisation' of blue-collar workers.[6] Such a development included widespread and highly active joint consultation as a supplement to collective bargaining, as well as numerous experiments with small semi-autonomous work groups, notably the famous QC Circles.

Thus, even without legislation, the array of participatory arrangements in Japan seems almost to equal West Germany's at the national, industrial enterprise, and establishment levels. What is different is the absence of a strong enough labour party that can take political power, although this may now be closer at hand, given recent developments in Japanese politics. Of course, many of the basic substantive and procedural rules of work in Japan were enacted as part of the labour reforms under the Allied Occupation – notably the Labour Standards Law, the labour relations acts, and social security – so that the need to struggle for legislative enactments has been less urgent than in some of the other countries. Notably, in the Labour Standards Law, there is provision for consultation between employers and workers or their representatives over workshop rules even in the absence of a union (the rules have to be at least the minimum regulations called for by the law). Given the vigorous role Japanese unions have come to play in representing workers' interests in the workplace, industrial democracy in Japanese industry may have been achieved even more deeply within the firm than the law originally envisioned.

With the recent formation of Rengo, the new and relatively unified labour centre, one of the aims of the movement is to strengthen labour's voice at national and industrial levels, where industrial democracy has been weakest. Rengo's hope is to follow the model of West Germany's DGB by shifting major collective bargaining issues from the enterprise to the industrial level, strengthening joint consultation activities at national and industrial levels, and helping to bring about unification of the non-communist opposition political parties. It is somewhat remarkable that the Japanese labour movement after decades of division and a long history of bitter ideological rivalry could achieve a semblance of unity, embracing two-thirds of organised labour and including both public and private sector unions. Several years will be required before it is known whether industrial democracy will be 'rounded out' to embrace the national and industrial levels but, with further structural change, this likelihood increases.

Threats to industrial democracy

Almost by definition, industrial democracy cannot exist without the self-organisation of wage and salary earners. Thus the forms of industrial democracy in a country will vary with the degree of autonomous unionisation, the levels at which unions participate in decision-making, and the range and importance of subject matter covered by such decision-making. Without independent self-organisation, democratically controlled, there is likely to be little spread of industrial democracy. In all the cases cited, this spread has been substantial but not comprehensive in every country.

However, after decades of union growth, several of the leading industrialised democracies are now experiencing notable declines in union membership density (measured by the percentage of union membership among employees eligible to form unions). Notably, these include the US, Japan, and the UK. Most of the other countries examined here show union density remaining at fairly constant levels. Sweden is the one nation that continues to gain, but it is now probably at an upper limit in the 90 per cent bracket – the highest in the democratic world.

Taken as a group, industrial democracy thus may have already peaked. The decline of union density in the US – from a high point of almost 35 per cent in the mid-1950s to about half that in the late 1980s, the lowest since 1945 – raises the possibility of American unions disappearing altogether or becoming so inconsequential as to represent but a very special interest group in the labour force although the absolute number of union members has remained almost the same.[7] Japan's density rate, too, has fallen from 35 per cent in 1970 to 27 per cent in 1988, also the lowest level in the postwar period. As in America, it is likely to fall further – again, absolute membership has fallen only slightly. In the UK, the union density rate has declined proportionately less, beginning from a much higher level of 59 per cent as recently as 1978 and dropping to around 45 per cent in the mid-1980s, about where it stood in the 1960s.

The decline of union density in these countries appears to have accelerated since the late 1970s, due primarily to the economic recession of the early 1980s, when there were rapid increases in unemployment in the most unionised sectors of these economies. Union membership rates, however, did not rebound with economic recovery, since there was now well underway a structural shift in employment, notably toward the white-collar service and small enterprise sectors, where union organisation has always been weak in most of these countries. Only the public sector, which tends to be highly organised, has sustained itself. In the US, for example, the public sector has shown sizeable absolute growth, while membership in the private sector has declined – no doubt as the result of later encouragement than in other countries of collective bargaining for public employees.

But still another important factor in accounting for the decline in density lies in the strength or weakness of legal and institutionalised procedures for organising unions and maintaining membership. Of the countries considered here, the US seems to be the most vulnerable in this regard. Under American labour relations law, at best a tortuous and difficult process awaits attempts by labour organisers to establish officially certified unions that employers

274

must recognise and bargain with. It requires petitions to the National Labour Relations Board with a sizeable number of worker signatures even to initiate the process; then a complex, argued determination by the Board of the 'appropriateness' of the bargaining 'unit' for which 'exclusive' union representation is sought; and finally, following an intense election campaign, the holding of a vote for or against the union – or among more than one union and no union if there are several seeking representation.

With the structural shift going on in the US economy, especially during the recession, numerous unionised firms were closed down or greatly reduced in size, resulting in considerable losses in union membership. As new firms or plants were opened in other sectors or even in the same sector, unions once again had to go through the legal process of obtaining recognition. (There is little automatic extension of union recognition in the United States.) Since employer resistance is allowed, at least within the limits of freedom of speech, and with a National Labour Relations Board becoming more sympathetic toward employers, the rate of organising success has fallen greatly – to less than half of the elections conducted. In other words, the union membership replacement rate has been far below what is required to maintain membership density. Perhaps what has been serving to prevent even a greater fall in union density in the US has been the spread of unionism in the public sector. The prevalence of the union shop and maintenance of membership provisions in the unionised private sector has also helped.

Canada's recent success in maintaining, and even slightly increasing, union density (almost 38 per cent) sheds light on the American case. Canadian labour relations laws are quite similar to the American, even in the procedure for obtaining union representation. Yet at certain points, especially regarding union petitions and conducting elections, the legal regulations are less stringent. As a result, it seems, the percentage of union election successes is much greater than the American.

Even then in the US, there is no automatic jump from success in unionising to collective bargaining or other institutions for union participation in management decision-making. In recent years, in one-third of the cases where unions win representation elections, employers have managed to delay making collective bargaining agreements. A number of American unions also have made bargaining 'concessions' to employers, particularly in the area of relaxing work rules, constraining wages and benefits, and permitting employers greater flexibility in human resource management – in exchange for greater job security and worker participation in decision-making. Perhaps, at best, these measures have served to maintain industrial democracy in America to a degree which has never been extremely high but intensely concentrated only through highly active collective bargaining.

It is not clear whether in face of the losses recently experienced, organised labour in America can make a successful comeback soon. Probably the spread of public sector unionism is reaching its limit. The traditional private sector unions themselves have embarked on new programmes to appeal to white-collar and service sector workers, including many part-time women employees, to accept unionism. So far there had been no major breakthroughs resulting from such efforts.

The other countries examined have much more positive legal and institutional support for unionising or representing wage and salary earners. None requires the laborious NLRB procedures for appropriate unit determinations and representation elections. The Japanese labour reforms, for example, allowed any two or more workers to form a union as long as it could show to the relevant labour relations commission that the union was democratically run and had financially responsible officers. Most unions in Japan were formed in this way, readily based on individual enterprise-level workforces.[8] No doubt the recent erosion of union density in Japan has been the failure to replace unionised enterprises and establishments that closed down as the result of structural change with new unionised enterprises with equal numbers of members. The slimming down of the number of regular or permanent employees with increasing numbers of part-time and temporary workers, especially women, ineligible to join the existing enterprise unions also probably accounts for a sizeable share of the union density loss. Again, as in the case of the US, the decline of union membership density in Japan has been stemmed by the prevalence of union shops. There is little evidence of fierce resistance or avoidance of unions by employers as widespread as in the US. Nor is there an unsympathetic set of labour relations commissions.

Still another factor must be taken into account in the Japanese case. Probably a number of non-union wage and salary earners about equal to those officially unionised are members of 'quasi-unions' or employee associations that have not sought 'union qualification'. These are usually voluntary organisations of enterprise level workforces which negotiate with management and participate in joint consultation and in semi-automonous work groups. They do virtually everything the officially approved unions do except seek official examination of their 'qualifications' to become *bona fide* unions under the law. It is not clear why they fail to do so, but probably they perceive it as unnecessary in order to obtain *de facto* recognition from employers. In fact, they usually are recognised as the representative bodies for workers under the Labour Standards Law and also have the right to strike. If difficulties do arise with employers, they can readily and voluntarily convert themselves into 'qualified' unions. This apparently is a source of some replacement for union membership losses, and possibly a reason why Japanese unions do not mount many organising campaigns, unlike America. On the whole, it is likely that by including the 'quasi-unions' industrial democracy in Japan is considerably more widespread than commonly recognised.

The UK has few legal procedures for establishing unions, but certain long-standing institutions serve to preserve widespread 'voluntary' membership. The tradition of craft unionism impels many workers to join the appropriate unionised groups to protect against encroachment on their own jobs and wages. The rise of the powerful shop steward system was a crucial element in this process. Closed shops also have long been prevalent in helping to sustain membership. Although a government hostile to unionism has been in power for the past decade and has stripped unions of some of their power, union density remains substantial, far above American and Japanese levels. With the unification of the EEC in 1992, we can expect a strengthening of industrial democracy throughout the member countries, including Britain.

Similarly, well established institutions protect the existing degrees of unionism in Australia, New Zealand, Sweden, and Norway and all show high rates of organisation. No doubt the Conciliation and Arbitration Commission systems in Australia and New Zealand assume that workers will join and remain in unions to make certain that they are blanketed in under the awards that favour wage and benefit uniformity among unionised employees. Moreover, with a Labour government in power in Australia that succeeded in establishing a social contract type of 'accord' with the unions early in the decade, there has been little erosion in the union density rates despite sectoral shifts and a somewhat alarming and persistent increase in unemployment.

The Scandinavian countries are famous cases where almost everyone is unionised. Perhaps longer than any of the other countries mentioned, industrial democracy has been firmly entrenched for half a century at all levels and in most sectors over all the important issues, including national economic policy and enterprise strategy. Forty-four years of Social Democratic rule helped assure the spread of unionism and industrial democracy. Even after the Social Democrats finally lost power in 1979, democratic union institutions have hardly been shaken – at least not so far. Industrial democracy seems to be thriving as before, despite attempts by Conservative governments to restore management 'prerogatives'.

Conclusions

The 20th century has been an era of industrial democratisation among the economically advanced market-oriented societies. Industrial democracy has been dependent primarily upon unionisation to achieve genuine worker participation in decision-making about rules affecting workers. While there are signs that this development has now come to a halt in several countries and may be reversed, in general, industrial democracy is well entrenched and institutionalised.

Each country examined here has developed its own forms of institutions for attaining industrial democracy. While all emphasise collective bargaining, there is considerable variety in other respects. Some can adapt more readily than others to changing economic and political circumstances without having to abandon unionism and the goal of industrial democracy.

Despite claims that industrial relations systems in advanced market-oriented nations are undergoing fundamental changes and require reconceptualisation, there is only limited evidence that the role of worker self-organisation is being seriously cut back in favour of non-union individual employee and small group participation. It is not likely that progress toward the goal of achieving industrial democracy has been permanently set back. Rather, especially in the US and Japan, it is temporarily being held in check due mainly to the on-going sectoral shifts in the economic structure.

Notes

1. Dunlop, J.T. *Industrial Relations Systems.* Holt, Rinehart and Winston. New York. 1958.
   See also Dunlop, J.T. and Galenson, W. eds. *Labor in the Twentieth Century.* Academic Press, New York. 1978.
2. Bamber, G. and Lansbury, R. *International and Comparative Industrial Relations.* Allen & Unwin, Sydney. 1987. pp. 3–29.
3. Kassalow, E.M. 'Industrial Democracy and Collective Bargaining: a Comparative View.' *Labor and Society.* Vol. 7. No. 3. July–September 1982. pp. 209–29.
4. For full reviews, see Bamber and Lansbury op. cit. and Juris, H., Thompson, M. and Daniels, W. eds. *Industrial Relations in a Decade of Change.* Industrial Relations Research Association, Madison, Wis. 1985.
5. Sturmthal, A. 'Industrial Relations Strategies.' Sturmthal, A. and Scoville, J.G. eds. *The International Labor Movement in Transition : Essays on Africa, Asia, Europe and South America.* University of Illinois, Urbana. 1973. pp. 1–33.
6. Koike, K. 'Internal Labor Markets : Workers in Large Firms.' Shirai, T. ed. *Contemporary Industrial Relations in Japan.* University of Wisconsin, Madison. 1983. pp. 29–61.
7. Kuchau, T.A., Katz, H.C. and McKersie, R.A. *The Transformation of American Industrial Relations.* Basic Books, New York. 1980.
8. For comprehensive materials on Japan, see Shirai (ed.) op. cit. (Note 6 above) and Shirai, T. and Shimada, H. 'Japan.' Dunlop and Galenson (eds.) pp. 271–322 (Note 1 above).

17 Management problems in using microelectronics in Japan, in comparison with West Germany and Korea

YOSHIAKI TAKAHASHI
CHUO UNIVERSITY

Introduction

The four following main topics in machine tool companies were studied, from the standpoint of international comparison, based upon the survey results of the research project at the Institute for Business Research.

(i)   What was the decision-making process for introducing microelectronics (ME) production equipment at the initial and present phases? Which people or groups and how many people or groups were involved in decision-making at each stage of 'initial proposal', 'discussion-elaboration of ideas', 'final decision' and 'realisation – material utilisation'?
(ii) What was the reaction of employees to the introduction of ME equipment in the initial and present phases?
(iii) Did conflicts take place when ME equipment was introduced? If conflicts took place, through which channels were they mainly solved?
(iv) How was the division of labour (programming, maintenance and operational jobs) among technicians, first-line supervisors and workers structured?

Responses to the questionnaire used were received between January and December of 1987 and the Korean research was conducted in 1988. The number of responses was eight (or six) from the Japanese and five from the German and Korean companies. Those who responded to the questionnaire were key people, like the president, the plant manager or the manager of the production department. Therefore the data in the responses depended upon their own observations.[1]

Decision-making regarding the introduction of ME

The first topic, see (i) above, was analysed not only in the initial phase of introducing the first ME machinery but also in the present phase of introducing FMC/FMS systems. The people or groups analysed belonged to the following thirteen levels:– (a) president (chief executive), (b) board director, (c) R & D department, (d) production and engineering section, (e) marketing and sales department, (f) personnel and labour affairs department, (g) production line middle manager, (h) first-line supervisor, (i) maintenance worker, (j) skilled manual worker, (k) unskilled manual worker, (l) works' council, (m) labour union (shop stewards).

From six Japanese cases, two kinds of typical decision-making patterns were found in the phase of introducing the first ME equipment. The first type is that the president or top management has a decisive influence on the total decision-making processes from the stage of the 'initial proposal' to 'realisation – material utilisation', with the assistance of engineers from the R & D department and the production engineering section. This decision-making pattern is found in four companies in which the stock is owned by the president's family. The aim of introducing ME equipment was to develop a new management strategy and to radically innovate in production technology. In one company which had such a typical decision-making pattern, the people of the marketing and sales department were fairly strongly involved in decision-making at the stage of the 'initial proposal' and the 'final decision' and this decision-making pattern is characterised as the 'top management initiative' type.

The second type is that the engineers of the production department mainly made the initial proposals, elaborated them and designed a final plan, with the assistance of the middle managers and skilled workers of the production line. After the final plan was formally decided by the top-management committee, production engineers also took the initiative at the stage of 'realisation – material utilisation'. This decision-making pattern was found in two companies in which the stock was not owned by the family. In these cases, the first ME equipment was introduced upon the initiative of production engineers who were looking for measures to rationalise the existing production processes in the plant. This pattern is characterised as the 'technicians' initiative on the shop floor' type.

Did both decision-making patterns change or not, when the introduction of ME equipment advanced to the phase of FMC/FMS systems? Comparing the research results, the following facts are found:- The first point is that the decision-making pattern of the 'top management initiative' type was not changed but was also maintained at the phase of introducing FMC/FMS systems. The second point is that, by contrast, the pattern of 'technicians' initiative on the shop floor' type was gradually changed in accordance with promoting the introduction of ME equipment. At the present phase of FMC/

FMS systems, the initiative in decision-making was taken by the staff of the production and engineering section instead of the technicians and middle managers on the shop floor, and the president also began to be involved at the stage of the 'initial proposal' on the one hand. But, this pattern was not changed into the 'top management initiative' type because the influences of technicians and middle managers on the shop floor were maintained on the other hand.

The influences of the labour union and of labour-management joint consultation on decision-making were very slight, and they had little influence on the stages of either the 'initial proposals' or 'discussion – elaboration of ideas'. In the case of the 'technicians' initiative on the shop floor' type, skilled workers were involved fairly frequently at the two stages before the 'final decision' and the stage of 'realisation – material utilisation', although in contrast the degree of their involvement in decision-making at each stage was as small as that of unskilled workers in the case of the 'top-management initiative' type.

In the five German cases compared with the Japanese cases, two typical decision-making patterns like in Japan could not be found. The fundamental characteristics of German cases could be derived from the research results. The first point is that there were two cases where the president exercised strong influence on the introduction of the initial ME equipment, while in the other cases the president did not significantly influence the process. But, it was common in both cases that the influence of the manager of the production line (*Fertigungsleiter*) was at least the same as the president's; in some cases it was even stronger than the president's. In contrast to the strong influence of the '*Fertigungsleiter*', the staff of the R & D department and the production engineering section did not strongly participate in the decision-making.

The second point is that at the phase of implementing FMC/FMS systems, the influence of the president, however, became stronger and also that the influence of the staff of the R & D department became relatively strong, even if the '*Fertigungsleiter*' was still involved in the decision-making. Especially the influence of the president on the 'final decision' generally became stronger than that of the '*Fertigungsleiter*'.

The third point is that as far as the first-line supervisor (*Meister*) is concerned, he was involved to a certain degree in decision-making at the stage of the 'discussion – elaboration of ideas' and 'realisation – material utilisation', although he did not strongly influence the stages of the 'initial proposals' and 'final decision'. The fourth point is that some workers were slightly involved at the stage of 'material utilisation', but had no involvement in decision-making at the other stages.

From the results of the five Korean companies we can point out the following characteristics:– The first point is that there were two cases where the president was strongly or fairly strongly involved in introducing the initial ME equipment and other cases where the president did not significantly influence the process except for the final decision process. However, it was common in both cases that the influence of the production and engineering section or the R & D department was the same as that of the president, and in some cases it was even stronger than the president's, as in the case of the German *Fertigungsleiter*'s function. Furthermore, it should be pointed out that Korean middle managers on the production line were fairly involved in introducing the initial ME equipment.

The second point is that in the phase of implementing FMC/FMS, the influence of the president became stronger for introducing ME equipment; but, the influence of the production and engineering section was still stronger than that of the president, and the middle managers on the production line were also fairly strongly involved. The third point is that the influence of supervisors, maintenance workers and skilled manual workers was fairly strong only at the stage of realisation – material utilisation in both phases.

Attitudes towards the introduction of ME

Analysing the reaction of employees in the Japanese companies towards introducing ME equipment, the attitudes of the staff and engineers of the R & D and production departments were positive from the initial stage of introducing the first ME equipment and became even more positive during the phase of implementing FMC/FMS systems. Although the attitude of the first-line supervisors was not so positive as the staff and engineers mentioned above, they were not against introducing ME in the initial phase and showed a more positive attitude in the more developed phase of FMC/FMS. Skilled and unskilled workers in Japanese companies were also not negative from the initial phase and the former showed a positive attitude to the phase of FMC/FMS. The labour unions in the Japanese cases had an attitude similar to that of the former employees and only one union was against introducing ME equipment in the initial phase. However, this union was positive towards the more developed phase of FMC/FMS.

Comparing the attitudes of the white-collar workers in the German and Korean companies with that in the Japanese cases, no clear difference could be found among the three countries; but, a small difference in the attitudes of skilled and unskilled workers could be found between Germany, Korea and Japan. German and Korean skilled workers were more positive towards introducing ME than Japanese skilled workers in the phase of FMC/FMS but German and Korean unskilled workers were not so positive as the Japanese in the initial introduction phase. Concerning the attitude of the German works' council, there were no cases where the works' council showed a very negative reaction. Although in the initial phase two cases showed a rather negative attitude, only one of them still did not change this negative attitude in the phase of FMC/FMS. On the other hand there was only one works' council which was positive in the initial introduction phase, but three works' councils became 'positive' in the phase of FMC/FMS (see Table 1).

Table 1 Attitudes towards the introduction of ME and FMC/FMS

	Initial introduction of first ME			Introduction of more developed FMC/FMS		
	Japan	W. Germany	Korea	Japan	W. Germany	Korea
R & D staff	1.5	1.3	1.4	1.3	1.3	1.4
Production Engineers	1.3	1.3	2.0	1.2	1.3	1.6
First-line supervisors	2.2	2.6	2.2	2.0	2.0	1.8
Skilled manual workers	3.0	3.0	2.6	2.5	2.0	1.8
Unskilled manual workers	2.7	3.2	3.0	2.5	2.8	2.0
Labour union, shop stewards	3.0	3.2	2.5	2.6	2.6	2.0

Note
Response scale used:– 1 = 'very positive', 2 = 'fairly positive', 3 = 'more or less', 4 = 'rather negative', 5 = 'very negative'

Conflicts in introducing ME and their resolution

In Table 2 the responses both from Japan, Germany and Korea are analysed in respect to whether or not any conflicts occurred when ME equipment was introduced in the companies, and if any, how they were solved.

No redundancy was found in six out of eight Japanese companies, and the other two companies stated that there was no conflict. Job transfers or reallocation of employees were implemented in half of the Japanese companies but some conflict occurred in one company. Similarly, education and training, introduction of shiftwork, and changes in working hours wereimplemented in these companies without conflict, because problems were solved through joint labour-management consultation. Change in the wage system was absent in the Japanese companies. After all, the personnel problems related to the utilisation of ME equipment were solved routinely

Table 2 Conflicts over ME introduction and their resolution

Type of conflict		conflict (A)					Method of resolution (B)					
		(1)	(2)	(3)	(4)	(5)	(1)	(2)	(3)	(4)	(5)	(6)
Redundancy	Japan			2	6							8
	Germany			5								5
	Korea	1			3	1	1	1			2	1
Job transfers	Japan		1	3	4							8
	Germany		3	2			1	2	3	1		
	Korea		2	3					3		1	1
Hiring specialists	Japan			3	4	1						8
	Germany			4	1					1		4
	Korea	2	1	2					2		1	2
Employee education	Japan			5	3							8
	Germany			4	1					1		4
	Korea					6						6
New health and safety rules	Japan			4	4				1			7
	Germany		2	3			1	1	1	1		2
	Korea			3	2			1	3			1
Introduction of shiftwork	Japan		1	4	3							8
	Germany		1	2	2				1			4
	Korea	1		1	3		1	1			1	2
Changes in working hours	Japan			4	4				1			7
	Germany		1	2	2						1	4
	Korea	1		1	3		1	1			1	2
Changes in payment	Japan			1	7							8
	Germany		2	2	1		1		1	2		3
	Korea	2		1	2		1		1		2	1
Others	Japan			2	6							8
	Germany			5								5
	Korea		1	1	1	2	1	1			1	2

Notes
(A)   (1) very conflictual, (2) conflictual to some extent, (3) not conflictual, (4) no such problem, (5) no answer
(B)   (1) collective bargaining, (2) works council, (3) supervisor, (4) personnel department, (5) others, (6) no answer

through this type of consultation and at the discretion of the personnel department.

More conflict was found in the German companies, compared to Japanese companies, although dismissal or layoff measures were not undertaken for excess workers. Job transfer or reallocation of employees was implemented in all five companies, with conflict occurring in three companies. Among them, one company solved it by consulting with the works' council, another solved it through consultation together with the discretion of the supervisor (*Meister*), and the last one solved it through collective bargaining and the discretion of the *Meister*. In respect to new health and safety rules, two out of five companies were faced with the works' council and the other solved it through collective bargaining and personnel management. Changes in the wage system were made in four companies and conflict occurred in two companies: both tried to solve the problem with collective bargaining and the discretion of the *Meister* and personnel management.

In comparing the cases of the Japanese and Germany companies, the conflictual situations that occurred were quite different. The reason for this may depend on the difference in character between Japanese joint labour-management consultation and German consultation with the works' council. As is widely known, the works' council in Germany is legally institutionalised in the co-determination system (*Mitbestimmung*), which has a long historical tradition. On the other hand, joint labour-management consultation in Japan is an informal system within the enterprise, and by maintaining good communication between the labour union and management, only negotiations on small matters are required.[2]

Negotiations between the works' council and management in Germany have to take place on various matters concerning labour conditions and result in compromise by mutual concession at the lowest. This situation leads to the occurrence of conflict becoming greater but the management side has accepted that the works' council has to pursue its own interests and vice versa. Things would not be able to proceed without the co-operation of the works' council, or at least could only do so at an unacceptably high cost.[3]

From the Korean responses to the same questionnaire, it was found that more conflict occurred in the Korean companies. In one Korean case dismissal or layoff measures were undertaken for excess workers but this conflict was solved by consultation between management and the labour union. Changes in the payment system also caused very strong conflicts in two companies, which were solved by collective bargaining in one case and by other measures in the other. The problems of hiring specialists occurred in three companies and were solved at the discretion of the supervisor in two cases. Changes in working hours and the introduction of shiftwork caused severe conflicts. Because a labour union was not organised in three of the five companies that responded to us, consultation between management and the labour union has perhaps played a more important role in Korean machine tool companies.

Differences in job organisation due to ME

According to various case studies and articles,[4] the division of labour between blue-collar and white-collar workers in Britain and France has been more distinct than that in Japan and West Germany. It has also been asserted that the transfer of techniques, or job delegation, has been implemented from technicians to maintenance workers, and from maintenance workers to operational workers, comparing the division of labour among them in the initial phase of introducing ME equipment with that in the more developed phase of FMC/FMS systems.[5] In order to make clear if there have been such different tendencies among British, West German and Japanese companies, the research put the question 'who was and is mainly in charge, and who was and is assisting for the following jobs:– (i) creation and development of basic programmes, (ii) correction and modification of programmes, (iii) setting programmes into the machines, (iv) trouble-shooting, (v) improvement of related tools and equipment, (vi) repairing equipment, (vii) operating, (viii) setting up, (ix) monitoring, (x) quality control.' Unfortunately only eight responses from the Japanese and five responses from the German companies were received, so that the validity of the analyses might be limited, but even if the sample is not large enough to obtain complete information, it may still be useful to analyse the results of the survey on the division of labour in Japan and West Germany respectively.

Concerning changes of people in charge of programming, maintenance and operation jobs, there was little change in job content between the time of the initial introduction phase and the developed phase. We could find two Japanese cases where the jobs of the 'creation and development of basic programmes' and 'correction and modification of programmes' was delegated from technicians to operational workers after five years. In four out of five German companies, the job of 'setting the programmes into the machine' was mainly done by operational workers, whereas there were three or four Japanese cases in which this job was carried out mainly by technicians, supervisors or operational workers. Therefore, the job of 'setting programmes' may not belong in the category of programming in West Germany.

In order to grasp the relationship in the division of labour among technicians, supervisors, maintenance, and operational workers, it is important to show who had been and was assisting each job of 'programming, maintenance and operation', with a comparison between the initial introduction phase and the more developed phase. The most interesting difference in employee teamwork between Japan and Germany concerned the question of who was assisting each job of 'programming, maintenance and operation' in the more developed phase.

Among the eight Japanese companies there were three cases in which operational workers assisted in the job of the 'creation and development of basic programmes' and also two cases where they assisted in the job of the 'correction and modification of programmes' in the more developed phase after ten years. And besides, Japanese operational workers were assisting in all three kinds of maintenance jobs in two to four cases in the present phase.

Compared with Japan, no case was found in Germany where operational workers participated as assistants or helpers in the job of the 'creation and development of basic programmes' and only one case was found where they assisted in the job of 'correcting and modifying programmes' and 'maintenance'. In contrast to the Japanese cases, four German cases were found where technicians or *Meister* assisted in the maintenance jobs and three German cases where they assisted in the operational jobs.

Concerning changes of people in charge of the three jobs in the Korean cases, outside specialists played important roles in the jobs of programming and maintenance in the initial introduction phase; but specialists in the company had gradually begun to take charge of programming and maintenance jobs. This means that it is not such a long time since ME equipment was introduced into the Korean companies where this research was conducted. Concerning teamwork, Korean supervisors participated as assistants in the creation and development of basic programming, correction and modification of programmes and other jobs. Korean supervisors have therefore played important roles in teamwork.

There has been a common style of division of labour in Japan and West Germany, so that the jobs of programming, maintenance, and operation have been implemented as teamwork by technicians, supervisors, maintenance and operational workers. Sorge and his colleagues have pointed to a difference between the Japanese–German case and the British–French case and stressed that these differences in the division of labour between West Germany and Britain depended upon other differences in national institutions, traditions of technical work and training systems. Maurice also mentioned in his thesis that the French and British form of the division of labour was different from the Japanese and German form in regard to the utilisation of CNC (Computer Numerically Controlled) machinery. Whereas education and training systems had been implemented internally in Japanese and Germany companies, such a system has not been established in France and Britain. Furthermore, job demarcation between manual or blue-collar workers and intellectual or white-collar workers has been distinctive in France and Britain, based upon the traditional, social and professional norms of these countries.

The research here can explain the difference in the division of labour between Japan and West Germany in that Japanese operational workers have participated, as assistants, in the jobs of 'programming' and 'maintenance' and learned from technicians how to do these jobs through on-the-job training, whereas German technicians or *Meister* have assisted in the maintenance and operation jobs and taught their subordinate workers about each job.

Why can such a difference be found between Japan and Germany, in spite of finding similar points such as:– (i) internal training systems, (ii) the major role of *Meister* or first line supervisor, (ii) negotiation or consultation between union and management at plant or company level? The most important reason must be that the wage level is directly linked with the content of the job of each employee in German companies; while in Japanese companies the wage level is decided by seniority, and job demarcation between employees is more ambiguous. In German companies qualifications have been more strictly structured, whereas in Japanese companies they have been more rough and have been decided based not only on the ability but also on the length of service of employees.[6]

Notes

1. Honma, I. and Takahashi, Y. *Microelectronics Technology Innovation and Business Administration.* (in Japanese). Chuo University, Tokyo. 1989.
2. Takahashi, Y. 'The Structure of the Enterprise Union and the Present Situation of Labour Participation in Japan.' Dorow, W. (ed.). *The Business Corporation in the Democratic Society.* Gruyter, Berlin/New York. 1987.
3. Bessant, J. and Grunt, M. *Management and Manufacturing Innovation in the United Kingdom and West Germany.* Gower, Aldershot. 1985.
4. Maurice, M. *New Technology and the New Model of the Firm – Change and Social Production.* Research Paper. Laboratorie d'Economie et de Sociologie du Travail, Aix-en-Provence. 1986.
   Sorge, A., Hartmann, G., Warner, M., and Nicholas, I. *Microelectronics and Manpower in Manufacturing.* Gower, Aldershot. 1983.
5. Itoh, M. *Technology and the Organisation of Human Networks.* (in Japanese). Japan Institute of Labour, Tokyo. 1989.
   Takahashi, Y. 'The Impact of Increased Utilisation of Microelectronics on Employment, Production Process, and Job Organisation – The Japanese Viewpoint.' Dlugos, G., Dorow, W., and Weiermair, K. (eds.). *Management under Differing Labour Market and Employment Systems.* Gruyter, Berlin/New York. 1988.
   Takahashi, Y. (1989). Job Organisation and Labour Unions' Response to Problems under Utilisation of New Technology, in: *Journal of Commerce (Shougaku Ronsan)* No. 30 – 4/5/6. Chuo University Press, Tokyo.
6. The above is based on the writings in Japanese of A. Ishikawa, and Honma and Takahashi op. cit. For reasons of space, it is not possible to include the complete Tables in English but these are available on request from the author at: Institute for Business Research, Chuo University, Higashinakano 742–1, Hachioji-shi, Tokyo, Japan.

18 Quality attitudes in Japan: a large scale exploratory study

WOLF D. REITSPERGER AND SHIRLEY B. DANIEL
UNIVERSITY OF HAWAII

It has been argued that Japanese successes in high volume repetitive manufacturing are significantly aided by the pursuit of superior quality[1] and that a quality focus is therefore important in carving and maintaining a competitive advantage.[2] Moreover, it has been suggested that this competitive advantage may specifically be based on the beneficial impact of quality improvements on cost or productivity or on a combination of both.

Thus, quality in manufacturing has received increasing attention because of successful new Japanese manufacturing techniques like 'Just-in-time' systems. These techniques demand and foster a 'zero-defect' environment, so costly buffer inventories, which are provided for expected scrap and defective components, can be reduced and ultimately eliminated. Companies pursuing a competitive edge by applying these manufacturing techniques need, as a consequence, to address quality as a strategic priority and precondition for the implementation of these systems.[3] Two prevalent models, static and dynamic views of quality, provide the decision frame for shaping action in this area.

Static and dynamic models of quality

Static optimisation views of quality are based on the Economic Conformance Level model (ECL). The ECL model is well known and has been accepted in American as well as Japanese industries for years. The model, as depicted in Figure 1, assumes there is a cost minimising conformance level that balances the cost of appraisal and prevention, which are normally associated with attaining higher quality, against the costs of failure, which are those associated with poor production quality. Lundvall and Juran, for example, define

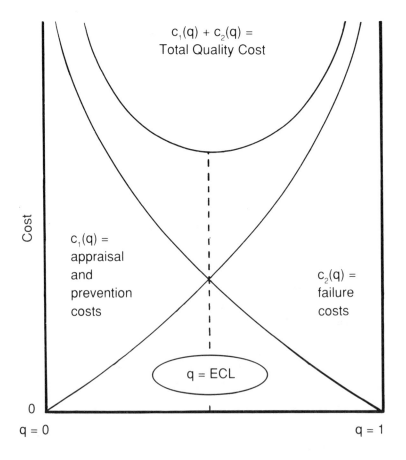

Figure 1 The economic conformance level model

appraisal and prevention costs as those arising from the inspection of purchased materials, inspection and test of work in process and final output, equipment maintenance, quality planning, quality training, process control, data requisition and reporting, and quality improvement projects.[4]

The other costs related to quality include failure costs for internal failure such as scrap, rework, retest, downtime and yield losses, as well as external failure costs such as warranty claims, complaint adjustments, and returned materials and products.

Appraisal and prevention costs increase with higher conformance, while failure costs are assumed to be zero if the process produces no defects (q = 1). Conversely, as appraisal and prevention programmes are deemphasised, higher failure costs are incurred. The relationships between these costs are shown in Figure 1.

Economically, rational behaviour dictates that firms may choose quality levels greater than the ECL, since the model does not account for market benefits associated with high quality such as higher prices or a larger market share. However, no economically rational firm would choose a quality level below the ECL, because the economic conformance model prescribes an optimal conformance level with a positive proportion of defects. Intuitively, this suggests that quality is costly. This contrasts with the dynamic 'quality is free' arguments of Crosby and Deming,[5] who advocate q = 1 or zero-defect as the optimal conformance level, and whose ideas have become more popular in recent years, because they are thought to reflect the assumptions on which successful Japanese industries operate.

Quality management hypothesis

A company's philosophy about quality is reflected in the attitudes of the operating managers who control the manufacturing process. For example, a dynamic quality orientation is indicated by the desire of operating managers to have top management leadership not only to endorse, but to lend strategic significance to the philosophy as well.

Similarly, the commitment operating managers have to quality are reflected in certain policies or beliefs, some of which are indicated below:–

- Reducing rejects does not increase costs, at least in the long run
- Acceptable quality levels (AQLs) are the sanctification of less than ideal production situations, and are not a superior tool in managing quality
- Management emphasis should be on defects and their causes, rather than on yields
- Acceptance of non-conforming materials from suppliers into the assembly process is to be avoided, even at the cost of a line stop

- Delivery of non-conforming products to customers is unacceptable, even at the cost of losing an order
- Quality problems on the line should be treated immediately at their source, even when this involves a costly line stop
- Quality is a production responsibility, rather than a specialised staff responsibility
- Pushing toward perfection in production is a desirable top management philosophy

Responses of adherence or rejection of these policies test the hypothesis that:– Japanese manufacturing managers adhere to the dynamic model of quality which is reflected in zero-defect notions.

To test this hypothesis 1,583 Japanese manufacturing managers in eight industries were sampled.

Questionnaire design

The data analysed in this study were collected as part of a broader study which examines the attitudes of personnel in a variety of Japanese manufacturing industries with respect to quality, inventory, flexibility and top management involvement. Data on the flow of information related to these operating priorities were also elicited. The questionnaire was composed of two sections: the first asked the respondents general information about their position, experience, company size and major product line; the second contained 36 statements concentrating on quality control, inventory management, Just-in-Time manufacturing and top management involvement in operations. Respondents were asked to express their agreement or disagreement with each statement on a 1 to 3 scale. The questionnaire was then translated into Japanese and the results were retranslated back into English. In addition, the questionnaire was pre-tested on a sample of manufacturing companies in Silicon Valley.

Sample selection

Companies were selected from the First and Second Sections of the Tokyo, Osaka and Nagoya stock exchanges, and from local market, over-the-counter, and unlisted companies. Since the concepts involved in Total Quality Control and Just-in-Time production are most applicable to repetitive assembly operations, 416 companies were selected from a variety of industries involving repetitive assembly. Each selected company was mailed a packet of twenty questionnaires, along with a covering letter that explained the study and requested that the questionnaires be distributed to various levels of manufacturing personnel. A total of 1,583 responses were received from 126 companies.

292

The responses were categorised into seven industry groupings, using the description of the major product given by the respondents.

The responses were fairly evenly divided between industries, with a high of 20 per cent of the responses from 20 precision electronics manufacturers and a low of 9 per cent of the responses from 10 computer electronics manufacturers. 70 per cent of the respondents were section managers, foremen, supervisors and technicians, 18 per cent were department heads, and 12 per cent responded from higher management levels and staff positions.

85 per cent of the respondents worked in factories employing 600 or more individuals. Chi-Square tests and cross-tabulations were used to pinpoint differences between industries. The Nonparametric Anova was applied for analysis of variance, whereas Duncan's multiple range test served to identify possible industrial groups. For the purpose of calculating means for the Nonparametric Anova and industry groupings, consecutive numbers of 1 (strongly agree) to 5 (strongly disagree) were used. For cross-tabulations and the Chi-Square test, 'strongly agree' and 'agree' were collapsed into the category 'agree', and 'strongly disagree' and 'disagree' were collapsed into the category 'disagree'.

Table 1   Response by industry

Industry	No. of Companies	(%)	No. of Responses	(%)
Computer Electronics	10	8	136	9
Precision Electronics	20	16	316	20
Consumer Electronics	18	14	248	16
Industrial Machinery	16	13	228	14
Precision Machinery	12	10	160	10
Automotive	10	8	180	11
Auto Supply	15	12	212	13
Other	25	10	103	7
Total	126	100%	1,583	100%

The quality-cost tradeoff

The issue of whether improved quality will always decrease cost, or whether there is some point at which quality improvement becomes costly has been widely debated. Consequently, six statements dealing with the quality-cost issue were presented to Japanese manufacturing managers to provide insights into their philosophies on this subject.

Table 2 summarises the responses to the topic:– 'Reducing defects in operations increases cost.' The majority of the managers disagree with this view. The number of respondents who believe that decreasing rejects increases cost, combined with those who are undecided on the issue, totals 40–50 per cent in all industries. This is an indication that although the 'quality is free' argument is shared by the majority of respondents, the proportion of those rejecting this notion is also considerable.

Table 2   Reducing defects increases cost

Industry	Agree (%)	Undecided (%)	Disagree (%)	Total
Computer Electronics	17.78	22.22	60.00	135
Precision Electronics	17.25	22.68	60.06	313
Consumer Electronics	19.03	23.48	57.49	247
Industrial Machinery	19.38	18.94	61.67	227
Precision Machinery	14.65	25.48	59.87	157
Automotive	17.78	21.11	61.11	180
Auto Supply	22.01	26.79	51.20	

Total 1,468
Chi-Square Prob = 0.649

No other statistically significant industry differences are indicated.

Another closely related issue is the use of 'Acceptable Quality Levels' (AQLs). Using AQLs is philosophically inconsistent with the 'quality is free' argument and is based on the assumption that errors are inevitable and economically justifiable.[6]

Table 3 shows the responses to the statement:– 'The AQL system is superior in giving the customer the quality he desires.' The evidence indicates a roughly even split between those who agree and disagree. A large proportion of industries, ranging from 33 per cent to 48 per cent, were undecided on this issue, which is puzzling, since accepting error as inevitable (the AQL system) is philosophically inconsistent with the dynamic views of quality and zero-defects which are prevalent in Japanese manufacturing.

Table 4 provides clarification of why this inconsistency may exist. Between 11 per cent and 21 per cent of the respondents believe that yields should be the managerial focus, while between 66 per cent and 80 per cent agree that the focus should be on defects rather than yields. This suggests a managerial focus on defect reduction which is consistent with zero-defect notions. Evidence supporting this concern with error reduction is also indicated in Table 5. Between 61 per cent and 83 per cent of the respondents disagree with the statement:– 'When quality problems emerge, line speed should be maintained and defective products should be repaired at a later state of production.' This indicates that Japanese manufacturers focus on immediate reduction of error at the source.

Table 3 AQL systems superior

Industry	Agree (%)	Undecided (%)	Disagree (%)	Total
Computer Electronics	30.32	34.11	35.66	129
Precision Electronics	29.93	35.86	34.22	304
Consumer Electronics	29.29	33.47	37.24	239
Industrial Machinery	36.74	39.07	24.19	215
Precision Machinery	37.09	41.06	21.85	151
Automotive	24.14	45.40	30.46	174
Auto Supply	27.00	45.40	25.50	

Total 1,412
Chi-Square Prob = 0.002

Table 4 Focus on yields rather than defects

Industry	Agree (%)	Undecided (%)	Disagree (%)	Total
Computer Electronics	18.25	14.81	66.67	135
Precision Electronics	17.31	11.86	70.83	312
Consumer Electronics	19.92	11.38	68.70	246
Industrial Machinery	18.39	14.80	66.82	223
Precision Machinery	21.02	13.38	65.61	157
Automotive	10.80	9.09	80.11	176
Auto Supply	11.54	17.79	70.67	208

Total 1,412
Chi-Square Prob = 0.002

It also shows that a majority of Japanese manufacturing managers are not willing to trade possible short term cost advantages for long range quality improvements and this idea is consistent with the general thrust of the literature and relevant in the context of the cost-quality tradeoff debate. There is evidence, however, that these 'Japanese manufacturing philosophies' are significantly more entrenched in the auto supply and automotive industries (Chi-Square P<0.000; Anova P<0.000). The auto supply industry is clearly singled out by Duncan's Grouping (see Table 5a).

Japanese manufacturing's determination to 'build quality' into their products and their willingness to accept higher short term costs in order to do so are reflected in Table 6. This table elicits responses on the tradeoff between the costs of a possible line stop and the acceptance of inferior components from suppliers to keep the line moving.

Table 5   Maintain line speed, repair later

Industry	Agree (%)	Undecided (%)	Disagree (%)	Total
Computer Electronics	22.06	16.91	61.03	136
Precision Electronics	18.04	18.67	63.29	316
Consumer Electronics	18.85	14.43	66.80	244
Industrial Machinery	13.16	12.72	74.12	228
Precision Machinery	22.15	10.67	67.09	158
Automotive	15.56	13.89	70.56	180
Auto Supply	10.43	6.64	82.94	211

Total 1,473

Chi-Square Prob = 0.000

Table 5a   Industry grouping for maintaining line speed

Duncan Grouping	Mean	N	Industry
A	949.63	211	Auto Supply
B	822.63	228	Indus. Mach.
B	784.57	180	Automotive
B C	756.48	244	Consumer Elec.
B C	735.75	158	Prec. Mach.
B C	733.99	316	Prec. Elec.
C	680.32	136	Computer Elec.

Nonparametric Anova Prob = 0.000

Table 6   Cost of line stop justifies occasional acceptance of slightly off-quality components

Industry	Agree (%)	Undecided (%)	Disagree (%)	Total
Computer Electronics	1.48	4.44	94.07	135
Precision Electronics	3.17	5.08	91.75	315
Consumer Electronics	1.21	5.26	93.52	247
Industrial Machinery	2.65	4.42	92.92	226
Precision Machinery	4.40	9.43	86.16	159
Automotive	3.33	3.33	93.33	180
Auto Supply	4.25	5.66	90.09	212

Total 1,474

Chi-Square Prob = 0.299

The evidence indicates overwhelming opposition to a quality-cost tradeoff in regard to inferior component input in the manufacturing process and this has been strongly corroborated by observations in Japanese factories. This finding is consistent with Garvin's suggestion that Japanese supervisors attribute quality problems primarily to product design and purchased materials.[7] The extensive efforts of Japanese manufacturers to avoid inferior component input has been documented in various other studies and our analysis supports these findings.[8] While an overwhelming majority of Japanese managers in manufacturing are unwilling to accept even 'slightly off-quality components', the question now becomes: 'Would they be willing to supply off-quality components or sub-assemblies under the threat of losing an order?'

The data provided in Table 7 show that between 51 per cent and 67 per cent of the responding managers would not deliver products that do not meet specifications but between 20 per cent and 32 per cent are undecided, and between 13 per cent and 17 per cent would deliver sub-standard components. Apparently, a greater proportion is undecided or unwilling to agree to a quality-cost tradeoff as suppliers to outside sources than as users of outside components and sub-assemblies. The Chi-Square indicates significant philosophical differences between industries on this issue. Precision electronics and computer electronics form a group in which delivery of products 'below quality specification' is more acceptable than in those groups where mass assembly is prevalent.

How do these findings fit into the context of current thinking? A continual reduction of defects leading towards a zero-defect goal is recognised by many as the essence of Japanese manufacturing management,[9] and the issue of the cost efficiency of this philosophy has led to considerable debate.[10] Hayes and Clark have provided evidence that reductions in reject levels from 1000 to 100 parts per million in 'elite Japanese companies' have still resulted in reductions in total unit cost; which supports the 'quality is free' argument. Tables 5 and 7 show that the majority of manufacturing managers operate on the basis of this philosophy but this rather large sample, which can be considered representative of Japanese assembly industries, reveals that there is substantial uncertainty and disagreement among Japanese manufacturing managers, and between some of the industries.

There are several explanations for these deviations in thinking among Japanese managers and one possible explanation is change. There is widespread agreement that the zero-defect movement has brought tremendous improvements in quality and productivity to Japan. Many Japanese manufacturers may have reached such high quality levels that only marginal improvements in quality and corresponding decreases in unit cost are possible. Therefore, they may have discovered that on the road to zero-defects there is an economic conformance level greater than zero-defects, which may require a change in their thinking to exploit this discovery and it is possible that the data here reflect this change.

Table 7 **Delivery of goods below specifications if not a quality problem for customers**

Industry	Agree (%)	Undecided (%)	Disagree (%)	Total
Computer Electronics	16.91	32.35	50.74	136
Precision Electronics	18.35	31.65	50.00	316
Consumer Electronics	15.32	21.77	62.90	248
Industrial Machinery	13.60	23.68	62.72	228
Precision Machinery	15.72	27.67	56.60	159
Automotive	12.78	26.67	60.56	180
Auto Supply	12.74	19.81	67.45	212

Total 1,479
Chi-Square Prob = 0.012

Table 7a **Industry grouping for delivery of goods below specifications**

Grouping	Mean	N	Industry
A	853.60	212	Auto Supply
A	828.02	248	Consumer El.
A	828.00	228	Indus. Mach.
A	825.78	180	Automotive
B A	765.11	159	Prec. Mach.
B A	711.57	316	Prec. El.
B A	710.43	136	Computer El.

Nonparametric Anova Prob = 0.005

Testing the following hypotheses may help to clarify this issue:– Those Japanese companies who are furthest down the road to zero-defects will be most likely to discard the belief in the 'quality is free' argument. They may abandon zero-defect philosophies and adopt the 'Western paradigm' of a quality-cost tradeoff. As a consequence, one would expect the zero-defect movement gradually to become obsolete in Japan as more manufacturers discover that quality is not free. In contrast, US management may have to adopt a zero-defect philosophy to catch up with Japan, and later rediscover the ECL model, once manufacturers have caught up with Japanese quality.

An alternative explanation for the possible deviation in thinking among Japanese managers is economy-related. Japanese manufacturers currently face very stiff competition and unfavourable exchange rates. For example, De Meyer et. al. found that Japanese competitive priority is price, while in the US and Europe the emphasis is on quality.[11] This may have triggered a greater scrutiny of the relationship between quality, cost, and a change in attitudes on this topic. Additional cost pressures from unfavourable currency fluctuations may also be responsible for the surprising lack of consensus on this issue (see Table 6). After all, AQL assumes an economically feasible error level and the sanctified acceptance of defects as a way of life in manufacturing. The Japanese may have discovered that this level is greater than zero, but much lower than US managers thought was economically feasible. However, a note of caution in interpreting the surprising results in Table 6 is in order. It may very well be that the AQL system is used only to assure compliance with customers, supplier contracts and specifications apart from the production process. Therefore the 'quality is free' argument may serve as a management tool, while at the same time AQLs may be a control device apart from the manufacturing process.

A third plausible explanation may suggest that there never was the widespread homogeneity of thought on the cost-quality tradeoff issue in Japan that one would tend to conclude from the literature and the findings of this study seem to support this contention. However, not much other support for this argument is available due to the lack of empirical evidence.

Conclusion

The study set out to shed light on two common assumptions about Japanese quality attitudes in manufacturing. First, it tested the common notion that Japanese managers have a dynamic view of quality which is reflected in 'quality is free' and 'zero-defect' ideas. Secondly, it sought evidence about industrial differences on the same topic.

Considerable evidence in support of the first hypothesis was found. Japanese attitudes do reflect a preponderance of zero-defect notions that support dynamic views of quality but there are at the same time substantial proportions of Japanese manufacturing managers who are either undecided or who concur with static optimisation views.

There are also differences in quality attitudes among industries which are often substantial and indicate that the assumptions may occur out of the homogeneity of such attitudes but this is not made apparent by the data; therefore, caution in generalising from data from single industry studies is essential. The lack of homogeneity in the findings is an indication that generalisation from the findings from case studies or industrial sub-groups may substantially bias understanding of Japanese manufacturing; and that much more research is needed to account for the heterogeneity in Japanese manufacturing that was brought out by the study.

Notes

1. Juran, J.M. 'Japanese and Western Quality: A Contrast in Methods and Results.' *Management Review*. LXVII. 1978.

Hayes, R.H. 'Why Japanese Factories Work.' *Harvard Business Review*. July-August 1981.

2. Feigenbaum, A.V. 'Quality: The Strategic Business Imperative.' *Quality Progress*. February 1986.

    Hayes, R.H. and Clark, K.B. 'Explaining Observed Productivity Differentials Between Plants: Implications for Operations Research.' *Interfaces*. November-December 1985.

    Reitsperger, W.D. (1986). 'Japanese Management: Coping with British Industrial Relations.' *Journal of Management Studies*. Vol. 23. No. 1. 1986. pp. 72–87.

    Wheelwright, S. 'Japan – Where Operations Really Are Strategic.' *Harvard Business Review*. July-August 1981.

3. Crosby, L.B. 'The Just-In-Time Manufacturing Process: Control of Quantity and Quality.' *Production and Inventory Management*. Fourth Quarter. 1984.

    Schonberger, R.J. (1982). *Japanese Manufacturing Techniques: Nine Hidden Lessons, in Simplicity*. Free Press, New York. 1982.

4. Lundvall, D.M. and Juran, J.M. (1974). 'Quality Costs.' Juran, J.M. (ed.), *Quality Control Handbook*. McGraw-Hill, San Francisco. 1974.

5. Crosby, P.B. *Quality is Free*. McGraw-Hill, New York. 1979.

    Deming, W.E. 'Quality, Productivity, and Competitive Position.' *M.I.T. Centre for Advanced Engineering Study*. 1982.

6. Hayes, R.H. and Wheelwright, S. *Restoring Our Competitive Edge*. Wiley, New York. 1984. pp. 362–3.

    Cole, R.E. 'Improving Product Quality Through Continuous Feedback.' *Management Review*. 1983.

7. Garvin, D.A. 'Quality on the Line.' *Harvard Business Review*. September-October 1983.

8. Takamiya, M. 'Japanese Multinationals in Europe: Internal Operations and Their Public Policy Implications.' *Berlin International Institute of Management*. 1979. pp. 79–86.

9. Ross, J.E. and Klatt, L.A. 'Quality: the Competitive Edge.' *Management Decision*. No. 24. Winter 1986.

    See also: Cole, R.E. op. cit.

                Reitsperger, W.D. op. cit.

10. Fine, C.H. (1986). 'Quality Problems, Policies & Attitudes in the United States and Japan: An Exploratory Study.' *Academy of Management Journal*. 1986.

    See also: Crosby, P.B. op. cit. 1979.

                Wheelwright, S. op. cit. 1981.

11. De Meyer, A., Nakane, J., Miller, J.G., and Ferdows, K. 'Flexibility: The Next Competitive Battle.' *Manufacturing Roundtable Research Report Series*. Boston University School of Management. February 1987.

Conclusion

MALCOLM TREVOR
NAGOYA CITY UNIVERSITY

At the level of the globalisation of competition, exemplified by Dr. Ohmae's 'Triad' concept, there is now considerable discussion as to whether the future will see increased openness or increased protectionism. Will the process of the freeing of markets continue, or will the much discussed emergence of three commercially defensive blocs – Japan, the EC, and North America – take place? In the latter case, the trend towards bilateralism that has already been identified will become more pronounced, and will oblige companies to rethink their international strategies.

In addition to the problems of managing overseas staff, which the recently arrived multinationals in particular have not yet solved, managers are faced with the problems discussed in Part 3 above, under the heading 'The Management of Change'. Technological change, changes in the structure of industry and employment, and such societal changes as ageing are powerful challenges to management's strategic insight and ability.

Companies are entering a turbulent period in which the uncertainty that many seek to avoid will increasingly make itself felt. Darwin's teaching that only adaptation can ensure survival will be visible again in failures among companies that do not adapt themselves in order to master what a well known book termed 'The New Competition'[1] – with a warning that competition is likely to become harder during the last years of the century.

In contrast to earlier views of international business as consisting mainly of exporting, or selling overseas through local agents, companies are increasingly taking the multinational path. Yet some of the old thinking persists and not all companies see the benefits to themselves and their competitive ability in becoming what Dr. Ohmae terms 'insiders'. Such companies are still oriented towards selling, without seeing that in global competition it is necessasry to know the international competitor, how he works and where he is likely to make his next move. As a videotape made by the British Chamber of Commerce in Tokyo for companies thinking of entering the Japanese market or of establishing their own branches in Japan put it, 'You can't afford to ignore Japan – because Japan won't ignore you.' In other words, managers should take the initiative and not wait for the competition to arrive in their home market.

A considerable amount has been written about the management of overseas staff, including the relatively recent phenomenon of Japanese managers controlling local staff in Europe and the USA etc. Some comments have tended to overemphasise the problems of communication and 'culture' – generally appearing to mean expectations, attitudes and normative or acceptable behaviour in the company. This has led to insufficient attention being paid to the structure of such overseas branches but Part 2 above on 'The Management of Overseas Staff' draws attention to such typical organisational problems, that can be found in multinationals of any nationality at certain stages, of the respective positions of expatriate and local managers, and the extent to which the latter have meaningful authority and can make substantive decisions, in a way that will satisfy their career aspirations.

The problems for Japanese companies overseas are merely the latest in the phenomenon of multinational spread, though not all Japanese managers necessarily see them in these terms. Elsewhere Dr. Ohmae has proposed that the Japanese companies should take such successful and accepted Swiss multinationals as Nestlé, Sulzer, and Hoffmann-La Roche as their models. In his view, 'Unlike Japanese multinationals abroad, they are hardly noticeable as a "foreign" company. They are quietly successful.'[2]

Adaptation, following the words of Peter Drucker quoted in the Introduction, is not a passive process so much as the positive, active formulation and implementation of strategies to deal with change or, in the case of overseas operations, with an environment different from that to which the company is accustomed at home. In 1981, for example, BMW established itself in Japan as a wholly-owned subsidiary, with its own distribution and service network. Currently it has 123 dealerships, and over 600 employees, and has increased its sales by 803 per cent in nine years; while the average increase for foreign cars in Japan, starting for various reasons from a very low point, was 373 per cent. BMW Japan has made a point of service and the supply of parts without delay, using computerised control, but it has still had to adapt to a type of market different from that in its home territory. The German head commented that, 'The Americans have complained about the distribution system here. We did not complain. We just left it as it is and started our own. This is part of our philosophy.' On the personnel side, the question, 'How is BMW different from Japanese companies?' elicited the response that, 'We want to be different from Japanese companies. We want to be attractive to young people, we want to be attractive to young women . . . We want to be attractive to people who are internationally minded, who like to meet people from other countries, who want to be something special or offer something special ... If we were to follow the old traditional Japanese way, then we would never get good people because these good people join the traditional Japanese companies.'[3]

In other words, BMW has used a new rationale for its Japanese operations and has not just assumed that it had to compromise with aspects of the local situation that it would have considered dysfunctional. The same can be said of Japanese manufacturing operations in Britain, for instance, where the companies have likewise been able to introduce successful innovations at Toshiba, Nissan and elsewhere.

The old saying that 'one swallow does not make a summer' is undoubtedly true in the sense that one success neither guarantees others nor points to an infallible panacea, least of all of the 'quick fix' type. Yet Braun electric razors held 40 per cent by value of the Japanese market in 1990: a successful penetration of the market that its Dutch manager saw as based on factors that included product quality, a series of popular television commercials running for eight years, plus the attention paid to Braun's own association of about forty of its most important wholesalers, which promoted its policy of becoming an 'insider'.[4]

At the time of actual or potential trade disputes, for which the protectionism and depression of the 1930s should act as a warning, managers need to avoid stereotypes; whether these are Japanese stereotypes of Europe and America or European and American stereotypes of Japan. More specific data and cases, not broad generalisations, are needed. More international comparative research needs to be done and the information that it provides made available to and used by company managers.

Multinational companies need qualitative data on overseas environments, as well as 'numbers', and in order to function effectively overseas their managers need to be properly oriented before they are sent abroad. Such a tool as a country-specific handbook, detailing labour markets, career expectations among local managers and employees, and management styles etc. found in the host country, can help managers going to a new overseas posting. It cannot only spare them 'culture shock', but can enable them to function more effectively more quickly wherever they are sent. Companies that have not yet recognised the benefits of this investment in orientation training would be well advised to do so.

Notes

1. Kotler, P., Fahey, L. and Jatusripitak, S. *The New Competition. Meeting the Marketing Challenge from the Far East.* Prentice-Hall, New Jersey. 1985.
2. Ohmae, K. *Beyond National Borders. Reflections on Japan and the World.* Kodansha, Tokyo. 1988. p. 4.

3. Seo, A. and Nidever, R. 'Taking on Japan: BMW Japan.' *Look Japan*. Toyko. November 1990.
4. Nidever, R. and Seo, A. 'Taking on Japan: Braun.' *Look Japan*. Tokyo. January 1991.